SACRED UNION

Awakening to the Consciousness of Eden

By TANISHKA

Volume Two: Red Tantra

Creating Sacred Union in Partnership

First Printing: 2014

ISBN: 978-0-9874263-3-8

Published by Star of Ishtar Publishing
P.O. Box 101, Olinda V1C 3788
Australia

www.starofishtar.com

Dedication

To those who are dedicated to restoring the sacred balance of opposites here on Earth.

Acknowledgements

I would like to thank the Christ, the Magdalene, Ishtar, Gaia, Luna and Sol for pouring their teachings through me as a channel, as well as their patience and faith in me to birth this book. I am also deeply grateful to all my clients who have entrusted me with their vulnerability enabling me to midwife this information from Source.

Endless love and gratitude to my Beloved, Michael for his willingness to process and move into deeper states of intimacy and ecstasy with me, as well as the incredible humility he instills in me through his acts of kindness and humor we see in our shared shadow selves. I would also like to acknowledge the opportunity he gifted me in embracing these practices wholeheartedly and his assistance editing these teachings.

I would also like to acknowledge a heartfelt thanks to my parents for teaching me so much about relationships, all my partners who schooled me through my apprenticeship in dancing with my shadow and a huge outpouring of gratitude to my daughter, Ariella who is 'steady, slow and wise' to coin her self-appraisal at age six! An ancient Tantrika, at eleven, she continues to be one of my greatest teachers.

I would also like to thank my beloved mentors, Kermit the Frog (my first 'Green Man'), Alice Bailey (for decoding the archetypal hero's journey), Stephen Robinson (my teenage poetry and drama coach), Jen Powell (who initiated me into Women's Mysteries), Warwick Sayer (my Astrology teacher) Evelynne Joffe (my Kabbalah teacher) and Osho (for making Zen and Kundalini Practices accessible through his legacy).

A deep gratitude to my Red Tent sisters, Annie and Elinor, for loving me through all my life transitions, Barbara and Tereza for their service as dream holders and the village who helped me balance parenthood with service to the greater good during my years as a sole parent: Deb, Karen, Bronwen, Wilma, Charity, Dani, Michelle, Evgenia, Kirsten, Echo, China and Lael - thank-you. A huge thanks to you too, Nick for your beautiful love as a brother in addition to your sound alchemy and graphic design. To Bel, for always making my work shine in Technicolor with your design wizardry, to Jane for her web support and good humor, and to Anne for being a total gun and the best VA anyone could wish for - thank-you for lifting the burden of endless admin off my shoulders and helping me get my message out to the world. A huge thank-you to Luanne for formatting my book so well and getting it print ready with such grace.

Table of Contents

SACRED UNION

by Tanishka

A Meeting
A Knowing
between kindred souls
that the time has come...

...for light to meet dark
for day to kiss night
for summer to know winter...

...so each may be student and teacher
aware of both strengths and weaknesses
willing to share all
to become what they are not
but promise to be
with a single intent...

...to illuminate all
when moon reflects sun
and sun shines on moon...

...to dance around the seasonal wheel
and surrender their fate
to the knowing of the ages
accepting only one
who's true spouse is the Great Beyond
having made the vow to serve
so that their journey through the cups
is offered up to all of humanity...

...drinking all that they have scryed and distilled
as a gesture of thanks
for all that they have known
in the presence of the other

 # The Path of Red Tantra

Creating Sacred Union in Partnership

The path of Red Tantra is the journey of the inner Queen / King - a phase which, chronologically, is activated in our life path during the ages thirty through sixty. This path of creating Sacred Union externally with another is only truly possible when we have learnt to balance our inner opposites. (This is the foundation work covered in the first volume of this series, 'Creating Sacred Union Within'.)

Given that we have been blindly navigating the terrain of relationships without the guidance of ancient wisdom to steer our ships, the majority of modern day relationships have not matured past the stage of falling in love with a projected ideal. This is illustrated in the Tarot as the coupling of the inner maiden and knight in the 'Three of Cups' card. This card depicts a level of relationship where we feel 'in love' with our own unexpressed aspects, which we project externally onto another. So we feel incomplete without them, hence the old relationship paradigm term: 'my other half'.

This relationship model is known as co-dependency, a dynamic where we rely upon 'the other' to do that which we think we are unable to do for ourselves. Understandably, this status quo eventually creates feelings of neediness, disempowerment, suffocation and resentment until we individuate from the other in order to grow into a fuller version of ourselves. If we don't use this time on our own to embrace the White Path of Tantra: Creating Sacred Union Within, we simply fall in love again with our projection of the perfect partner and then reject them when we realize they too, are human and incomplete.

Unconscious Partnerships Play Out in Three Stages

1. **The Honeymoon Phase**. This is when we fall in love with our opposite or disowned self externally in someone else. Our euphoria is fueled by the expectation they can save us from the suffering we have unconsciously created for ourselves. This is when we revert back to 'baby speak', giving each other pet names as we take it in turns to soothe and parent each other's wounded inner child, in exchange for affection, reassurance and the perception of emotional security. At this stage of relating, we unconsciously try to get from our partner what we feel we didn't get from our parents.

2. **Polarization**. This is when we lean on each other's strengths to the point where we completely avoid doing those activities we don't feel confident doing. To disguise our growing sense of disempowerment, we start to develop a sense of superiority about the tasks we are good at. This leads us to minimize and judge the tasks our partner does, so resentment grows and the passion dies. When we don't appreciate and respect one another, we end up bickering like siblings. Such a dynamic creates unconscious competition with each other, undermining any effort to co-create something lasting and sustainable. For example, both parties putting each other down (either directly or indirectly to their friends or shared children) to bolster their sense of self-worth.

3. **Rejection to Reclaim Personal Power**. This is when we have become so polarized that we feel righteous and superior towards our partner. To avoid taking responsibility for our own imbalance, we blame our opposite for sabotaging our happiness and then break away in order to reassert our sense of authority over our

own life. It is women who are usually the first to leave. Not because they don't love their partner but because they don't know any other way to end the destructive dance of polarization and conflict. This stage can be very frightening when we love our partner, but feel we are betraying our own values by staying with them. This stage is inevitable if we value truth and recognize something needs to change, if we are to grow. So rest assured, if you are currently in this place of needing your relationship dynamic to change...you are ready to enter the new paradigm of Sacred Union.

Unconscious relationships occur when we operate on default; governed by the conditioning and role models we received growing up. To create a new model of healthy relating which is mutually uplifting, honoring and supportive, we first need a template before we can create it.

Before we can enter a dance of conscious partnership with another, we must first develop a strong sense of selfhood. This individuation stage is necessary if we are to grow beyond co-dependency. This independence enables us to consider what life would be like without 'the other' so we can consciously choose to be with them from a place of empowered sovereignty, rather than need. For, unless we first commit to ourselves and our own values, we cannot truly commit to someone else.

When we find ourselves at a crossroads in a relationship, contemplating the question, 'Should I stay or should I go?' we are really ready to embrace relationship as a path of spiritual growth. This is because we have grown beyond the illusion of unconsciously expecting our Beloved to be our savior. In order to have a conscious relationship with another, we must first have a conscious relationship with ourselves. Without this precursory stage of self-love and empowerment, our commitment to another is built upon a shaky foundation, instead of one based on self-understanding and love. For more info about marriage to self, read volume one, 'Creating Sacred Union Within'.

Newsflash: Fastest Honeymoon on Record!

Every relationship goes through these phases, however, the more self-aware we become, the faster we shift through them. So while the 'honeymoon phase' may have lasted a year or two in previous eras, now it may last only a week or two. So a long relationship is not necessarily a measure of a 'successful' relationship, as we have been taught to believe.

In the path of Red Tantra, instead of trading our partner in, only to repeat the same process with someone else, we strive to take responsibility for embodying our disowned selves. We do this by acknowledging our partner as our teacher. Their role is to mirror everything we are unable to see and accept in ourselves. That doesn't mean the reflection is a complete mirror image!

We are attracted to our opposite as their energy helps to complement and model how we can become more balanced. So they may act out a core wound in the opposite way to us. Our challenge, is to focus on the underlying issue and not the symptom; otherwise we simply escalate the drama of opposites.

If we subscribe to the concept of a holographic universe, whereupon we experience reality according to our projections (a theory first made by Albert Einstein and later explored by quantum scientists), those closest to us often reflect our subconscious beliefs about ourselves and life in general. So rather than judge their behavior, we seek to question what disowned aspect they are reflecting back to us. This perspective engenders gratitude rather than reactivity.

The Key to Everlasting Love

For a relationship to grow beyond the honeymoon phase and survive the polarization phase with grace and mutual respect, we must enter into a sacred practice, which assists us to see and own our disowned aspects. This shifts the focus from egos blaming each other to one of personal responsibility. Such a discipline ensures both parties remain humble, open and receptive and therefore available to love and be loved. Without an agreement to regularly face the other in complete transparency, all the unconscious thoughts, words and actions will be projected onto the other. These accumulate over time, destroying trust and mutual respect, making true intimacy on any level impossible.

This process needs to be holistic (honoring of the whole self or soul), rather than just a psychological negotiation, which is what can occur in traditional couples counseling. A soulful approach encourages couples to 'get out of their heads' and into their hearts. For, viewing a situation from a rational perspective of right and wrong can further entrench polarization. Instead, this is when both parties need to be encouraged to reconnect with their feelings. This can only be done when they acknowledge their compensatory behaviors, such as disassociating, blaming, judging, competing or numbing themselves to avoid feeling their disowned vulnerability. Only then, can they connect soul to soul.

When we view our relationship as a path to enlightenment, we become gracious about the lessons learned through our human flaws and hurts. So instead of becoming increasingly bitter and cynical about love, marriage or an entire gender, we come to appreciate how every experience in our relationship is highlighting what we need to do to resolve our own inner conflict and imbalance. It is this shift in our perspective that restores harmony as we genuinely feel gratitude towards our partner. Instead of fearing the cost of their human flaws, we come to appreciate how both their weaknesses and strengths serve us. This does not mean staying in an abusive situation where one partner is looking at their unconscious behavior and the other isn't.

Sacred Union is built upon a mutual commitment to grow through self-awareness. If both partners aren't willing, you have to face the truth that you're not in a partnership, you are in a parent / child dynamic, which is unhealthy and will limit your personal growth. It is only when we honor ourselves by saying, 'No' to situations that don't honor us, that we then attract situations that do - whether that ends up being with our current partner or with a new one. We must identify what we don't want, before the space can be created for what we do.

When both parties make this commitment to self-growth, irrespective of their partner, transcendent love is possible. If an agreement is made to do a Sacred Union practice simply to please or appease the other, then the dynamic of parent / child will continue. Without this mutual commitment to honor self and other by regularly owning our shadow, we unconscious wound each other. So we owe it to ourselves and to our partners, to be willing to take responsibility for ourselves, otherwise we remain in a marriage of convenience, staying together for fear of not surviving alone.

Making a commitment to embrace our relationship as a path to wholeness makes it possible for us to feel truly safe, loved for who we truly are, rather than pressured to be perfect or face rejection. The only essential ingredient is that both partners are willing. Given the payoff is a truly soulful connection and multi-orgasmic sex, whereas the alternative is divorce or a cold war, it seems an obvious choice!

How the Path of Red Tantra Can Help You

Couples: The practices in this volume will assist couples who have been experiencing increasing polarization and conflict with each other, by providing a template to see and honor their partner as their mirror and teacher.

Singles: For those who have left co-dependent relationships or have been working alone to create inner balance, this volume will provide you with the tools to establish and sustain a new model of conscious partnership. This includes a step-by-step conscious courtship guide to assist you in establishing a conscious partnership.

Families: This path creates a strong foundation for families, by ensuring the wounded inner children of the parents don't get projected on everyone else. This commitment to be transparent and self-responsible creates a safe group dynamic. Such a practice deepens intimacy and trust, to help withstand the external pressures of children, who also trigger our unhealed aspects.

So, as you can see, regardless of our current relationship status, when we have a map for conscious relating, we can anchor it in our own lives and avoid enacting the legacy of wounds from our ancestral lineage. By learning to dance harmoniously with our opposite, we balance ourselves and create something that can endure the constant cycle of change.

> *'Tantra means 'to weave'. When something is woven, it is strong. It is now time to weave together all our disparate parts internally, so we can live in a truly interwoven way with those around us.'*

> Tanishka

# Relationship Revolution

Why Relationships Are Evolving or Dissolving

Identifying What We Don't Want

Like many folk, I grew up in a family where my parents had not embarked on a path of emotional / psychological soul-healing to address the wounds of their respective inner children. This meant they unconsciously projected their negative expectations onto each other, recreating and exacerbating the wounds they had received in childhood. This is the unfinished karma (past life experiences) we reincarnate to heal. So my training as a Tantrika started here, observing what not to do if you didn't want vinegar put in your coffee! (True story.) And like so many children, my expectations of partnership were anchored through this role-modeling - witnessing the cold wars, blame games, sarcasm, criticism, competition and resentment which escalated to a bitter divorce.

Many years later I found myself working in the family law courts, watching long queues of estranged couples getting their divorce paperwork hurriedly stamped, without any of the pomp and pageantry that had created their legal, wedded union. Like a fly on the wall, I sat next to the magistrate to record the proceedings for the transcripts, watching the end of the road for polarized parents who had declared war upon their opposite over cash, assets and children.

I saw disempowered men try to dodge maintenance, and disempowered women try to extract every cent possible for fear they couldn't create an income in their own right.

Equally, I have seen women rightfully demand that their tireless work as housekeepers and primary care givers be financially recognized, and devoted fathers picketing for their legal right to have equal access to their children. Having been divorced myself, I also know how gut wrenching it is to try and explain to your two year old that Mummy and Daddy won't be living in the same house anymore. Let alone how that defining moment makes you determined to never re-create the same circumstance again.

Acknowledging the Cost of Unconscious Relating

Most primary relationships in our families of origin have been immature and dysfunctional - a fact made evident by the success of 'The Simpsons' - the longest running U.S. sitcom of all time, voted by Time magazine as the best TV show of the 20th Century. This show lampooned the unconscious family dynamics which struck a chord with millions who identified from their personal experience. This pop culture phenomenon played the role of 'group therapy' for the masses, enabling us to laugh at our collective interpersonal shadow. The protagonist, Homer, the iconic 'everyman', is named after the Greek playwright who wrote down the collective psychodramas to empower the people. Everything has its reason and season, so rather than watch it for another twenty years, laughing at our caricatures and doing nothing to change the dynamic in our personal lives, we must now transform our destructive partnership and family dynamics by adopting a fresh approach.

Understanding the Past So You Don't Recreate It

As part of our personal preparation for adult relationships we need to consider and understand the wounds we received in childhood so we don't 'act out' our unresolved negative expectations from our family of origin. It is our unconscious words and behaviors that wound our partner and children, eroding trust and harmony. That said, no one is perfect. So don't expect yourself to be completely healed before attempting intimacy with another. (Particularly after a messy break-up.) However, the more self-aware we become, the more we can identify our triggers, making us less likely to project our past wounds on to our partner. It is self-awareness that minimizes our potential for conflict and drama.

Partnerships are built upon the foundation of our inner union with ourselves. Families are then built upon this scaffolding, so we need to spend time and energy investing in our primary relationships with ourselves and our partner, especially after the added pressure of children. Accessing relationship resources and support is imperative if we want to create healthy partnerships, not just as a final act in the drama before lawyers are called.

Reading insightful books, attending personal growth and relationship seminars, online courses and regular journaling all help us deconstruct and understand our interior thoughts and feelings, so we have greater awareness of the fears which can underpin our external actions.

Given we internalize both of our parents as we grow up and they become our template for our feminine and masculine self-expression, 'running away from home' to create a happy family will not work unless we take the time to examine our inner templates. Yes! The days of expecting someone to rescue you from the pain of your past, in the form of a 'white knight' or 'good woman' are long gone. As now we start to acknowledge we must find that 'white knight' or 'good woman' within ourselves, if we wish to attract it externally in a partner. (For more details on how to heal these inner gender imprints, read volume one, 'Creating Sacred Union Within'.)

Nuclear Families - Sound Like a Toxic Way to Live?

Unfortunately, in our current societal structure of 'nuclear families' living in separate homes - often miles from extended families and soul brothers and sisters, we can find ourselves feeling very isolated from support when we most need it. This is the main reason many new parents find themselves feeling overwhelmed by fears, insecurity and depression as they struggle to adjust to non-stop responsibility without the backup of other adults to help shoulder the load or debrief with on a regular basis. When babies are born, the need for routine keeps most new mums housebound. This is because babies and young children need the stability of routine. So women often struggle to adapt as they lose their independence and juggle doing all the chores required to run a household, such as shopping, cooking and cleaning, while being full-time care givers who are sleep deprived and nursing their own unresolved birth trauma with a cocktail of post-natal hormones.

Similarly, new dads are often stretched by the pressure placed upon them to provide the additional resources needed to care for their dependents, in addition to being greeted by a demanding household upon their return each night. This transition is summed up beautifully here...

'A baby is like a hand grenade thrown into a marriage.'

Susan Maushart, *'The Mask of Motherhood'*

This quote illustrates the findings of her research which revealed conflict escalated in marriages by 87% on average, after the birth of the first child. The primary cause of conflict was over the division of labor - squabbling over who was doing more and who felt more tired or had the worse end of the deal. So, regardless of what the young, hip and upwardly mobile couple thought life would look like after baby, nothing can quite prepare for the shock of polarizing into the gender roles appointed to them by nature and the subsequent re-enactment of their own parental drama. This slap upside the head with a cod is further compounded when they realize how unsupportive our individualistic, synthetic and commercially-driven culture is, toward those who embrace their natural cycles, such as those who opt for parenthood.

'It takes a village to raise a child'

African proverb

In traditional cultures, this additional responsibility of child rearing was shared amongst the tribe, as each family had a small separate dwelling on shared land, so additional support was only a few steps away. The community also accepted the responsibility for providing, which eased pressure on couples integrating this major life change.

In direct contrast, most local town-planning laws in the West inhibit our natural instinct to live on shared land and pool our resources. Such inter-dependent community models ease personal burdens considerably by minimizing privately-owned resources and the cash needed to purchase them, in addition to reducing the need for personal domestic labor. I'm not suggesting communism, where a model of community is imposed upon the people. Rather an appreciation and awareness of the gains sought when we live more interdependent lives, in a spirit of community that is directed by free will.

Without this, the sense of overwhelm, stemming from the stress of always trying but failing to meet all our needs, keeps us too manic to think clearly, accessing ingenuity to problem-solve our own immediate concerns, let alone the problems of society as a whole. Understandably, the common response is to distract oneself with substances and virtual realities ranging from social media, celebrity gossip, reality shows, porn, computer games, movies, soap operas and pulp fiction rather than take life-affirming action to re-structure our lives.

Where's My Happily Ever After?

Our modern culture, particularly in the West has focused more upon the desires of youth than it has upon the needs of older members of society. This is because young singles have an impressionable mind and a disposable income, making them a prized target market for advertisers. Since, when we're young, our focus is more on developing a persona based on what other people think, this emphasis on the youth culture results in external (ego) desires having more importance than internal (soul) qualities, which we develop as we age. Since inner riches can't be bought and sold as commodities, they are dismissed or minimized as having little or no value. As a result, we are encouraged to search for and find the perfect mate, then live 'happily ever after'. This unrealistic ideal leads us to feel like a failure if we struggle after the big day!

Our patriarchal culture has been shaped by the unconscious masculine, which is goal-oriented, so we have been encouraged to achieve status symbols rather than to master life lessons. This is why people throw a lot of money at weddings and baby showers but then offer little or no support after the celebration. Whereas, ancient cultures valued and honored the need for mentoring and marking of all milestones as they prized the soul's inner journey above the accumulation of external wealth, status and power.

Rites of Passage are the teachings and initiation ceremonies which prepare us for each of our life transitions. They are called 'rites' as they are our birth rites - which constitute our basic human right to have access to the wisdom we need so we can make the best possible decisions to steward our lives. In the absence of this necessary life training, we have been more susceptible to the propaganda of corporations that don't have our best interests at heart.

In addition, our myths, legends and folktales have been distorted, so they offer no authentic moral, but instead indoctrinate us to make lesser decisions. For instance, maidens are taught to not trust elder women who have knowledge of the mysteries, boys are taught to slay dragons instead of taming them. Girls are taught to look for a 'Prince Charming' instead of a man who is authentic. We are taught a prize catch is the wealthiest man in the land - a notion which puts pressure on boys to make money their greatest priority, and on girls to 'land a man' who can take care of them financially. Everything echoes this early conditioning. For example, songs like, 'Diamonds Are Forever' or 'Diamonds are a Girl's Best Friend' suggest a woman needs wealth over relationships.

Without ancient customs like initiation into Red Tent moon lodges, when girls start cycling with the moon, so they can sit with the older women once a month and learn how to become women who seek to fulfill themselves and contribute to the greater good, we end up with an epidemic of young women referring to themselves as 'girls' and sporting the word, 'Princess' on their bumpers - both on their cars and track pants.

Fortunately, female comedy writer / performers like Gina Riley and Jane Turner from the ABC's TV series, 'Kath and Kim' and Ruby Wax, Jennifer Saunders and Dawn French from BBC TV's 'Absolutely Fabulous' have created much-needed satires about women who refuse to grow up. They accurately lampoon overindulged 'high-maintenance gals', who expect to have their every whim catered to, with the implied threat being, they'll take their 'trophy bride / celeb' status elsewhere if their demands are not met.

At the other end of the spectrum, we have the pathetic 'good girl'. An equally tragic casualty of this 'eternal girl' conditioning who does everything for others and asks nothing in return, while silently hoping one day, all her dreams will come true and she will be rescued by a man who will whisk her away to a large townhouse with servants. Toni Collette in the film, 'Muriel's Wedding' springs to mind by way of an example.

Author's Note...I find it curious that the patriarchal pap which kept women casting men as their savior God, starting with JC - is such bitter irony, given how tirelessly he worked to awaken people to take responsibility for themselves!

De-coding the Creation of a Bridezilla!

So what happens when a 'Peta Pan' (eternal princess) decides to tie the knot? A bridezilla is born! Yes, her wedding is not really about her long-term partnership and new life chapter, it's all about her! It is her swan song, her 'Total Girl' event which declares to every other girl in the land, 'I am the supreme princess. I am the 'alpha chick', the one in the glass slippers! I am the most beautiful girl in all the world'. It is essentially a diva performance fueled by tulle and satin to prove her taste is as good as a blue blood! So the ultimate proof of her value as a woman is really as unstable as a coke-addicted child star.

The words, 'perfect wedding' are the giveaway. Anyone who is trying to create perfection is attempting to pull off a head-trip rather than focusing on the simple truth of the heart. This mindset leads the emotionally immature bride-to-be (often encouraged by her mother / mother-in-law / matron of honor) to focus on planning the 'perfect wedding' usually at a cost to her relationship with her partner. For when so much attention is given to the wedding dress, the shoes, the shade of napkins and floral arrangements, but not to the 'state of the union', we end up with one third of western marriages filing for divorce and many others settling for immature co-dependent partnerships as the status quo. So while I can understand modern couples dismissing the 'pre-nuptial' couples counseling with a celibate priest, I would encourage spending less on the party favors and more on developing relating skills, such as self-awareness, emotional maturity, assertion techniques, personal boundary setting, conflict resolution and healing fears of intimacy. For the more one addresses their inner fears and insecurities during a major life change, the less likely they are going to feel out of control and consequently try to control everything around them.

Immature men, on the other hand, swing between finding a woman to look after them and possessing a love object that says to the world, 'I must be quite a man to have a chick like this on my arm!' Again, both serve a purpose to the unconscious ego, which is why men operating on this level of awareness are quick to seek out a replacement model when a relationship ends, just as one would replace a lost, stolen or broken appliance.

Ultimately both genders, when immature, focus on what the other person will do for them and their external appearance, both of which bolster their ego and social status. Traditionally for women, this means a man who will foot the bill for her new shoes, living room blinds, car, spa treatments and holidays. Whereas for men, this means a woman who will cook him comfort food, clean the house, run his errands, wash his dirty clothes and do the lion share of child rearing. One provides while the other nurtures. This level of partnership has an expiry date...as the disowned self grows increasingly frustrated and resentful.

Are You Ready for Change? The Warning Signs of Relationship Breakdown

For Women...

Statistically, it is women who instigate marital break-up. (Source: http://www.aifs.gov.au/institute/pubs/WP20.html) This could be because statistics show men are healthier and live longer when in partnerships, whereas women's health and wellbeing declines. This paints a fairly transparent picture, illustrating that it is women who are more likely to forgo their needs in relationship. So it makes sense women tend to be the ones most likely to initiate change, when the alternative is to continue to compromise their needs in order to uphold a partnership which isn't mutually supportive - emotionally and psychologically, in order to reap material security for them and their children. So while women may try and make a relationship work for as long as they can, when the cost becomes personally too unsustainable they put an end to it, to preserve life.

The feminine governs emotional / spiritual growth, so girls mature emotionally quicker than boys, which prepares them for their role as mothers, assisting their children to express themselves and understand their emotional responses. With few rite of passage ceremonies in our modern society to assist boys to emotionally mature into men, and a culture that shames men for expressing any emotion other than anger, many unaware men unconsciously seek out women who will process their emotional states for them. This emotional immaturity is then compounded by our socially-sanctioned 'drinking culture' that not only encourages alcohol consumption as a way of disassociating from one's feelings, but also affirms alcohol as an intrinsic part of male bonding rituals and national identity. (i.e. you're not an Aussie / German / Scot etc. unless you can down a beer in less than a minute.) This leads immature men to seek out partners who will not question their habit of unconsciously suppressing their emotions with alcohol or other recreational drugs on the premise that 'everyone else is doing it'.

This dynamic often works temporarily, as women will mother their partners until children come along. Then it becomes painfully obvious to women, post motherhood, that they no longer have the capacity to continue patiently holding the space for all of their partner's emotional states and emotional dependence without an equal exchange of emotional support and maturity offered in return. To be fair, there are many substance-abusing women whose emotional immaturity impacts on their partners and children, especially in the West where many women are disconnected from their feminine nature. This leads them to deny their need for addressing their emotional needs and forming ongoing structures of emotional support such as Red Tent sisterhood circles to process their emotional states. Women, however, do possess a natural propensity for emotional intelligence, which is why men as a group are more likely to suppress their emotions with alcohol than women.

The epidemic of breast cancer in the West also indicates just how much societal pressure is placed upon women to nurture the needs of everyone around them, relegating their own needs till last, to the point where they seldom get met. (For more info about the holistic perspective on the cause of breast cancer, I recommend reading, 'The Body Is the Barometer of the Soul' by Helen Noontil or 'You Can Heal Your Life' by Louise Hay.)

Women usually leave a relationship emotionally before they leave physically. They do this by shutting down emotionally if they feel hurt or unappreciated by their partner. When shut down emotionally, women retreat into their heads, becoming increasingly anxious, distant and critical. This is usually when they feel like they have to 'wear the pants' and be in their masculine polarity, organizing everything, so their capacity to also be in their feminine polarity declines and they resent having to nurture everybody's needs.

When women shut down emotionally, they are unable to open sexually to their partner, as sex for women is an internal act. Unless their inner self feels seen, heard, honored, safe and loved by their partner, they can't open to greater states of vulnerability and surrender with them. If women attempt to over-ride this internal self-preservation instinct, their body will often respond on their behalf, manifesting physical symptoms such as recurrent yeast infections to keep potential invasions of imposing, dishonoring energy at bay. This is a phenomenon I have seen countless times with female clients.

When a woman has left a partnership emotionally, she will start to leave mentally by planning a life of increasing independence until finally, she leaves physically by creating her own security, so she can take care of her own needs (and her children). Women who are very polarized in their feminine energy (nurturing, emotional, home bodies) will often take longer in this third phase. This is because they're developing their 'inner masculine', finding the will and confidence to physically leave an unsupportive relationship.

Women who find they are regularly shutting down from them partners emotionally therefore need to acknowledge there is a need for mutual honesty, transparency and growth if all their emotional concerns are to be heard and addressed, or they will continue to shut down in other ways, leading to a complete relationship breakdown.

For Men...

Men who are not feeling happy in their partnerships often start feeling trapped, confined and resentful of the obligations and responsibilities associated with their partnership. This leads them to withdraw. For instance they may work late, socialize more with their friends, indulge in escapist activities like video games, porn, social media or use substances such as drugs and alcohol. Many men leave their partnership physically and mentally without even realizing they've done so. Often this occurs when children come along as an unconscious reaction to the increased responsibility of fatherhood. This is because most men have been under-fathered, with little or no male mentoring, initiation into manhood or introduction to an experience of authentic brotherhood. This leaves them unable to acknowledge their deep insecurities about their own value and abilities as a man. So they respond by trying to get approval for their manhood from their partner or they disassociate and leave the majority of parenting to them, lest they get it wrong. This sense of separation with their spouse and children continues to widen if they don't recognize the need for assistance in dealing with their underlying fears and issues.

The masculine governs rational / material growth so boys mature rationally quicker than girls, which prepares them for their role as fathers. As the protector / provider, they will use their problem-solving abilities to acquire what their family needs on a physical level to survive. Just as women carry the load emotionally for their immature husbands, men carry the load financially for their immature wives. This is equally true in same sex relationships, depending on which partner embodies more feminine or masculine traits.

Those with excessive feminine energy will often crave another child just as their youngest reaches school age to unconsciously avoid looking at their own ability to turn their gifts into a viable income for fear that they don't have what it takes. This places extra strain on their partner to provide even more by compensating for someone who wants to just be taken care of.

Brother / Sister Circles

This dysfunctional relationship dynamic of compensating for and parenting the underdeveloped child self in one's partner will reduce as we reclaim the ancient practice of sisterhood and brotherhood circles. Structured as simple sharing circles, where each takes it in turn to speak their truth and be witnessed, these monthly gatherings provide a forum to face oneself regularly with the support of peers, confronting personal insecurities. Through this practice, one cannot then continue to avoid taking action and being accountable for oneself, which replaces the unconscious tendency to blame those closest to you. Known in ancient times as moon lodges and sun lodges, they are a key component if we are to create authentic lives of integrity. I speak more about these practices in chapter four and run an online course to teach modern men and women to create these community-building circles in their own neighborhood. For more info see the resources page.

Changing the Mold

Men who witness their own urge to disassociate can transcend this default setting by questioning their resistance to intimacy and responsibility. This can be done through journaling, discussing it with a trusted friend or mentor, or ideally, through regular attendance at a men's circle. For, while shutting down emotionally or avoiding intimacy can be dismissed as 'normal male behavior' because it is what the majority of Dads have modeled in generations past, it is dysfunctional. The pay-off for men sharing their true thoughts and feelings to themselves and those around them, is authentic relationships where they feel loved for who they are, rather than what they do. Unlike the men of the previous era who felt like mere 'walking wallets' to their families, with no real love and passion to come home to, due to their inability to connect.

Another way for a man (or masculine dominant woman) to feel truly powerful is to identify the unconscious ways they need others to validate their virility (external power to pursue, charm and seduce another). For example

- Flirtatious gesturing, including suggestive glances, comments or body language. This is done to reassure the ego, who is asking, 'Am I attractive to you?' When we see and know our own worth, we don't seek such external reassurance.

- Pursuing a love object who's a challenge to possess. This potential conquest releases endorphins so they feel alive, so it is referred to as, 'the thrill of the chase'. Those who are actively pursuing their purpose in life regularly take risks in honor of a much greater quest, so have no need to assert their virility in this way.

- Seducing or intimating others to assert their dominance and control. One does this in an effort to gain the upper hand for fear of being out of control.

- Covert behaviors, such as using pornography, illicit substances, engaging in illegal practices or forbidden sexual liaisons. These are akin to the inner teenager sneaking around to passive-aggressively assert, 'I am clever enough to do what I want.' Such acts of defiance come from an unconscious need to assert one's individual will and see if they'll survive, if they do. This dynamic occurs when men feel like boys at home, so they misbehave to prove to themselves that 'she' isn't in control of him - 'she' being the partner they have projected 'mother' on to.

Such behaviors are often a reaction to one's partner shutting down emotionally or sexually, often due to their emotional insensitivity or immaturity. To avoid this wounding scenario escalating, both parties need to openly discuss their hurt and concerns, so they can take responsibility for taking the necessary action to address the wounds unconsciously motivating the destructive behavior. If couples can embrace such potential crises as an opportunity for growth, one avoids anchoring a pattern of continual betrayal of self and other through a cycle of hurt and reaction.

A Word to the Wise...

So guys (and masculine dominant women), if you start to notice in yourself the desire for seduction to boost your sense of self, examine the emotional cause of distance between yourself and your partner and be proactive in discussing your desire to reconnect emotionally. Don't just do something nice for her and then feel dejected when her icy facade still doesn't thaw. Tell her how you feel! This is what will melt the ice queen you once knew as a hot tamale. This is what takes real courage, emotionally. (A challenge when you've been brought up having acts of physical bravery affirmed!)

On a positive note, risking rejection by addressing the cause will empower your masculine sense of self. Unlike sneaking around flirting with other women, which initially may grant you a temporary ego boost, but will undermine your ability to problem-solve as it creates a split within your psyche. Leading a double life (from the double-edged sword of the mind) will only make you feel more like a naughty boy than an empowered man who deals with his challenges head on.

A man who is centered in his heart's truth addresses his fears in the present, which continually builds his personal power. This is what gives a man great presence, when he dares to give his reality all his commitment and focus. Anything less is the cowardice of a boy who is unconsciously looking to others to validate him as a man.

Women (and feminine dominant men), if you feel yourself withdrawing, closing down like a flower shutting its petals or a drawbridge clanking shut, depending on the degree of hurt - speak up! Don't just implode, grow a hemorrhoid and sulk. For unless you risk further hurt by being completely honest, you won't know whether true resolution and growth is possible with your partner, which will prolong or continue doubts. The longer this unhealed situation persists, the more anxious and emotionally unbalanced you will feel within yourself, further undermining your ability to act appropriately on your behalf.

Similarly, if your male (or masculine dominant) partner confides in you that they are having doubts about your relationship or feels attracted to another, don't shoot them down in cold blood as this takes real courage. Instead, breathe and acknowledge your own reaction. Then commend them for their honesty and commitment to truth. Sure, you may need to buy yourself some time to deal with your own reaction before you can discuss solutions, but do recognize that this moment offers real transparency, so it is a window for growth. It's how we respond that determines whether our relationship will transcend the challenge or be destroyed by it.

Can You Handle the Truth?

Ultimately, there is no higher honor one can bestow upon someone than their deepest truth. It is singularly the most important quality one must observe, if we are to be in right relationship with ourselves and those around us. It is the cornerstone of the emerging consciousness of Sacred Union. For when we lie to ourselves, we lie to all of existence. Equally, we cannot lie to another without lying to ourselves.

Denial serves no purpose whatsoever, it only prolongs and accumulates more suffering. To make the shift to realize our human potential, we must simply awaken to and honor the truth. This means supporting those who dare speak the truth, be it in our personal lives or publicly to support those who risk all, to alert us to injustice. (Edward Snowden and Julian Assuage come to mind.) This means acknowledging what is true for us in each moment and speaking our truth and acting upon it. For only when we walk in truth, can we honor those who speak their personal truth to us, even if it's not comfortable to hear.

> 'Eden is not a place. It is a way
> of being, which is transparent.'
>
> Tanishka

For us to have truly blessed, graceful and loving interactions with others, we must be completely honest with each other. We need to share how we truly feel, and mean what we say. As a culture, we have been so afraid of being emotionally, psychologically and energetically naked, that we have made it

25

illegal to appear in our natural physical state in front of one another. When we have nothing to hide, image will become a thing of the past, along with all the industries that pray upon our insecurities, urging us to enhance our image.

No relationship can survive without honesty. No civilization can survive without honesty. No human being can survive, if they are not honest with themselves.

Suffice to say, we must each be prepared to look like a 'fool for love' if we are to truly open our hearts to give and receive love. It is the first principle, the first vow of conscious partnership. It is the sacrament of the base chakra, our physical energy center, and our survival depends on it.

♆ Transcending Co-dependent Gender Roles

From Wedlock to Empowered Inter-dependence

Since the sexual revolution of the 1960s, many have rebelled against the polarized gender roles that have been modeled to us throughout the Piscean Age (1 AD - 2000 AD). As a result, many have gone to the other extreme, creating a cultural case of unconscious transgender identity. For example, many men have rejected the role of the traditional male in their quest to distance themselves from the unconscious masculine role models who they viewed as being imbalanced and completely lacking in feminine qualities. Unfortunately, many have 'thrown the baby out with the bath water', rejecting their masculinity altogether due to a lack of positive male mentors who could model the empowered sacred masculine.

Many boys also witnessed their mother's anxiety within their household while growing up which led them to anticipate their mother's needs in a bid to make them happy. This habitual pattern can make it near impossible for a man to identify his own needs or make a decision, as he has no idea what he really wants. In relationship, these men often strive to please and over-give, becoming martyrs for a cause as they strive unconsciously to be 'the perfect little man' to strong women (or feminine dominant men) onto whom they transfer their feelings from their mother.

The Disempowered Masculine

The legacy of this childhood dynamic is known culturally as the SNAG (Sensitive New Age Guy), a passive man who unconsciously seeks to please in all his adult relationships. This inhibits his ability to share his authentic thoughts and feelings for fear of making others unhappy. Typically, men with such a disempowered masculine will seek out dominant women to win their approval in an unconscious attempt to heal their mother / son childhood wound. This results in them being agreeable rather than authentic, so their female partners eventually reject them for being insipid and not 'manly' enough. This is because women unconsciously want a man to be personally empowered enough in his masculinity to assert his own direction.

For men who grew up feeling unable to express their rage at their fathers and society for oppressing the feminine, adopting a passive approach to life was an understandable survival strategy. Now, however, it is time to confront the fear of rejection and commit to speaking their naked truth if they want to enjoy healthy relationships with women where they are not being dominated, abused, bullied or continually rejected for being 'too nice.'

If men in relationships unconsciously embody the 'shadow feminine' by being passive rather than assertive (the 'positive masculine'), they will be reluctant, unwilling or afraid to take the lead in decision-making - for example, never taking the initiative to suggest a holiday destination, restaurant or making a surprise booking. This passivity means it falls to their partner to 'wear the pants' by organizing everything. Over time this leads to resentment - even in women who prefer to be dominant, lest they feel unsafe and out of control. They will lose respect for their partner, viewing them as another dependent they must think for and organize. This resentment is what kills a woman's sex drive.

The feminine wants to trust she can completely surrender to the masculine. If she feels she can't trust him to function as an independent adult, she won't entrust her deepest vulnerabilities into his safekeeping. What's more, if she's the one making the lion's share of decisions and organizing their shared life as the dominant, active polarity, she is not going to be overly receptive. For receptivity is the feminine polarity, so a woman who's operating out of her masculine won't be approachable, let alone receptive to his tentative advances. Similarly, standing up to a woman who's in 'manic mode' may be scary but ultimately it will help calm the beast as she will be grateful to have help and respect you for being proactive. In homoerotic unions, the same dynamic occurs as all coupling, regardless of physical gender, embodies this interaction of these gender poles, with one operating more out of their feminine and the other the masculine. So, better to risk making plans that your feminine counterpart disapproves of, than never daring to take the initiative at all!

Case Study of a SNAG

I once met a beautiful man who touched my soul because he truly saw and honored me and the sacred feminine, but unfortunately this had come at the cost of his masculine. Standing beside him, I often felt I had more testosterone than he did. So while I thoroughly enjoyed his company as a brother, there was no attraction due to his lack of male mojo. The degree to which he had been emasculated was evident in how he drove, walked, ran etc. For example, he was erratic and indecisive rather than trusting his instincts to lead or take a risk. He slouched and schlepped, rather than walking with a straight back and a sense of purpose, because he was yet to find one. (A man without a purpose is lost and his posture telegraphed this.)

When I observed him speaking with his 'trad male' unconscious brother, he became tongue-tied and unsure of himself as he could feel his brother's judgment and dismissal of him as a man. He even craved sugary treats like a woman to self-soothe his inner child, unlike a traditional unconscious male who would be inclined to use alcohol or work to distract and shut down his sensitivity. He then revealed to me how he had been a big pot smoker.

Author's Note: Marijuana increases a man's passivity, so dependence on this dependence is common amongst men who have rebelled against their father's insensitivity, embodying more of their feminine nature than their masculine. This tendency is compounded by the 'stoner lifestyle' of being a 'night owl' so they are powered more by the lunar light of the feminine than the solar light of the masculine.

After years of pot abuse it was as if he was perpetually stoned, despite being clean for a year because he embodied the qualities one exhibits when under the influence of that plant deva. Unfortunately, pot smoking has become a pandemic amongst men since the 1960s due to their unconscious effort to connect with the feminine within. When this is done consciously, men awaken the archetypal energy of 'The Green Man', the masculine aspect who governs the heart. Embodiment of 'The Green Man' connects a man to the Earth Mother and her natural cycles. Whilst it does offer a shamanic doorway out of the limited viewpoint of the rational mind, for many, it becomes a habitual smokescreen to avoid taking responsibility for oneself and the state of one's life.

For a man to empower his masculinity, he needs to detoxify from his self-deceptive, co-dependent relationships with feminine plant devas who offer him an unhealthy substitute for intimacy, with a clear vessel for the sacred feminine. Attuning to the solar wheel, arising with the dawn will also help him dismiss melancholic feelings of pessimism and self-doubt.

The Connection Between Piercings and Gender Disempowerment

My SNAG friend also shared how he had pierced the head of his penis with a gold bar, an act that he'd been inspired to do by an ex-female lover who was into body piercing for erotic pleasure. It struck me like a bolt of lightning that his piercing symbolized how he had crucified his masculinity to win her approval and ever since this metal object had continued to disempower the flow of energy in his magic wand. (In magical traditions, it is understood that metal obstructs the flow of body chi, which is why wands are traditionally made of wood or crystal rather than metal.)

A few days before this conversation, another brother had his tongue-piercing fall out while speaking to me and he acknowledged it was as a result of what I'd said when addressing a group of young men about porn addiction. So he concluded he no longer needed his piercing.

It then occurred to me that body scarifications were signposts indicating where one was literally scarred and disempowered. This is because the body holds within its cells that which we have not expressed. So when we have healed an issue, the body will often reject the piercing. I found it interesting that my friend told me initially the piercing in his penis was exciting, offering heightened sexual pleasure, but then he forgot about it as it felt numb.

This is because there are two paths to ecstasy - devotion or destruction. If we engage in a behavior that is dangerous or self-abusive, it will initially offer us the thrill of excitement, but will ultimately deplete us, leaving us shut down or numb, so it takes a greater and greater risk to top the previous high. This is why people become addicts, always needing a greater flirtation with the dark to make them feel truly alive, since they are numbing themselves to avoid feeling their insecurities and emotional pain. This tendency is illustrated by sexual addicts who ram larger and larger objects into themselves, or experiment with asphyxiation to feel a euphoric high, or cutters who accelerate self-harm flesh wounds, or substance abusers who increase the dosage.

The Disempowered Feminine: Ball-breaking Amazons

Equally, many women have become so focused on achieving external power by acquiring financial autonomy that they discard men who don't measure up to their rational ideal as inconsequential. This attitude signals they are operating more out of their masculine polarity than their feminine, with a tendency to view others in terms of what use they are to them. This occurs when women focus on acquiring security above everything else, which stems from a fear that they can't rely upon the masculine to provide and protect them. This creates an inner sense of competition as they try to prove to men that they don't need them because they are 'as good' or 'better than men'. This results in them unconsciously striving to be 'taken seriously in a man's world', an unconscious ambition that leads them to undervalue and diminish their feminine qualities, like compassion. Hence many security-driven women seek out a man who lives up to their checklist, rather than begin the process of loving the imperfections in themselves before seeking a mate.

Many women are also piercing their erogenous zones, such as their labia and nipples. This fashion trend is more prevalent in gay and lesbian communities where there is often more overt wounding and rejection of their foundation gender.

Culturally, we are so disconnected from the feminine realm of nature that we now have a pandemic of infertile Western women seeking out man-made science to conceive. In addition to modern women being so disconnected from the lunar cycle, this sad state of affairs can also be attributed to aberrations of nature including our widespread use of plastics, pharmaceuticals and agra-industry toxins in our water, synthetic lighting and technology undermining healthy endocrine function, EMF pollutants distorting natural biorhythms and GMO contamination of our food supply.

When a woman connects to nature and her natural cycles, she becomes more receptive as she becomes more connected to her sensual needs and the extent to which her emotional state informs her health. When a woman is operating out of her masculine polarity, she leads from her rational self, which often disconnects her from the natural world, seeing it as less important than the world of men - civilized society. This is why only seeking to address infertility with practical methods such as IVF often serves to create more hysteria for the inner feminine. To watch me speak about this phenomena visit

http://goo.gl/CLn1cy

For a woman to re-empower her feminine polarity she needs to start by sighting the moon every night to regulate her endocrine system, and remove herself from over-exposure to fluorescent light which plays havoc with female hormones. Ensuring one sleeps during the 10pm to 2am lunar zenith is also key as this is when our endocrine system resets and our body detoxifies and repairs. If we then exacerbate late nights with caffeine and high GI foods upon waking, we place even more stress upon our feminine cycle. For more info on restoring endocrine health, read 'Womancode' by Alisa Vitti.

I have also witnessed women fall pregnant after getting a puppy or kitten, getting into their garden and regularly attending Red Tent women's circles to empower their lunar / psycho-emotional self. These lifestyle adjustments are best made in addition to acupuncture and herbs, which are helpful in rebalancing female hormone levels and promoting healthy flow of chi. Even learning a partner dance, such as salsa can assist masculine-dominant women to follow and passive men to lead. Anchoring this in the muscle memory of the somatic body is a great start to re-empowering one's female foundation gender.

It's Written in the Stars

There are no mistakes in the divine plan, so it is both timely and necessary that women have risen up since the twentieth century to express their truth, values, traditions, ideas and talents. A trend that has been further activated by the two Venus transits we experienced in 2004 and 2012 when the planet, Venus crossed our sun, illuminating the strengths of the feminine while inciting rage at how the sacred feminine had been denied. In the wake of this transit, we have seen many respond to the inner call to take action on restoring the balance on our planet, be it in their own lives, their community or on the global stage.

The solar feminine is the warrior aspect of Venus, which a woman must develop if she is to mature from the maiden / princess aspect of Aphrodite, who seeks validation for her love and beauty, to the self-assured mature Queen who has learned to make self-honoring decisions so she can confidently shine as a star. This is the embodiment of the mature Venus, known in ancient Babylon as Ishtar, which means 'star'.

The ancients revered and studied the stars as they understood the significance cosmology played in charting their course through the natural cycles which impacted their everyday lives. The ancient myths were the teaching parables for the psychodramas evoked by passing celestial events.

For example, in the myth of Ishtar, she, as the Queen of Heaven descends through the seven veils of illusion (the seven dimensions of understanding symbolized by the chakras in our human energy field which are governed by the seven inner planets). When she arrives in the human realm, she is naked and vulnerable, stripped of her otherworldly powers. This describes what occurs in the microcosm when we incarnate and forget ourselves to be all knowing divine beings. It also describes what happens in the macrocosm, where we cyclically descend into the dark astrological ages, followed by the light. This phenomenon is known as the precession of the equinoxes.

We are emerging from a descent through the dark age of Pisces into the 'Golden Age of Light' known as the Age of Aquarius. This return into the light was symbolized by the divine cross being intercepted by the cross of matter on the 21st of December, 2012, which formed Ishtar's sacred symbol, the eight-pointed star on the galactic equator. This signaled her return to the Great Above, taking up her rightful place in the Heavens. This heralds the resurrected Goddess re-emerging after much suppression within our World Soul.

As outlined in volume one, Ishtar ascends to her rightful place by making self-honoring choices that enable her to bridge her way home by climbing the inner Tree of Life. This process of journeying up through the major energy centers (chakras) to become self-aware is de-coded in my first two books so I won't extrapolate on that here.

We can, however, see the return of the empowered sacred feminine through the widespread global embracing of yoga, holistic healing, Goddess fashions, women's spirituality, sacred space interior design and projects which honor community, the earth and her natural resources at an ever increasing rate since the shift in 2012.

Reaching for the Stars!

This is an exciting time to be on the planet with so many heeding the call to play their part in restoring the balance. It is important to note, however, that this process of ascension to merge with the light of the divine must start with the foundation of reconnection with Mother Earth through positive self-care. Without this adequate grounding, like Icarus, we will blow the circuitry of our nervous system as our kundalini (life force) accelerates beyond what we can integrate, and we experience symptoms ranging from mania to psychosis. (For more info, refer to Volume One.)

So too, a woman cannot be truly powerful, out in the world effecting sustainable change, if she has not first healed her foundation gender, which is her connection to the natural world and her body. We do this, first and foremost, by parenting our inner child whose unresolved emotions will cause illness in our bodies if we deny them. Only then can we reach skyward by developing our own inner masculine, without becoming unbalanced as an 'imitation male'.

Meanwhile, the men on our planet are reaching deep into themselves and the Earth, to become more grounded, humble, connected with their hearts, bodies and children, by embodying the archetype of the Green Man. This is the aspect I mentioned earlier, who lives sustainably in accordance with nature, a direct contrast to the cultural modeling our men have received growing up. This takes courage when we consider they were conditioned to emulate the patriarchal Sky Father who was silent, strong and all-powerful, ruling sternly from above, disconnected him from his heart and those around him. With the return of the Green Man into our collective psyche, we are seeing more men dropping their kids off at school, pushing prams and finding ways to leave the rat race and work from home. As men seek to balance themselves by embodying their inner feminine, it is imperative they don't recreate the dynamic of being the domestic servant by polarizing in their feminine at a cost to their masculine. This is where attending regular men's circles can support and encourage men to share their heart's passion with the world so they can identify and pursue their true purpose rather than just settle for any job to provide for their dependents.

The symbol of the six pointed star which is the symbol for the New Age illustrates how men are retreating down to the womb of Mother Earth to heal, embodying their disowned feminine, just as women are rising up, by embodying the traits of their disowned masculine as torch bearers, leading the way to restore balance.

This Sacred Union symbol illustrates two intercepting triangles, which represent the integration of feminine and masculine polarities. The feminine triangle points down toward the Earth and the masculine triangle points up toward the sun. This symbolizes how women need to connect with the Earth and the wisdom of their bodies as a foundation before seeking success out in the world, and how men need to find their purpose before they can make a commitment to raising a family. This is a time in our evolution of each seeking the opposite within to become whole.

So it is both timely and necessary that Earth-connected women are soaring upward and outward externally, embodying the two sides of Ishtar, the warrioress / lover to share their understanding with the greater good. Just as we need our men to be present in their hearts on the home front, directly involved in the raising and mentoring of our collective children. Where possible, the ideal is for both genders, irrespective of sexual preference, to find a balance between both nurturing (the feminine) and providing (the masculine).

By exploring these extremes, rejecting our foundation gender, then accepting responsibility to heal it, we can consciously choose to embody the gender into which we incarnated. Only then can we create partnerships that are not a reaction against our parental and societal conditioning.

The Key to True Love

Healing the Brother / Sister Connection

In 2008 I received a transmission, that it was time to awaken the Grail codes on the planet. (Coincidentally I saw two others had received the same message the same week!) The Grail is the quest for ultimate truth. A truth, which, when realized will restore peace on Earth.

Not entirely sure what this transmission referred to, I followed my inner guidance to create Grail circles for men and women to balance their feminine and masculine energies in accordance with the sun and moon signs occurring at each full moon. At the completion of the final circle, after we'd journeyed around the complete astrological mandala, I received the following message:

'We all need to learn how to do brotherhood / sisterhood before we can journey sacred union with our beloved.'

This is brotherly / sisterly love - known as agape love. Agape love is what we give freely without expecting anything in return. So instead of sizing up members of the opposite sex in terms of personal gain, categorizing them as a potential conquest or threat, we instead adopt an attitude of being open hearted, giving of ourselves freely. The process to awaken this love is done in three stages:

1. Learning about the Archetypes

The universal aspects that make up our psyche are called archetypes. They have been personified in myth, as Gods and

Goddesses. Deconstructing their myths enables us to understand how we re-enact their universal stories in our own lives. So by using archetypes as a map of our feminine and masculine psyches, we can empower each facet. This means we experience less conflict, both internally and externally. Archetypes are associated with the fourth dimension which is governed by our fourth chakra, the heart, which is the central chakra. Applying this framework of understanding means we can be more centered as we take responsibility for the sum of all our parts. This process of self-awareness opens the heart and is essential to balancing our masculine / feminine halves. (For a full explanation of the feminine and masculine archetypes within your psyche see volume one.)

2. Same-sex Sharing Circles

Before we can interact harmoniously with our opposite gender, we first need to first heal our foundation gender. This is accelerated through participating in sisterhood circles for women and brotherhood circles for men. This process of sitting in circle, taking turns to speak one's inner truth, in a space of mutual respect and reverence, anchors an experience of being seen, heard, accepted and loved by reflections of our own gender. Whilst a simple process, it opens our heart to brotherly / sisterly love, through shared trust and intimacy. It also enables us to feel held and supported, which can be profoundly healing if we didn't feel truly seen, heard, understood and supported by our parents. For unless we can open our hearts and share our vulnerabilities with our brothers and sisters, we won't feel empowered to share our deep fragility with our opposite.

Sharing circles support our wellbeing on all levels. It is what we naturally do as human beings, without the distraction of TV. We gravitate towards each other and sit in a circle to share our thoughts and feelings. We are communal by nature. Without this intrinsic human need being met, we experience increased stress levels, community breakdown, family breakdown and mental health disorders.

How Sharing Circles Assists Our Mental Health

In our human energy system, the sacral chakra (our emotional center) is located in our belly, below our solar plexus chakra (our lower mental center). This placement indicates we must first address our emotional wounds before we can heal mental health issues, such as depression and anxiety. Our culture has denied the importance of our emotional needs, due to the dismissing of anything feminine as less important. As a result, both men and women have been emotionally abused or neglected to varying degrees. The emotional center is where our inner child sits within our personal energy field, so when this aspect becomes overwhelmed with unresolved emotional experiences, our constructed persona literally falls apart as the mental self can no longer, 'keep it all together' creating what is referred to as a 'mental breakdown'.

Sharing circles create a safe container for sharing all of our unresolved emotional experiences, so they don't accumulate and overwhelm us. This emotional clarity creates mental clarity, supporting our ability to function mentally. For a sharing circle to be a truly safe space it needs to be facilitated by one who has journeyed to the depth of their own emotional wounds so they possess the compassion, empathy, reverence and receptivity to intuitively guide participants through the unexplored areas of their psyche with gentleness and strength. It is through this combination of qualities that participants feel safe enough to open and let go and experience their vulnerability. The relief in sharing taboo thoughts, feelings, memories, hopes, dreams, regrets, fears and experiences creates an immediate bond. This is developed through the shared experience of personal self-expression, which generates humor through the recognition of similar feelings, compassion for the suffering of others and gratitude for insights others provide. All of which engenders trust in ourselves and the process of life. This is both life-changing and life-affirming, gifting participants confidence they take into the world to effect even greater positive change.

A circle creates a vortex of energy, with no beginning or end. Within that energy field, we are innately guided to move and share the focus, attention and energy. This promotes a paradigm of relating where everyone gets their needs met. When we have an experience of our authentic needs being met socially, we can recreate this dynamic in other settings.

'The Red Tent' was made famous by the novel of the same name by Anita Diamant. Like all great works of fiction, it had such a widespread universal appeal because it rang true, as if channeled intuitively. It illustrated how central the custom of the monthly moon lodge was to the sisters of the Biblical, Joseph. 'The Red Tent' is now a global movement as women heed the inner calling to gather and remember their sacred customs and teachings.

To me, the popularity of this book and the subsequent global embrace of this phenomena is proof that this ancient feminine custom is an intrinsic and natural function of a conscious humanity. It is a practice we have known in multiple civilizations and lifetimes, despite it not being documented by patriarchal historians in their 'his-tory'. For so many around the globe to be intuitively following their inner guidance to create the same shared experience affirms 'The Red Tent' is a place within us. It is our womb, simply externalized for us to create and receive the mothering we need to grow on a cyclic basis.

As we awaken to the understanding that men also have an inner feminine which requires the same emotional support, for our boys to grow into emotionally intelligent men, more men's circles will form, similarly out of an intuitive need.

3. Soul Friendships with the Opposite Gender

Given how polarized we have historically been in our gender expression, the majority of folk are heterosexual. This has hindered our ability to form heart-centered friendships with members of the opposite sex without the agenda of our lower selves rearing its head. (Pun intentional.)

In an unaware society, the majority of folk operate out of their lower selves which are governed by their lowest three energy centers. This means, they base their reality only on what they perceive through their physical senses of: sight, touch, taste, hearing and smell. These are therefore the means through which they assess a potential mate. So someone operating from their lower self looks for someone who, primarily looks and smells good and the unconscious mating dance begins.

The Bonding of Lower Selves through Un-sacred Sex

In this 3D mating ritual, a couple bonds very quickly in the lower three chakras. This means they have sex, bonding their primal animal selves. Since we are alchemical beings, this act enmeshes us energetically at the base chakra. This energy center governs the fight, flight or freeze survival response, which links our survival fears to our new partner, creating a sense of physical dependency. This is why those with a strong base / sexual connection can't bear to be physically apart for long and often move in to co-habit very quickly, so they can take care of each other physically.

Once bonded physically, they fuse in the sacral chakra, (the emotional center), taking it in turns to soothe and take care of each other's inner child so they feel mothered or fathered.

The more the bond strengthens emotionally between a couple, the more they are likely to start fuse in the solar plexus, echoing each other's views and opinions. Unifying their viewpoint affirms they are not alone, so in finding agreeance together they feel righteous, as if anyone who differs with them, is wrong. By bonding in the lower mental plane, they feel more secure about their identity and beliefs. (This is akin to merging with the group mind of a religious group or football club, to increase one's sense of personal identity and power.)

Needless to say, when your primary connection with the opposite sex is polarized through these lower centers, you're going to attract or repel strongly like magnets. (If you recognize yourself in the above description, don't worry as we must identify with our shadow, if we are to take responsibility for ourselves and grow.)

When we only relate to the animal self, child self and ego in the opposite gender we get a distorted view of them. For example, so long as you both are fused and feeding off each other like leeches during the honeymoon phase, you affirm how much you love and adore the opposite sex. Then the disowned self surfaces, disgruntlement grows into despair and you reject the opposite sex in favor of your same sex friends. That is, until you miss the excitement of dancing with your opposite and seek out a new dancing partner for another round which ends the same way. Not surprisingly this see-saw approach deteriorates one's confidence in dancing harmoniously with members of the other camp. This is reversed with homoerotic individuals who reject same sex lovers to hang out with their opposite sex friends.

The answer is to zip up your lower chakras and meet members of the opposite sex through your heart and upper chakras. So what does that inner dialogue look like?

Heart: 'Who are you?'

When we meet someone from this center we are genuinely interested in getting to know them, in a spirit of acceptance without seeking anything from them. We then relax and share our true essence with them, rather than trying to impress them with information such as: what our ego knows, what we've done, what we have acquired or by how we look.

Throat: 'What experiences have you weathered?'

When we meet someone from the throat center we willingly share our inner truth, which includes our vulnerabilities, with complete transparency. This invites them to do the same. This does not mean playing the victim in an effort to evoke pity and be taken care of, but rather being honoring of each other's sensitivities. This is the second gate of truth, which ensures safety and mutual respect for each other's human fragility.

Third Eye: 'What are your perceptions?'

When we meet our opposite from the third eye, rather than regurgitating the facts from the morning's headlines and sharing gossip, we ponder our existence together and the reality that lies beneath the external circus. We genuinely want to know how they see life and the universe so we can potentially broaden our understanding and know them more deeply by seeing reality through their eyes.

Crown: 'What is your bliss?'

When we seek connection from our spiritual center we are wanting to know them as an emanation of the divine. We do this by asking what makes them feel divine - at one with creation. Connection at this gate is an invitation to inspire each other so both feel uplifted by the experience of meeting the other. Not competitively, but as divine complements.

'Do to others as you would have them do to you.'

Jesus. Luke 6:31

Only when we can truly meet and appreciate the opposite gender as their soul selves can we restore our trust in the opposite sex. When we discover the joy of connecting with our soul brothers and sisters, we become more aware of the strengths and beauty in our own inner masculine and feminine. We also gain more insight into every man and woman, which enhances all of our relationships.

Without the distraction of seduction in friendships, or the unconscious projection of our partner as our savior, we can see our opposite as our teacher and mirror. This creates a safe and mutually honoring dynamic. This attitude engenders compassion for our opposite, dissolving the sense of superiority and judgment we may have harbored toward the opposite sex as a form of self-defense.

Compassion is the quality we must develop if we are to break the pattern of unconsciously using the opposite sex for our own ego gratification. This attitudinal shift opens up our sensitivity to every brother / sister we meet, so we perceive them as a whole person, rather than a potential conquest. This is a necessary step before embarking on a conscious courtship, as it breaks the unconscious pattern of falling for someone who feels like home, which is someone who'll re-wound us unconsciously in the same way our parents did.

So if we are to break the destructive pattern of re-living our dysfunctional childhood story, of what relationships look, sound and feel like we must abstain from hunting for Mr / Ms Right. Then we stop the unconscious bonding of lower selves, which creates co-dependency. By creating conscious friendships with the opposite sex, we experience transpersonal love, by taking personal responsibility for our own shadow and wounds. This makes it emotionally safe to share our vulnerabilities and insights, while learning to honor our authentic needs, setting boundaries as needed. This experience creates trust in ourselves to not compromise our truth, when interacting with our opposite.

Once we take the dominant connection at the base out of the equation, we can connect in the upper chakras as those aspects are not overshadowed by the demanding lower emotions of the inner child or the sexual addiction of the animal self. This creates a more mature soul connection...like a perfume which has an exquisite aroma, because the base notes are complemented by middle and treble notes. Vibrationally, this kind of relating, where we meet at various energy centers, creates a harmonic connection similar to the resolution of a musical chord in comparison to the dissonance of three consecutive notes being played!

This is a literal truth, as each energy center within our bodies resonates to the musical notes of a scale. This awareness helps us cultivate friendships with the opposite physical gender that literally restore harmony! To anchor this consciousness, I recommend referring to men as 'brothers' and women as 'sisters' (if they are not your lover) and just watch how friendly the world becomes!

To watch my You Tube video on Healing the Gender War visit: http://goo.gl/lHzL1g

How Forgiveness Opens the Soul's Higher Heart

When we can see our brothers and sisters with compassion, we can more easily forgive those who have hurt us in the past. This includes our parents, ex-lovers and even ourselves. For when we truly listen to the experiences and perspectives of a man or woman, with no ulterior motive, we see empathize with them, as we place ourselves in their shoes. It is this approach from which emerges the unity consciousness of 'I Am' when we truly see ourselves reflected in the other. When we open to the perception that, 'I am you and you are me' we awaken the higher heart chakra. This is the energy center located between the heart and the throat. Then, like a flower, our unconditional love for humanity unfolds. This is true agape love - selfless, unconditional love without an agenda. It is the flowering of our consciousness, which starts with compassion for ourselves and then blossoms into compassion for others.

Help from Above

In 1977 the planetoid Chiron was discovered in our galaxy. In ancient mythology, Chiron represents the archetypal energy of brotherly love. As explained in volume one, he is the masculine aspect who governs the throat chakra. His purpose is to transform our wounds into understanding, so we can then teach others from our personal experience. He connects us with our vulnerability, awakening our tenderness and sensitivity, so we can be a true friend to ourselves and others.

Awakening this aspect enables us to live in peace and harmony, which is the lesson of the Aquarian Age (2012-4012 AD). The first step lies in acknowledging our human frailty. For when we connect with our vulnerability, we share more of our inner self with those around us. This creates true emotional intimacy, which is the foundation for conscious community. Before we integrate this aspect, we operate from ego, trying to prove how well we are doing on our own, by projecting a confident persona. It is inevitable that this mask falls as we mature emotionally and psychologically. As a result, many were brought to their knees to confront their own vulnerability in the lead up to the birth of the Aquarian Age on the 21st of December, 2012.

Ever since the discovery of Chiron in 1977, the focus on our personal healing has increased, along with the number of self-help book titles now readily available. One can also observe how those born after 1977 have this aspect anchored within them, resulting in many of our youth dedicating themselves to serve in the healing arts. Those who denied their emotional vulnerability have manifested physical illness or injury as a catalyst to connect with their human frailty.

Because the archetypal energy of Chiron governs the throat, we will also see an increasing number of opportunities for people to let their voice out. Whether that's voicing their opinions on social media, the resurgence of folk music, community choirs, sound healing or devotional chanting events.

All of these activities help to clear energy blocks in the throat chakra, which assists authentic self-expression, including our deepest vulnerabilities. Clearing this gate also assists in healing the union of brother / sister within. Once we harmonize these opposing gender polarities the feminine / masculine energy meridians can flow unimpeded into the third eye (brow chakra) which is where the inner serpents, Ida and Pingala meet to create sacred union within.

☤ How Porn Disempowers and Addicts

The Truth about the Shadow Side of Sex

Porn is programming that anchors an unrealistic expectation of erotic human interaction. It does this by preying on the fantasy of complete submission. This fantasy stems from the natural core desire of the feminine to submit in complete trust to the masculine, and equally from the natural core desire of the masculine to have the feminine completely trust and submit to the masculine.

In an uncontrived situation, a feminine individual completely surrenders to the masculine individual when they trust their partner emotionally, psychologically, physically and energetically. This enables 'her' to let go and become completely receptive to the active masculine. It is a dynamic which occurs organically between two consenting and empowered adults, regardless of gender, if the masculine dominant being has proven themselves to be trustworthy by communicating 'he' truly sees and honors all aspects of 'her' being.

Porn takes this innate yearning within us and manufactures a scenario where the feminine is not seen or honored, but consents anyway, compromising 'her' innate value as a being in her own right. Regardless of the nature of the acts engaged in, this portrays the feminine in a degrading situation. To the masculine, it sends the message that they should be able to find a woman (or toy boy / lady boy) who is willing to submit to them, regardless of how he relates to her.

For women, it sends the message that a sexy woman is one who is disempowered. This is the opposite of the truth. The more genuinely self-accepting and empowered a being is, regardless of their gender, the more attractive they are to others.

This anti-feminine propaganda is created by the collective unconscious masculine who feels powerless, due to a lack of male mentoring, initiation rites and men's circles. Those operating out of a disempowered male psyche fear someone operating out of their feminine will see their weaknesses and reject them. Hence the need to create a fantasy of a woman who will fall for their constructed persona, without question.

A mature, self-aware woman will see and name a man's shadow. That's the role of the feminine in the age-old story of the sexes - a man will meet his fate. Fate being a woman who will insists he must grow if he is to win her hand. She does this by pointing out his disowned aspects - his shadow. As illustrated in the fairy tale, 'Peter Pan'. The story about the eternal boy who won't grow up. He meets a girl, Wendy, who encourages him to accept his shadow. She does this, not to emasculate him, but out of love, so he is whole and human and can grow beyond the world of delusional dreams and potential with the other 'lost boys'. This story illustrates the immature masculine who's not prepared to face and heal his inner conflict of opposites. This results in him continually running from intimacy and responsibility. His unresolved issues play out externally as constant battles with his 'dark father' (Darth Vader) portrayed by Captain Hook. Peter Pan is a modern day portrayal of the ancient mythic protagonist, Eros - a beautiful boy who was self-centered and didn't know himself because he had never faced himself in the mirror. This is the role of a conscious partner, just as the moon reflects the light of the sun. So when his partner, Psyche (meaning soul) tried to hold the light of truth up to Eros, the eternal boy he always ran away...and she heartbroken, descended into the underworld to find self-love.

Men and women have re-enacted this universal story throughout the past few millennia of patriarchal consciousness. As a result, many women have compromised their authentic selves in an effort to appear unthreatening so they can keep the affections of their immature man. This has meant relegating their emotional needs and mothering their men. The women who played the role of the 'good girl' or 'good wife' never grew up either. Instead they behaved in a submissive way to ensure they were taken care of financially. They ensured the status quo by staying silent or only venting their true frustration to their girlfriends, rather than risk speaking directly to their mate, to avoid taking the risk of being rejected for their true self.

Why We've Seen an Increased Prevalence of Porn

We have been experiencing a rapid awakening in consciousness. Ever since the Aquarian Age energies were felt during the cusp which started in the 1960s ushering in the collective return of the archetypes of Lilith and Pan. This primal force of authentic self-expression shook the foundations of our 'civilized' world, demanding power to the people.

This awakening was exacerbated by the rising of kundalini (primal feminine energy) from within the center of the Earth herself. This energy began to rise in 1980, a phenomena which was measured by scientists, who observed the Earth's heartbeat (known as the Schuumann's resonance) was quickening. If we view this from a cosmological perspective, Gaia, the Earth Mother was waking up her children from their sleep state, to remember the totality of their identity.

We see the evidence of this phenomena in the increased environmental awareness which has sparked a growing number of Earth festivals, tribal fashions like dreadlocks and tattoos, people learning, owning and making indigenous instruments like didgeridoos and drums, organic whole food cafes, adobe mud brick housing, recycling and wildlife conservation initiatives, eco-tourism and sustainable educational programs. Such cultural trends indicate the positive re-emergence of the base chakra archetypes: Pan, the nature man who is not afraid of the wild, befriending his own beastly instincts and Lilith, the wild woman, whose power is her connection to the Earth and her natural cycles.

With the re-emergence of these primal aspects within our psyche, more men have acted out their primal urges, seeking out partners with no sexual shame or inhibition. Meanwhile, women have started to awaken their erotic nature and along with it their authentic power, resulting in them saying, 'No' to situations that don't r-e-s-p-e-c-t their truth.

So modern day men are responding to an increased surge of kundalini, in conjunction with conservative sexual taboos relaxing, without the empowerment of their authentic masculinity. So they feel the growing need to assert their masculinity while fearing humiliation by a growing number of women who have awakened to their power. In addition, there is an increased accessibility to sexual images through the internet.

Identifying the Cycle of Porn Addiction So You Can Get Off the Rat Wheel

Unfortunately, many 'civilized' men have sought out their need to explore their inner Pan in a covert way. Such as exploring their sexual fantasies online, rather than discussing their authentic erotic desires with their partners. Similarly, many women who have not empowered their inner wild woman, scapegoat their partners for 'not growing up' rather than own their own shadow. When both of these aspects are disempowered, it creates a cycle where she rejects him for not being mature, so he rejects her by fantasizing about compliant girls. The more we consciously embrace the positive traits and qualities of Pan and Lilith, the more authentic and empowered we feel, resulting in unbridled erotic intimacy, which only occurs in unions that honor a deep sharing of truth.

Honoring Lilith and Pan

As with any aspect, the more we embrace it in a healthy and loving way, the less it expresses itself in a distorted and destructive way. To empower these primal aspects we need to first understand them. Below is just a quick thumbnail to recap - for a more comprehensive overview refer to volume one.

Lilith is the authentic wild woman. She is the aspect of a woman who activates a man's self-awareness by making him aware of that which he doesn't see in himself. This is what awakens his journey up the inner Tree of Life to become enlightened. She is the serpentine Goddess of kundalini, the awakener. Instead, she has been cast as the harbinger of doom, amidst the distortion placed upon the collective feminine as 'evil temptresses' not to be trusted. This was a deliberate act, to keep men unaware and therefore submissive to the shadow elite, who perpetuated fear of growth with threats of Hell and damnation. In ancient mythology, Lilith was the original woman who was rejected by her partner, Adam for not being agreeable and compliant. The patriarchs replaced Lilith with Eve as a prototype for she was a girl who never demanded he grow up. Understanding this story as a dysfunctional template for human relating, is essential for both men and women who want a foundation for a new template of conscious, mutual growth, based on trust and respect.

Lilith is the primal, erotic feminine who men are instinctually attracted to. She is often depicted as dark haired, opinionated, physically liberated and unashamed. She represents the lower nature of the feminine, like a lioness or wild cat. She is the Sphinx who guards the temple - a woman's body, which is a vessel for the divine feminine. When the Lilith aspect is consciously awakened within a woman, like the Queen of Sheba, she will pose a riddle to those who seek entry to her palatial interior. They must answer correctly or entry will be denied. In other words, a man who is not capable of honoring the feminine within himself, won't have the awareness to honor it in her. (More info about the riddle of the Queen of Sheba in the later chapter, 'Words of Wisdom From The Holy Couple.')

Pan is the authentic wild man who has been demonized as 'the devil' in monotheistic religious doctrines. He is a part of us, regardless of our gender. He is simply our primal masculine expression. When empowered, he has a genuine reverence, understanding of and affinity for the natural world, including his counterpart, Lilith. When he is suppressed, he fears nature, so reacts by trying to dominate the natural world, which includes the chaos of the feminine. This attitude of domination ultimately threatens both his survival and the survival of his habitat as one cannot live out of alignment with what is natural and thrive.

Both of these aspects, when integrated, enable us to be our natural selves, honoring our innate truth. Eroticism and truth go hand in hand. So long as there is denial or deceit in our relating, we will limit our unbridled erotic expression and connection. Truth is the ultimate aphrodisiac. Truth is the highest form of love and the greatest honor one can bestow on another. Until we make that shift to being completely naked and honest with ourselves and each other, immature women will suppress their frustrations (and passion) by mothering men and immature men will reject intimacy with 'real women' in favor of girls they can dominate. Ultimately the empowerment of these aspects unblocks our self-expression at the first gate - the base chakra. This frees us to transcend power plays and stand naked in every sense, risking all for truth.

How Porn Impacts Upon the Masculine

Porn is masculine domination propaganda which repeatedly shows images of a thin, hairless, doll-like girl compliantly satisfying every whim of a man's lower nature, without asking anything in return. This feeds the illusion that the ideal woman is not real - i.e. curvaceous and hairy (symbolizing a mature and fertile natural woman). Instead, it imprints the synthetic notion that the ideal woman is completely artificial. She is bleached, waxed, tanned, plucked, dyed and acting the way she thinks he wants her to act. She is an illusion, the great deceiver! (Evil laughter...Whoa Ha Ha!)

With porn, a man can project upon a woman, whatever thought responses he wants her to have. In return, he can temporarily delude himself that the onscreen woman is offering herself to him without asserting any conditions so he feels the unconditional love he felt as a baby. (We feel this unconditional love as babies because our ego has not developed so our parents reflect back to us our own open-hearted acceptance of them. As our ego develops, we challenge them with our own individual thoughts and needs and subsequently feel the loss of their unconditional love.) So those who are emotionally immature unconsciously seek out someone who will love them, without asking anything in return, like an infant.

It isn't just porn that perpetuates the false expectation of a man finding a compliant girl who will try to keep his affections by always being nice and serving everyone else at a cost to herself. It is anchored repetitively in our collective psyche through the media, including ad campaigns, commercial films, TV, radio and magazines. One only needs to apply the Bechdel test to modern day prime time TV and box office films. This test asks three questions of a film:

1. Are there at least two women featured?

2. Do they have a conversation - about something other than a man?

3. Are they referred to by name?

(N.B. The original 'Bechdel Test' (/ˈbɛkdəl/ bek-dəl) asks whether a work of fiction features at least two women who talk to each other about something other than a man.) http://en.wikipedia.org/wiki/Bechdel_test

One man publicly questioning this is Colin Stokes, whose talk on You Tube is well worth a watch: 'The Hidden Meanings in Kids' Movies' by Colin Stokes: http://goo.gl/pYelBV

Six Ways Porn Is Debilitating for Men

1. Energetically he will become dependent on a machine for arousal.

2. His opportunities for real affection and intimacy will decrease.

3. He will become less able to relate to and connect with real women.

4. He will seek darker and more taboo fantasies in an effort to feel the same rush he felt initially by engaging in this forbidden fruit, leading to inner conflict, shame and guilt.

5. He will experience an increase in erectile dysfunction as there is no transmission of kundalini life force to activate his inner fire.

6. He will feel depleted and tired due to his constant need to ejaculate, which expends his life force.

For more great insights and scientific proof on how harmful porn is watch these great Ted talks on You Tube:

'Why I Stopped Watching Porn' by Ran Gavrieli
http://goo.gl/MwZV6k

'The Great Porn Experiment' by Gary Wilson http://goo.gl/EAiPSt

The Global Cost of Porn

Most porn users are unaware that by focusing on this disempowering fantasy, as they generate their sexual chi, they are unwittingly engaging in a form of black magic. Those who practice the conscious use of energy, know when one raises sexual energy, while focusing on a desire, as they release the energy raised, with a focused intent, they literally charge that idea into manifested form. This principle is used by advertisers, evangelical churches and entrepreneurs - getting people so excited, they buy or donate!

But I'm not Hurting Anyone!

Literally 'getting off' to fantasies of domination and degradation of the feminine keeps the patriarchal (unconscious / dark masculine) consciousness anchored, within both the individual and collective psyche. This is an act of abuse, to self and other when one considers the energetic ramifications of this dark ritualistic behavior. Those who don't acknowledge the energetic nature of the universe, excuse this shadow indulgence with the excuse, 'It's not hurting anyone - what I do in the privacy of my own home!' Unfortunately, when one is unconscious of the effects and underlying intent of their thoughts and behavior, they deny any accountability, a hallmark of the immature masculine ego.

The feminine is one half of us and all of existence. So when we engage in misogynistic behavior we are undermining and wounding our own inner feminine which is what men need to embody, to feel whole and create enduring partnerships. Continuing to hurt one's own feminine self, by feeding the neurosis of the dark masculine only hurts oneself. For men who habitually indulge in this cyber dependency, in favor of human interaction, end up becoming more machine than men. (The pathetic image of 'Darth Vader' jacking off in front a computer comes to mind.) Symbolic, when we consider the box office success of the films, 'Transformers' and 'Iron Man' and how our superheroes look darker and more armored with each successive Hollywood remake.

Use 'The Force'

Raising energy sexually is one of the most powerful ways to charge an intent. This is why so many magicians and Tantrikas focus on positive images as they release their orgasmic energy for personal or global healing. (More about sex magic in the later chapter, 'How To Be a Sexual Activist'.) Like batteries, we can amp our wattage by lighting the spark in our base energy center, then direct it up through higher and higher substations (our chakras) to fuel the earth grid of the global soul, our collective consciousness. Unlike, those who engage in porn for personal gratification, who charge the collective energy grid with a false and destructive paradigm, using only their base energy. That paradigm being, the distortion of Sacred Union to one of sexual slavery. The irony being, those who fantasize about having a sexual slave, are the ones who become enslaved in their minds.

Anchoring this misguided perception of relationship creates an addiction, because it is ultimately, unfulfilling. For when the energy generated stays centered in the base chakra, it creates a physical dependency. Since the energy doesn't travel up the central nervous system during an act that offers only physical stimulus, it is in no way renewing, only depleting. So the majority of men on our planet are giving their life force into the black hole of cyberspace, which is why they keep returning, to try and recoup their energy, which creates an addiction. It's akin to someone with a gambling addiction, trying to get something back, when the odds are stacked against them. So instead they release all their energy, for no return. This creates a cycle of powerlessness. As the men are expending their true power (kundalini) on something which disempowers them.

A Personal Note to the Guys...

So guys, if you're generating your life force and then blowing it on some mirage of an artificial woman, be mindful you are also inviting a reflection of this into your world. Since we live in a holographic universe, 'like attracts like' so if you're charging up the notion of a fake women as your ideal turn-on, don't be surprised if the women you're attracted to in reality, use seduction to take your life force in various forms, such as money, assets, or children.

More importantly, this vibration you're attuning to prevents an honest and naturally sexy woman walking into your waking world. So don't continue to put all your sperm into the porn 'slot machine' because, just like a pokies machine it will never give back to you exactly what you have put in. (Slots / pokies: more trashy sexual innuendo here than an episode of 'Benny Hill') This unconscious mindset keeps one enslaved to a machine - a computer. It is akin to having sex with a robot. Better to have sex with your toaster as you'd at least see your own reflection to generate some self-love rather than giving all your energy to the manufactured images which are manipulating you on screen. Quite simply, porn is for sex addicts who are afraid of real women. So face your fear and you'll have the best sex of your life!

Like the adage, 'where there's fear there's power'. When we face our fears, we take back our power, whereas when we avoid them, our sense of powerlessness increases. This is why an empowered man has no interest in porn. Porn is only used by immature men who have unresolved feelings of hurt and anger towards the feminine. This is why they indulge in an act of passive aggression rather than risk direct confrontation and rejection. So rather than feeling bad and trying to give up 'cold turkey' if you want to free yourself of this addiction, equip yourself with the understanding, confidence and skills to interact authentically and intimately with the feminine. I recommend reading up on the shadow feminine, reading men's empowerment books and attending men's circles. On my website you'll find the men's empowerment books I recommend as well as my first book, 'The Inner Goddess Makeover' which is an easy to read road map of what makes women tick and has helped many husbands better understand their wives.

How Porn Impacts Upon the Feminine

A large number of women are in the position of feeling resentful that their porn addicted partners are cheating on them, while questioning whether they have any right to feel justified in their anger, since the 'other woman' is an image. This confusion stems from our cultural denial of that which exists, but can't be perceived through the five physical senses, leading to a negation of the energetic realm. So while we maintain a denial that sex is only a physical act, rather than acknowledging it is also mental, emotional and energetic, we downplay the ramifications of porn upon our real life relationships.

I recently saw an article written by a male psychologist on a website for new mums which assured women they should be grateful if their husband was indulging in porn rather than having an affair or visiting a brothel. This attitude is so detrimental to partnerships as it justifies the unconscious behavior of the masculine, when a woman is at her most vulnerable. This is when she needs her partner to grow up and step up into conscious manhood to assume his new role as a father.

Engaging in pornography undermines one's soul connection to their partner, as it demonstrates a complete disrespect, both personally and to the feminine. Fantasizing about having sex with a fantasy woman, is a sign that a man is feeling disempowered in his masculinity, if he is attempting to bolster it by having a nameless woman degrade herself for him. This urge to seek out a fantasy interaction with an illusory woman is a sign that a man needs to address his fears and unresolved wounds.

When a man is watching porn, he is raising his sexual energy by engaging with the astral body of the woman he is fantasizing about. For the porn star, her ego is receiving male attention and energy en masse, which feeds her ego and affirms she is God's gift to men, bolstering her self-image and confidence. She has no personal association or connection so gives nothing in exchange like a female Eros, the beautiful boy who was so self-absorbed, that those who fantasized about him wasted away to nothing.

Any sexual act with another is exactly that, an exchange of sexual intent and energy. Whether one party is self-pleasuring, witnessing a sexual act or being the muse, inspiring it. Sex creates an energetic transmission which links the energy fields of all who are participating, with their highly charged sexual energy - even if they are not in the same location. This bonds sexual participants to one another in ways they aren't consciously aware of, as they emit energy like an umbilical cord into the astral plane to connect with their love interest. So self-pleasuring as you fantasize about someone charges and feeds a sense of emotional dependency and energetic addiction. It is also why people who engage in this behavior, find themselves daydreaming about their fantasy lover as their fields are linked in the astral (also known as the second dimension). This is the realm of fantasy, addiction and delusion, where one seeks to lose themselves temporarily by distracting themselves from their real life problems. By avoiding the underlying issues they aren't open to the insight needed to create practical solutions, so they continue to indulge their flights of fancy. If this continues, one becomes so separated from their conscience they end up completely disoriented, unable to discern their life path and purpose. This loss of one's soul connection is illustrated in the story of 'Alice in Wonderland' where she becomes fixated on external stimulus, following the signs that say, 'Eat Me' 'Drink Me' to the point of personal chaos.

A Personal Note to the Women...

The more your man is lost in this netherworld of illusion, the less chance you have of resolving the real issues in your partnership and the more you will come to resent him for not being clear, focused and present and available to you and your children. Porn will continue to undermine the quality of your relating if you don't risk confrontation and rejection, to share how you feel about it and set boundaries accordingly to honor yourself.

The Playboy Bunny Youth Culture

Many Gen Y girls (those born 1981-2001) are trying to emulate this immature male fantasy of the porn star, as they see how many men desire it. This is evident in the number of girls dressing like playboy bunnies and branding their cars with porn star / Playboy iconography. This is because their unconscious Aphrodite aspect seeks to become the ultimate catch a man could have. Unfortunately, they do not realize they are setting themselves up to be abused psychologically, physically, emotionally and energetically by playing this role.

Many men prey on young girls, because young girls are less likely to have developed the self-understanding to assert their truth and needs. This is because unconsciously, they want everyone to like them. During a girl's maidenhood, she is in the process of individuating from her mother, so she is likely to do the opposite of everything her mother advises in an effort to assert her own feminine identity. This tendency puts young girls at risk from sexual predators who want to act out their domination fantasies with a real girl who won't say no.

That is, disempowered men who are seeking to feel virile and powerful, through degrading the feminine.

Today pornographic imagery is so prevalent, that pubescent boys and girls, when exposed to pornographic images, naively assume it is what adult sexuality looks like. As a result young boys expect girls to be free of pubic hair and compliant with all the sexual behavior they have seen modeled in porn. Equally, young girls dishonor themselves by complying, thinking this is what is expected of them, if they are to be desired. This shadow sexual behavior results in physical, emotional, energetic and psychological abuse. As a community of adults, we need to respond by providing a model of sacred sexuality to our youth, instead of either trying to enforce moral chastity or condoning sexually explicit fashions and behaviors. Especially given the additional pressure of corporations whose advertising campaigns prey upon this demographic, encouraging their rebellion to boost sales.

In our current social climate young girls unconsciously aspire to emulate 'Eve' - the prototype of a nubile girl who is sexually available, regardless of whether her sexual partner is able to truly see and honor her true self. This makes young women as vulnerable as sitting ducks in hunting season when the pornographic conditioning boys receive creates an expectation that it's okay to humiliate or hurt a girl for your own personal pleasure.

Nearly one in five women experience rape at some point in their lives, with 1/3 of those rapes occurring in college aged females, according to the Centers for Disease Control and Prevention (CDC). 2014.

Furthermore, the social conditioning aimed at young women through the media prevents them from embodying the aspect of Lilith, who connects them to their natural self and authentic urges. This sets a young girl up to believe if she wants to be loved, she shouldn't speak her truth and set boundaries accordingly or she will be rejected for it. This conditioning starts from the moment she can talk, with fairy tales imparting that if a girl gets too big for her boots, she won't fit into Cinderella's glass slipper and win the heart of Prince Charming.

Fortunately the rules are changing as women awaken to their inner power. So now there's a new league of empowered women who aren't shopping for a Prince. These are women who are looking for a King, a man who understands and honors the feminine within himself and is therefore capable of honoring the feminine externally in others. This emotional maturity is essential in a man, if a woman doesn't want to be continually put down, mocked, minimized or rejected for being an authentic woman.

Add to that, single motherhood is now at an all-time high with more women preferring to face life alone with the sole responsibilities of child-rearing and income provision, rather than compromise their truth to stay in a partnership with an unconscious man. This often occurs when children come along and women realize they don't have the energy to parent their partner as well as their children.

Women who stay with emotionally immature men often immerse themselves in their relationships with their children rather than deal with the lack of fulfillment and passion in their primary partnership. These are 'Eve' dominant mothers who prefer to not 'rock the boat' by speaking their truth, lest they risk their financial security. As a result they invest less energy into their partnership and more into their parenting. This leads them to unconsciously strive to prove their worth by being the perfect mother. Sadly, this creates a dynamic where the children dominate because she is so needy of their approval that she is unable to set appropriate boundaries and discipline them when required, since they are her primary source of love.

The Dark Road Towards Pedophilia

In mysticism, it is the fateful meeting with the authentic feminine (Lilith) that the hero needs to see his own shadow and mature. If unconscious men reject real women in favor of girls who are acting out a fantasy of a hairless sexual doll (Eve) they will only ever feel powerful in the presence of unaware girls. (The term, 'girls' applies to women of all ages who have not begun the journey to truly know, understand and heal themselves.)

Without a solid foundation of true intimacy, such immature unions quickly disintegrate into resentment and blame. This is when the rose-colored projections start to dissolve and each party unconsciously tries to manipulate the other. When an unconscious relationship breaks down, our culture does not encourage us to take time to reflect and grow emotionally and psychologically. Instead, we are pressured to take steps to emphasize our 'best assets' and resume our search for Mr or Ms Right.

Subsequently, a dangerous pattern develops with immature men seeking out younger and more naive girls to seduce and dominate as a compensation for their deep lack of personal empowerment. It is this dynamic which creates a society where pedophilia is rife, as unaware and wounded adults seek to possess the innocence they have lost, externally in another. So rather than take responsibility for healing their wounds to reclaim their own emotional innocence they seek out those who seem unaware of the human shadow. Contributing to this trend is our lack of rites of passage which impart the wisdom needed to transition from one developmental stage to another. An essential ingredient if one is to mature emotionally and psychologically.

Viagra: Medicate Rather than Mature

Similarly, men who run from facing and owning their weaknesses feel so powerless in the face of an empowered woman that they find it hard to get and maintain an erection. This leads them to seek out sexual encounters with women who won't point out their shadow traits, such as a mistress, sex worker, young girl or virtual lover. This is also why Viagra is in such high demand. Instead of men attending men's circles and healing their masculinity by understanding their wounds, they attempt to address the symptoms with a 'quick fix' pill rather than heal the root cause, (pun intended).

Unaware folk are only capable of engaging in domination sex. Sex acts based on an ego 'performance' rather a true and honest exchange of naked souls. The latter is an interaction akin to the infinity sign, where both parties allow the energy to move wherever it wants to go. Personal awareness, empowerment and self-acceptance allows both parties to lead and submit without a self-consciousness thought.

Those who have no concept of sacred sexuality have no idea what they are missing because they have never experienced that level of liberated and ecstatic, sexual freedom in complete communion with another. Without entering into such a creative dance, they miss the kundalini activation and expansion of consciousness that conscious sexual communion offers. For if we don't understand and express all of our archetypal selves, which govern our major energy centers, when we climax, it's just a physical release. In other words a 'fuck' is exactly that - one person 'fucking' another over by ejaculating all of their pent up stress, anger, resentment and disappointment into a receptive vessel. Whether that's a tissue, the shower recess or their partner. (And we wonder why women of a certain age would prefer a cup of tea!)

There are equally many unaware women who only perpetuate this type of friction based sex. That is, rubbing their sexual nerve endings in their genitals to create electric inner heat as a pathway to releasing stress. As a result they also become addicted to this vampiric sexual exchange, equating exhaustion and relief with pleasure. So they never explore the expansive bliss of a yin orgasm which can leave them sighing, moaning and murmuring for hours. (This is what follows when one's sexual energy reaches all the way up to the crown chakra. For more info about the yin orgasm read volume one.)

Let it be said, however that lusty lower sexual expression is great as part of a well-balanced sexual diet, but just on its own is not fulfilling. This is illustrated in the myth of Ishtar (the Babylonian Venusian Goddess who governs sacred sexuality and governs the crown chakra). When she descends to the Great Below she meets her twin sister, Ereshkigal (her shadow side) who is addicted to friction based sex, but never feels fulfilled. In the later chapters I'll introduce you to ways you can expand your sexual diet with a love arts banquet!

The Gift of Sexual Initiation

When a man has sexual intercourse with a woman who has opened her major energy centers he will receive what's known in Sanskrit as 'Shaktipat.' This is when his own dormant kundalini serpent is awakened by the energetic transmission he receives when she climaxes while inside her. The more surrendered in love and perfect trust she is, the greater the charge he will receive. This will undoubtedly be the best sex he has ever experienced, but afterwards he will have to face and integrate the shadow aspects that his own meridian of light - the serpent of consciousness awakens in him.

For a man who is ready and humble, a meeting with an awakened woman is a gift that will accelerate his own awakening, if he has the good sense to not reject her for being the one who unleashes all he has not resolved. Let it be said, however, that just because a woman looks like a

Goddess, does not mean her kundalini is awakened. Yes! Contrary to the advertising campaigns, designer clothes, a tight ass and large earrings do not make a woman a Goddess! The telltale sign that a woman has awakened her Shakti (serpentine Goddess mojo) is that she will experience kriyas up her central pillar. These are rushes of energy which surge up her central nervous cord along her spine causing spasms in her physical body. To activate this current of energy a woman must do the inner work of understanding the seven feminine aspects which govern her major energy centers. (My first book, 'The Inner Goddess Makeover' is a DIY workbook for women wishing to do this, a process which is intensified when journeyed one aspect per month in circle with other women, who reflect and accelerate one's self-understanding.)

Vestal Virgins and Whores

In ancient times women who served as sexual priestesses were honored for this role, serving in temples as vestal virgins, hierodules and geishas. These women opened men to experience and connect with their souls. They did this through art, which is the language of the soul, including the art of lovemaking. Hence they were schooled in the sacred arts of dance, music, poetry, sacred space, altar making, flower arranging, wine appreciation and sacred sexuality, enabling them to inspire men's souls with acts of beauty.

The women who dedicated their lives to sacred service in the community were the custodians of culture. Their proficiency and appreciation for the arts provided a bridge to men's hearts. For men, being in a sacred feminine temple space and experiencing these refined offerings helped to civilize them by reconnecting them with their hearts and subtle senses, so they were true gentlemen. This is why men were said to go the temple after returning from a battle, to 'take the war out of them' before they were considered ready to reunite with their families. Not all men would engage in acts of sacred sexuality, they would simply have their humanity restored through multiple acts of kindness, beauty and healing, reducing the likelihood of post-traumatic stress being enacted upon their loved ones.

Unfortunately in modern times this sacred profession has been reduced to girls performing degrading acts often naked in public or performing base sexual favors in exchange for money. As a result, they become embittered toward their clients, as they become the constant receptacles for the toxic energy and words of men filled with unhealed wounds toward the feminine. Just as Babylonian hierodules provided many forms of love in addition to erotic coupling, modern sex workers also play many roles including that of emotional confidante. To ensure customer relations, many mother their clients emotionally by listening to their complaints about their partners and agreeing with their viewpoint. This ego stroking helps unconscious men feel validated and justified in their decision to seek out paid sexual services. Payment enables a man to feel that he is in control and calling the shots. It also means he doesn't have to truly give of himself. This transaction ensures he can be her sole focus, like he was with his mother when he was a baby. This is why so many men paying for sexual services seek out large breasted women. There is a huge need for sacred sexual healing professionals to redress this cultural denigration of a once honored calling.

⚕ Understanding the Power of Attraction

The Ebb and Flow of the Mating Dance

In order to understand the dynamics of the mating dance we first need to establish which gender is dominant within us. For our physical gender does not necessarily mean we are playing that gender role within the mating dance.

Below is a questionnaire I have devised to ascertain which gender polarity is currently dominant within you.

Gender Polarity Questionnaire

Simply use a pencil and ONLY tick which statements most apply to you. Be as honest with yourself as you can to get the most accurate result. You may also wish to ask others who know you well to fill it in on your behalf as sometimes we can be blind to our own shadow.

How would you describe yourself?

Someone who is...

___motivated to take action

___has a strong work ethic

___is always busy

___is organized

___has a structured life

___focused on making money

__has a sense of purpose

__can stress about time

__tends to show affection with material gifts

__can be disciplined and expects others to be too

__needs their space to be neat and clean

__happy just being, rather than doing

__expressive with their emotions

__focused on friends and family

__is not very ambitious

__is comfortable with chaos and mess

__is able to really rest and relax

__is accepting of others

__shows affection with touch and spending quality time

__can be scattered, without clear direction

__is able to go with the flow and surrender

What qualities do you attract in a partner?

Someone who is...

__motivated to take action

__has a strong work ethic

__is always busy

__is organized

__has a structured life

__focused on making money

__has a sense of purpose

__can stress about time

__tends to show affection with material gifts

__can be disciplined and expects others to be too

__needs their space to be neat and clean

__happy just being, rather than doing

__expressive with their emotions

__focused on friends and family

__is not very ambitious

__is comfortable with chaos and mess

__is able to really rest and relax

__is accepting of others

__shows affection with touch and spending quality time

__can be scattered, without clear direction

__is able to go with the flow and surrender

To Score: How would you describe yourself?

If you ticked more of the traits in the first section, your masculine self is dominant. If you ticked more of the traits in the second section, your feminine self is dominant. If you ticked an even amount in both sections, you are pretty balanced. However, ideally, you'll have more ticked in your foundation (physical) gender.

To Score: What qualities do you attract in a partner?

This section provides a fail-safe cross check because you will attract your opposite. So if you ticked more answers in the first section, you attract more masculine traits in a partner signaling that you're operating more out of your feminine, despite how you see yourself. Whereas if you ticked more answers in the second section, you attract partners with more feminine traits indicating that your masculine polarity is dominant.

Understanding the Mating Dance and the Pull of Opposites

There are three stages to empower one's manhood just as there are three stages to empower one's womanhood. Only when we understand these three phases can we understand the dynamics of why we attract the partners we do, and how we can change the mating dance so both are empowered.

Stage One Man

Unconscious Masculine Dominant

This phase describes a traditional male who leads with his masculine polarity but has not yet developed his inner feminine qualities. He embodies the positive masculine traits, such as decisiveness, action, courage and the ability to provide and protect. However, without the balance of his inner feminine, he will also express excessive masculine traits, such as aggression, dominance, cynicism and acting without thinking. If not balanced, these traits will, over time, alienate him from women and undermine his partnerships.

Stage Two Man

Unconscious Feminine Dominant

This phase describes a man who has rejected being a traditional male so he leads with his feminine polarity, often to win the acceptance and approval of women and feminine dominant men. This means that he expresses the positive traits of the feminine, such as consideration for others, emotional intelligence, nurturance and creativity. However without the balance of his positive masculine, he will embody a lot of shadow feminine qualities such as being indecisive, directionless, unmotivated, passive-aggressive and manipulative.

Note: This second stage is one of individuation and transition. It is a temporary stage, however, many men remain in this stage long-term, excusing their behavior with spiritual jargon like, '*I prefer to go with the flow*' or '*I don't do time*'.

Stage Three Man

Conscious Masculine Dominant

This final phase describes a man who has been through the first two stages. Instinctually, he leads with his masculine, which is positively anchored as he has sought understanding, healing and empowerment of his masculine selfhood. This is complemented by his inner feminine, which he has developed by embracing his own descent to confront his human frailty, birthing a greater humility and spiritual understanding of himself as a soul. Only when a man has undertaken the personal growth to get to this stage will he attract a woman who is leading with her empowered feminine.

Stage One Woman

Unconscious Feminine Dominant

This phase describes a traditional female who leads with her feminine polarity but has not yet developed her inner masculine qualities. This results in her embodying positive feminine traits such as receptivity, nurturing, patience and creativity. However, without the balance of her inner masculine, she also expresses excessive feminine traits such as victimhood, indecisiveness, passive aggression and financial dependence. These traits will alienate her from men and undermine her partnerships with men.

Stage Two Woman

Unconscious Masculine Dominant

This phase describes a woman who has rejected being a traditional female so she leads with her masculine polarity, often to win the acceptance and approval of men and masculine dominant women. She expresses the positive traits of the masculine, such as a strong sense of purpose and direction, decisiveness, optimism, financial stability and courage. Since she is not balanced by the positive feminine, she will embody a lot of shadow masculine qualities such as being aggressive, cynical, judgmental, acting without thinking and insensitivity. Note: This second stage is one of individuation and transition. It is therefore meant to be a temporary stage, not one in which women remain, excusing their behavior with rational jargon. i.e. 'I have to survive in the real world.'

Stage Three Woman

Conscious Feminine Dominant

This final phase describes a woman who leads with her feminine polarity because she has actively sought to understand and empower her feminine sense of self. She has also cultivated her inner masculine by developing her talents, intellect, self-worth, enabling her to take calculated risks on sharing her gifts with the greater good. This gives her a sense of balance. So while she honors her instinctual foundation gender, she is also aware of, and honoring of the masculine, both internally and externally. Only when a woman has undertaken the personal growth to get to this stage will she attract a man who is leading with his empowered masculine.

How Gender Imbalance Undermines Partnerships

Below is a thumbprint of how both genders, when disempowered, impact on the quality of our relationships.

A Disempowered Masculine

- A partner who never makes a decision but instead always defers to the other, avoiding responsibility.

- A partner who has not found their life purpose.

- A partner who just adheres to the status quo rather than asserting their own thoughts, opinions and ideas.

- A partner who still worries about their father's opinion of them, or focuses on trying to get the approval or recognition of their worth from others.

- A partner who has trouble standing up for themselves.

- A partner who is disorganized, messy and unreliable.

A Disempowered Feminine

- A partner who needs to be in control.

- A partner who constantly analyzes and criticizes others, undermining the efforts of others.

- A partner who always needs to be right.

- A partner who disassociates to avoid feeling.

- A partner who is obsessed with doing, and finds it hard to stop, relax and just 'be'.

- A partner who can be rigid about adhering to rules, structures and routines.

How These Internal Dynamics Affect the Mating Dance

Men in the second stage, who are operating more out of their feminine than masculine polarity, take a passive role. Whilst men do need to develop their feminine traits to be well-rounded human beings, this should not be at the cost of their foundation gender.

In other words, for the masculine within us to be empowered, we need to feel the courage of our convictions and possess enough sacred solar fire to take action when appropriate. When a man has empowered masculine energy, he will lead a courtship by initiating action. This takes confidence, which is one of the most sexually attractive qualities a person can possess. (This is not to be confused with a show of bravado, as this has the opposite effect, telegraphing a lack of maturity.)

When a man pursues a genuine love interest and is intuitive enough to attune to and read whether the recipient is equally receptive, his advances will be welcome. If, on the other hand, he is trotting out seduction methods, with no real attuning to, or connection to the other party, he risks humiliating rejection.

This is because those with a developed feminine are highly intuitive, so they will immediately sense a premeditated and impersonal agenda. This is often the courtship method adopted by many stage one males. Being driven by their ego, they assume their prey is too naive to detect their game-play, which is insulting. This is why men using pick-up lines in bars get the 'death stare', a drink in the face or a public insult. Unfortunately, it is the fear of this social ridicule that scares second-stage men into not approaching women at all.

Men need to simply trust that by speaking to women with no agenda, they will naturally open up to each other and connect on all levels. This is what leads someone to feel excited, lit up internally and keen to pursue a deeper connection. The more aspects we uncover in ourselves, the more chance we have of genuinely connecting with a wider cross-section of people, and more deeply with a prospective partner. Whereas, if we only relate to another's appearance, they sense we have no genuine interest in them as a person, just the image we are pursuing.

The Ultimate Turn-on for a Man

The ultimate turn-on for a man (or masculine dominant woman) is someone who is truly receptive to him. So guys, if you want women (or feminine dominant men) to be open to you and warmly receive your ideas, suggestions, opinions and desires, you first need to develop your own ability to be receptive. That means truly listening and perceiving the subtleties in life such as body language, intuitive thoughts and gut feelings.

The Ultimate Turn-on for a Woman

The ultimate turn-on for a woman (or feminine dominant person) is to be deeply desired. So, if a man is stuck in the second stage, unable to take the initiative in pursuing a woman, she will tire of him and settle for a man whose advances excite her. One only has to look at our anatomy to see how this is true on an energetic level.

The Ins and Outs of Attraction

A man's appendage protrudes, so his role, when empowered in his masculinity, is to take the active role in seeking union with his opposite. (To be crude: like a plug seeking a socket.) This means speaking his intent, expressing his appreciation of her and initiating a courtship. If he is passive, he will attract women whose feminine is disempowered so they lead from their masculine polarity. Until he heals his masculinity, he will repel women who embody the positive expression of the feminine.

The feminine, on the other hand, is magnetic and receptive so her role is to attract rather than pursue. This means, attending to her needs and creating a welcoming environment internally by healing herself to become loving and open, which will be reflected in her home. So when a woman searches for love externally, actively pursuing a mate, she will inadvertently attract passive behavior from males and men whose masculinity is disempowered. Until she heals her femininity, she will repel men who embody the positive expression of the masculine.

We are all made up of feminine and masculine energy, so we will always attract someone who complements our energy. So if you don't like the type of people you're attracting, seek to heal your gender imbalance. (I've created a 'Sacred Union' oracle deck so you can get a snapshot of the state of your own 'inner marriage' with practical tips on how to empower each of the archetypes that make up your feminine and masculine halves. (See Resources page.)

Opposites attract, just like magnets. The masculine pole is positive and the feminine pole is negative. The more we are polarized in one gender expression, the more intense the attraction will be, but with that comes a susceptibility for intense conflict. When we heal both genders within us, the spark of attraction is there without the conflict, as we lead with our foundation gender in a really positive way.

It's all a matter of balance. The more a woman is polarized in her feminine by being passive and agreeable, the more she will attract an alpha male who needs to feel dominant in every situation to assert his masculinity. Equally, if a woman wears the pants by always taking the lead, organizing everything because she needs to feel in control to feel safe, she will attract only emasculated partners, those whose masculine polarity is impaired. So too, if a man is polarized in his masculine by being dominant and dictatorial, the more he will attract a submissive woman who loses his respect due to her own lack of confidence and self-respect. If a man is passive, always doubting himself to make the right decision, he will attract domineering women into his life that he feels pressured to please in order to keep the peace.

The Power of Attraction

Why is it some women have men flock to them, just as some men make hordes of women go weak at the knees? To answer these questions we simply need to understand what each gender polarity finds attractive. Let's look at the masculine polarity first.

What Attracts the Masculine

The masculine focuses more on the external than the internal, which is why men (and masculine dominant women) are more likely to be aroused by erotic images, films and performances. This is also why men are often very attracted to women who have fit and healthy bodies. A woman (or feminine dominant man) in good physical health suggests to their reptilian brain they have good genes for mating, regardless of whether they are looking to father children or not. This is not a conscious thought and therefore not a conscious choice.

Breast Men

Similarly, an unconscious man might consider himself a 'breast man' as he has made an association as a very young child that a loving woman offers him large breasts for comfort. Alternatively I know of one man whose mother was unable to breastfeed due to her traumatic birth and post-traumatic stress, which contributed to his desire for a woman with a very ample bosom. Breast obsession is also common in men who are emotionally immature as they lack the means to self-soothe themselves emotionally when they feel upset. So, like an infant, they will hit the bottle and try to snuggle up to a 'double D' woman in a bar.

Leg Men

Similarly, the attraction to long-legged women can be formed in early childhood, by young boys looking up at their mothers and wishing to be picked up and held, leading them to idolize women who recreate that unconscious fantasy of receiving that maternal love all to themselves.

Fuller Size Lovers

So too, men who are attracted to very large women have equated love and happiness with the softness of women, who, in their early childhood could surround them in their nurturing embrace.

The Return of the Soul Man

Ideally, men will seek to move beyond shopping for a type, based on their physical assets. The degree to which a man can do this indicates his emotional maturity. If he develops his own inner feminine, he will naturally start to value and seek out more of an inner connection with prospective partners, rather than just unconsciously focusing on the exterior traits associated with their wounded inner child's search for the 'all loving mother'.

When a man matures emotionally, he is far less inclined to compartmentalize women by valuing, rating or pursuing them according to their individual external features. This is the behavior of the 10% rational mind rather than the 90% soul. So, such pre-requisites indicate the psyche of a boy residing in a man's body, which unfortunately has been encouraged and socially sanctioned during the past six thousand years of patriarchal consciousness. The evolved or conscious man who has awakened his inner feminine will feel genuinely aroused by finding out what a woman thinks, perceives and feels, in addition to how she looks, smells and moves.

Homoerotic men on the other hand, hunger for the love of the masculine. If we seek that which we feel we do not possess within, in order to feel whole and complete, it may suggest they were raised in a gender dynamic where their Father embodied more of his feminine traits, and their Mother, more of her masculine qualities. For example, they may feel more attracted to heart-centered men and repulsed by aggressive women. Alternatively, this hunger may stem from the other extreme, where their Dads felt shut down, distant and emotionally unavailable, leaving their inner child with a deep need for male love that was never met in their early development. One could speculate on the wounding that underpins the opposite desire, suffice to say, if operating from the masculine polarity, homoerotic men will equally value, rate and pursue men for their external traits such as 'tight buns, a big package, nice pecs' etc. Similarly, the more they develop their emotional intelligence the more they will seek out partners for what's on the inside, rather than focusing primarily on the outside.

Unfortunately, this propensity to focus on the external is specifically what has made men more susceptible to being externally programmed through visual autosuggestion of pornography. A phenomenon that has undermined men's primal erotic response. Ultimately, a man (or masculine dominant woman) desires a feminine partner who feels loving to come home to. Someone who can help them to grow inwardly by opening up their inner world of feeling, perception and understanding of themselves and the meaning of life. Someone who can help them to be more in their heart than their head, enabling them to come home to the true essence of their inner self. So, rather than for a girl (or nurturing man) to mother them, they will have awakened their own inner feminine and be looking for a woman (or feminine dominant man). If embraced consciously, they become an external reflection of their own inner feminine who can inspire and model positive feminine choices for them.

What Attracts the Feminine

Women (and feminine dominant men) focus more on the inner qualities of a person, so they'll take more notice of what they say, how they express their feelings and their vibe (energy). So it makes sense women are attracted to men who have spent some time getting to really know themselves and have the confidence to express their innermost thoughts and feelings. This is why those who are feminine dominant swoon for musicians who bare their soul in their music. They seek a meeting of souls, a soul mate union with a man (or masculine dominant woman) who has sought out meaning beyond the material world.

This is why women are more likely to prefer erotic fiction or romantic films as a pathway to arousal, as these love arts focus on the inner world of the characters. Those ruled by their feminine relate to the protagonist's feelings as inspiration for their own fantasies. Whereas external images that show everything and leave nothing to the imagination seem base by comparison, so rob a woman of her ability to fantasize, which is her greatest turn-on. Unfortunately, this is why women (and feminine dominant men) are more prone to scenarios of unrequited love, if their penchant for fantasy leads them into delusional states about men (or masculine dominant women) who neglect them emotionally or don't even know they exist.

This need to elevate the mundane world into something magical is because the inner realms of existence rule the feminine where mythical, celestial and elemental beings exist in the other dimensional planes. This is why girls love fairy tales that acknowledge these parallel realities, and swoon when a man does something romantic, because he has demonstrated an affinity with her feminine realm where the key focus is love. To have a man in this mortal realm reflect her deep personal values is like having a fantasy fulfilled. That, being one who is so moved by love that they risk rejection to express it.

It also takes creativity to express one's romantic heart; creative thought to hatch the idea and then ingenuity, skill and daring to pull it off. To be creative one must enter a space where they are at one with the creative source of all life...the animating presence of the divine! In other words guys, the more creative you are with your date nights, birthday ideas, unexpected surprises on a Friday night, the more your feminine partner will see, adore and worship you as a God! (Likewise, if you let your inner Adonis atrophy once you get the ring on or mortgage signed, she will view you more as a mere mortal and fantasize about other men like silver screen Gods.) This is why women develop crushes on the same heartthrobs that feature in many romantic comedies, as repeatedly they fulfill her fantasies of a man who will go to great lengths to show their beloved the enormity of their feelings. It is this willingness to express their heart, their true essence that will melt the heart of a woman. So, obsessing over the pursuit of washboard abs, a great salary or sports car is more likely to impress your mates and superficial girls rather than a woman who wants to see and know the real you.

One lovely example I recall of a man of average looks and a low income enchanting a house full of women was when I was in college. He was the partner of one of my housemates. He arrived at the front of our house on the morning of her birthday with a birthday card he had made from plywood and painted - it was eight foot tall! It wasn't expensive, it wasn't even painted that well but it was larger than life, it was ridiculous and it was a statement to the world that he loved her and he didn't care who knew. It filled all five of us young women with joy, having proof that loving men existed - not to mention a memory we'll never forget. What this delightful young man demonstrated was a comedic device known as exaggeration - doing something deliberately larger than expected to the point of ridiculousness. This silliness appeals to the magical child within, lightening our spirits with the fifth element, Spirit - the element of surprise.

'Comedy is when you expect something to break and it bends' - W.C. Fields

In fact, given what most women want is a man who will risk looking like a fool for love - I recommend seeking inspiration from the world of comedy for those seeking to woo their partner with romantic gestures. (Again this is why romantic comedies are bankable commodities with the female demographic.) This is because this genre evokes the archetypal fool, one who expresses all of his selves without any self-conscious fears about what other people think of them. Only a man who truly knows, and is comfortable with, himself can do this. This is essentially a man baring his soul, his innocence, which is the exact opposite of what men in the patriarchy era were conditioned to express.

How to Increase Your Feminine Magnetism

As stated earlier, the feminine polarity is magnetic, so those who wish to attract an empowered masculine partner (or more proactive behavior from their existing partner) are best advised to resist the urge to pursue the masculine as this only repels them.

Instead, women do best to focus on enhancing their natural feminine energy flow, which is inviting rather than demanding. By being community-minded in their approach, sharing and networking to get all of their needs met with grace, women feel abundant and therefore able to give freely. By focusing on their heart desires, they nurture themselves and radiate love. This amplifies the light of their inner Venus, which attracts others to their inner spark. When the flow of love is directed inward, it magnetizes more loving energy to be directed towards them, following the same current.

If we were to view the flow of feminine energy, this is how it would look:

The feminine energy field flows outward from both arms, as if seeking to gather and embrace energy back to the center. This is why it feels so feminine and nurturing to wear a robe or wrap yourself in a shawl or blanket as this mimics the feminine flow of energy.

Picture the shape of the feminine current of energy as it moves from the heart, down the heart meridians in the arms, out to welcome and embrace life, returning to the heart. So too, women who focus on gathering to themselves what they truly need, remain centered in the heart. This empowers their feminine polarity, which attracts those in the masculine polarity to them like bees to a honey pot. The more loving women are toward their male partner, the more inclined he'll be to do things for her, especially if she expresses her gratitude with warmth and affection.

To further amplify your feminine magnetism, connect to the sensual realm of Mother Nature and the mystical realm of Grandmother Moon. Attuning to their rhythms and expressing their qualities further assists the amplification of one's sacred feminine essence.

To connect with the Earth, I recommend doing the 'Tree Meditation' as a daily morning practice. (See Resources page)

Ways to Entice Your Lover (for Women and Feminine Dominant Men)

To enhance your feminine chi, consider how you can increase your receptivity to love, relaxation and pleasure. Here are some practical suggestions to flow with the feminine so you can attract masculine energy which complements your feminine essence.

- Consider how can you create a sanctuary, a temple of love within yourself and within your home, that feels good to come home to. A place / energy others will want to visit, including your Beloved. You can do this by creating sacred space using natural objects of beauty and art. For instance, in your home, drape fabrics to soften hard geometric lines, use warm inviting color tones and engage the senses with essential oils and fresh flowers. Create a home that relaxes those who enter and reminds them of the importance of pleasure.

- Become involved in regular communal practices that help you to embody the sacred feminine such as Red Tent women's circles, Goddess workshops, belly dance classes, women's retreats, yoga classes, art therapy classes and dance meditation events. These practices help you to open like a flower so your inner gifts blossom and your energy is receptive.

- Anoint yourself behind the ears with your own yoni juice (the nectar of your temple gates). Since the olfactory sense is the most primal, as it governs the base chakra, it is your scent and not something manufactured, that is guaranteed to tantalize and entice a lover.

- Taste your own yoni nectar to imbibe feminine chi, grow and eat culinary herbs you have fertilized with your moon flow (your diluted menses and yes, you wash them first). Also eat as many alkaline foods as possible to enhance your feminine beauty and strengths.

- Wear clothes you feel beautiful in, especially fabrics that feel sensual to touch. Opt for clothes that drape your curves, rather than dissecting them into geometric shapes with tailored clothes.

- Exercise to release your endorphins, as genuine happiness is magnetic.

- Spend time with your favorite friends, especially those who you laugh a lot with.

- Spend time doing things you love.

- Pamper yourself often.

- Visualize your partner doing to you the acts of love you most desire. Try doing this when lying next to them in bed and watch as they receive this suggestion telepathically and respond!

Actions Women Can Take to Demonstrate How Much They Love Their Man (or Masculine Dominant Woman)

Show your love through small actions and your attention to detail, as men express their love through their actions, so they will understand this love language more than you telling them how you feel. For example, cook their favorite meal, buy them a silk smoking jacket and slippers to relax in, or massage their feet at the end of a day. Here are some other practical suggestions:

- Welcome your lover with deep gratitude and joy.

- Wear something you know will arouse them.

- Take them a cold iced tea or homemade lemonade if they are working outdoors.

- Send them sexy texts saying what you want to do to them when they get home.

- Encourage them to have a weekend away fishing with their friends or a night out with their male friends on a regular basis.

- Encourage them to pursue their talents and hobbies i.e. by displaying them.

- Gift them oral pleasure to unwind and relax.

- Give them space when they get home from work to transition, such as showering.

How to Increase Your Masculine Potency

The masculine energy moves outwards in a direct line like a penis, an arrow or a hero going straight to his goal without hesitation. The more a man dares to trust himself by taking risks, the more attractive he is to those in their feminine polarity.

The masculine energy field protrudes out like an arrow from the center. This is why men want to get out there and make their mark, focusing on their target.

This is because a man who shines embodies the qualities of the sun, which is the sacred masculine principle. He radiates confidence and belief in himself. So the more a man leads the dance, pursuing a woman (albeit respectfully, rather than with an attitude of arrogant domination), the more she feels confident to submit to his will. What she is responding to is the size of his golden rod of light. In our culture obsessed with the external, we have misinterpreted this as the size of a man's phallus; whereas true manhood is found in a man's energetic connection with the sun or Divine Father.

Men can also strengthen their pillar of light by doing the '*Tree Meditation*' daily to anchor the light of the sun in their light body. (See Resources page)

Watching the sunrise / sunset is also helpful in awakening the sacred masculine codes within, and doing the annual 'Kingship Rite' to commemorate the birth of the annual sun cycle - a practice which is outlined in my online course for men. (See Resources page.)

Ways to Pursue Your Lover (for Men and Masculine Dominant Women)

Ultimately, it doesn't matter what you do but how you do it, as women love surprises, so she'll just love you for making the effort. Men are electric so they shine most in their essence when they are doing, creating, planning and leading. So if a man burns brightly out in the world but then comes home and sits passively in front of a TV, she will feel less attracted to his light, as she only ever sees it when it is dim.

Whereas when a man takes the lead and surprises her with an unexpected act of love, he will reap the benefits, as she will shower him with acts of kindness and affection (and probably sexual passion inflamed by her renewed love for him!)

The key is whether he is truly doing it with her in mind or whether it is really something for him. For instance, on the Australian reality show, 'Don't Tell the Bride', men were asked to plan every aspect of their wedding, which would be revealed to their bride on the big day. Watching this show was traumatic as every groom blew the budget on excessive Buck's turns, adrenalin-pumped pre-wedding holidays and bar crawls with their 'Best Man', followed by novelty-themed venues, which were against the express wishes of their partners. All of this meant skimping on the time, effort and money invested in their partner's bridal shower and dress. We then watched the U.K. version and were pleasantly surprised to see the exact opposite; sensitive men who outdid themselves with attention to detail, love and creativity, eager to make the most of the opportunity to show their beloved how well they knew them and appreciated every little thing they had done for them in the past.

So - observe what she likes, then surprise her with it - she will be deeply touched as you demonstrate you truly know her and value her for who she is, not just for what she does for you. She will feel cherished, and assured you truly see and understand her. These are the kind of romantic gestures women hope to hear when they ask, 'How did he propose?' They want to hear to what lengths he went to declare his love or what small things he did that were filled with great meaning. Here are a few magical, romantic suggestions to enchant and touch your feminine lover's heart:

- Buy her flowers often and for no particular occasion.

- Surprise her with an opportunity to dress up by getting tickets for the theatre, opera or masquerade ball. You may even take her to a lovely boutique as a surprise and watch her try on dresses a la 'Pretty Woman', or give her beautiful lingerie in a fancy box with tissue wrap.

- Send her to a Day Spa or arrange to have a mobile massage therapist give her a treatment at home.

- Buy her a book you know she wants to read.

- Take her to a restaurant that has ambiance such as dining al fresco surrounded by fairy lights, in a cozy booth by candlelight, or a moonlit picnic on the beach or in a park - with or without a waiter or musicians.

- Run her a bath with candles and a glass of wine (with sultry Latin music, Enya or Crowded House).

- Show her you are sentimental with a slide show of memories. Do remember and celebrate your milestones, such as wedding anniversaries (and not with a perfume your assistant chose) as marking growth is important to the feminine.

- Organize a weekend away (without asking her to book it, or seeking her opinion on where to go.) Do however ask her casually before making the booking if she's got anything planned for her weekend so as not to double-book.

- Wash the dishes without being asked, fix something around the house or wash her car. In the book, *'Reclaiming Goddess Sexuality'* by Linda Savage, she explains how the fastest way for men to get more sex is simply by doing more housework! Stats show women do the lion's share of housework, despite working comparable hours to men. This phenomenon is known as 'The Second Shift'. So, if a woman is exhausted from doing menial chores, she ain't gonna feel too darn sexy.

Author's Note: Whilst I am advocating you fill her life with a little magic to show her you still have the spark of love in your heart well lit for her...I don't recommend telling her you want to treat her like a princess. This is a creepy way of saying, 'I'm emotionally immature so I'm going to put you on a pedestal and project on to you that you are perfect'. This is not real, balanced or sustainable and is a statement used more by stage one macho guys who undermine their partners by treating them as little girls. Instead, I recommend relating to your feminine partner as your best friend, your Beloved, your Queen, your Goddess. This honors both her human and otherworldly selves in equal measure.

Whilst women dream about being with a man who will demonstrate he values the feminine realm of love, fun, play and magic, they need to be with a man whose foundation is grounded, practical, strong and confident in the outer world. Without this strong masculine expression, they won't feel attracted to him. This is why women are attracted to men who have mastered a skill, fathered a project, travelled to other cultures, taken risks on their ideas and talents, and found their purpose beyond the accumulation of wealth.

A woman wants to feel as if a man can broaden her world. So it is not the money that women are after, but the perception that a man can offer her opportunities to see and experience a world bigger than the internal and domestic one she is comfortable with.

As I stated earlier, women love romantic comedies because ultimately what touches their heart is a man whose soul is bigger than his ego's pride, a man who'll risk looking like a fool for love. So here are a few suggestions if courting or wishing to maintain the affections of a woman or feminine dominant man:

Exaggeration: express your heart's appreciation of them with larger than life gestures, such as lighting a hundred candles or filling their room with flowers. This could be hiring a costume to wear for them on Valentine's Day such as dressing as the God of Love, Adonis, (a la Fabio) complete with mock Euro accent. Alternatively, you could make them a tapas meal and perform your own foot stomping version of Flamenco as their red-hot Latin lover, wearing only a black G-string, Zorro mask and cape. Remember, if your goal is to be an idiot you can't lose!

Extreme Underplay: make something miniature for them like a tiny box with your personal scent captured inside or with your belly button lint that won't take up any room in her luggage and can be sneaked in if she has to go on a work trip...or get hold of her iPhone and take some silly photos of you expressing your love when she's asleep and downplay it by not telling her. Then patiently wait for her to find it in her own time or send her a text during the day asking her to check her virtual gift.

Personification: this is when we give inanimate objects and/or animals human qualities (i.e. by sticking your finger in the head of a prawn / shrimp and using it as a puppet a la Steve Martin's performance in the film, 'Dirty Rotten Scoundrels'). You could sing a love song using her cat or stuffed animal - there's a lot of comedic scope here for inappropriate behavior. Email or make her a card with an image of an animal, which you caption with something personal, or tie a love note to her dog to deliver to say sorry after an argument to acknowledge you would like to come out of the doghouse.

Rhyming Words / Couplets: instead of just writing in a card, make up a short poem, which is easy and childlike if you rhyme every second line. This is also an easy way to compose a song to serenade your love. You could even ask a cake decorator or florist to deliver the message for you. Try spelling it out in candy, nuts or pasta on the kitchen table for them when they arrive home.

Do think of the consequences of your actions, so don't write your love message on the bathroom mirror in your partner's best lipstick or leave them to clean up after your prank. You may even wish to create a birthday rendezvous, where you tempt her by sending her on a treasure hunt, ending at her favorite store. To do this, ask the staff at a handful of stores / cafes to give her a rhyming couplet note which sends her to another shop and so on. Alternatively, this could be done in different rooms, leading in to the garden, so at the end of her goose chase she finds you with a surprise dinner for two.

Now if your ego arks up and says, 'All these grand acts of love I'm meant to do! What do I get in return?' Fear not...Romeo, as when a woman feels truly cherished, she will unleash adoration in ways that will tempt you to send me a thank-you note! Just as any great lover knows, if you attend to a woman (or feminine dominant man) with true generosity of Spirit, the outpouring of love you receive in return will leave you breathless! So give without the expectation of receiving, because the feminine is highly intuitive and can perceive a power deal being brokered, even if she doesn't speak it. She'll just shut down little by little, until you're shut out by the ice queen, wondering what went wrong.

Things Men Can Say to Demonstrate How Much They Love Their Woman (or Feminine Dominant Man)

Someone with a feminine essence yearns to hear their masculine counterpart express their innermost thoughts and feelings. This helps them to feel deeply connected to their partner. When women feel a deep inner connection with their partner, they feel moved to express that externally with acts of love and affection.

A word to the wise: never lie to your feminine partner to get in their good books. Just as they can detect when they're being played with actions loaded with an agenda, they can also spot insincere words at a thousand paces. I offer these sample statements in the hope, they will attune more men and masculine dominant women to seeing and appreciating the individual beauty of their feminine partner without them feeling as if they're only wanted for their boobs, blow jobs and home cooked meals.

- *'That color looks great on you.'*

- *'I love you in that top.'*

- *'I love the smell of your hair.'*

- *'Thank you for that beautiful dinner' or say what you liked about her meal.*

- *'I love how funny you are.'*

- *'I dig your perspective on things.'*

- *'I love the feel of your body.'*

- *'You look GOOOOOD today, honey.'* (Nice when spoken with an Afro lilt in your voice - if you have no idea what I mean, I recommend you listen to some Al Green.)

The Ego Versus Soul in Relationships

Transcending 'Can't Live With You, Can't Live Without You'

Can't Live With You, Can't Live Without You

If you're in a relationship where you feel an intense attraction that triggers you constantly, the connection is very karmic. That means you have big lessons to teach each other, which you were unable to resolve in other incarnations. If you're both willing to do a hieros gamos practice, to own your disowned aspects at each of the seven gates, I recommend staying to embrace the opportunity to do the shadow work. (Only on the condition you are not in an abusive relationship.)

The hieros gamos is a seven month process, entered into during the dark months of autumn / winter, when our shadow behavior surfaces due to the weakening solar light. It involves self-reflection at new moon and transparent sharing of one's shadow at full moon. This is why the ancients would commit to journey with a partner for a year and a day; it was an agreement to complete another cycle of the hieros gamos.

If it is not possible to work together to own your respective shadow traits, I recommend separation to avoid going round in circles, like the film, 'Groundhog Day' re-enacting old wounding scenarios. Although the pull of these karmic connections can make it feel impossible to walk away from, I see it as one of our final lessons in leaving the Underworld of living in only the 3D reality. We do this by simply choosing to walk away from the drama.

For, we have been sold the notion that drama is love. It is not. Just because something is intense, doesn't make it right. In fact, those who generate a lot of energy within us, promoting a strong sex drive and big emotions, are there to stir up our energy so we can deal with what we haven't resolved. It is not their responsibility to quell the storm raging within us, it is ours. That said, it is very easy to put all our efforts into 'making it work' externally in an effort to restore harmony and inner calm, but this is a distraction from healing ourselves.

The ultimate lesson lies in facing the fear, 'Can I live without you?', daring to confront the possibility that we are alone, separated from love. Only by moving through this fear, can we take back our inner power. We do this by reconnecting to the infinite source of love. By focusing on our connection with Spirit, we find the strength to individuate from one we have bonded to in the lower chakras. Easier said than done. In fact, it can take many attempts, breaking up and getting back together, until eventually the battle between higher and lower self is spent and our light prevails. In this scenario, each round of conflict and reflection makes it easier to commit to our path of highest growth, as we discover more inner strength by developing the strengths of our inner opposite. The more whole we become, the less dependent we feel.

Should I Stay or Should I Go?

The key to discerning whether your relationship is spiraling your energy lower or higher is to observe whether your self-care increases or decreases when you are in partnership with this person. Everything is a mirror, so if you are being honored externally in a loving way, you will treat yourself accordingly, whereas if you are not being honored, you will start to make an increasing number of self-dishonoring choices. For instance, your diet may become less nutritious, you may take up a toxic habit, you may stop seeing your friends, or spend less time doing a hobby you love. The way to summon all your energy back, so you have the strength to leave this kind of love addiction scenario, is to reclaim all the activities that are self-honoring and fill you with joy, as well as routines that restore you to optimal health.

We often choose partners who feel like home. If we grew up in a dysfunctional family dynamic, this means we find a mate with whom we recreate similar dynamics. The intensity we feel with them is often due to the unresolved issues they trigger within us. So, leaving this dynamic is akin to our inner child making the conscious decision to leave home. This can only happen when we develop our other archetypal selves who champion and reassure our inner child that we have what it takes to look after our needs. The home we are leaving is our 3D home, created by our wounded child's expectations of others.

Connecting with Mother Nature and Spirit reassures our inner child. They awaken our sense of home within our heart (like Dorothy in '*The Wizard of Oz*'), so we can feel at home within ourselves and not seek another to take care of us. ('*The Tree Meditation*' mentioned earlier, done as a daily practice, helps to strengthen this connection to the universal Mother / Father and our sense of home within.)

The Kama Sutra, the ancient Hindu manual on courting and relationships, identifies the following, as signs that a union is not honoring and must end:

- Your lover promises you everything but gives you nothing.

- They say one thing yet do another.

These points both illustrate one who is not walking their talk, one whose lower and higher selves are not working in alignment. To stay with one who is not capable of walking in truth means you are deceiving yourself, should you continue to choose them, over your own highest truth. Only when we love ourselves, can we identify that which is not loving behavior from others. Only when we make the commitment to make self-honoring choices, can we leave a situation that diminishes our light. We can still love someone but not their behavior. Leaving them does not mean we stop loving them. It simply means we love ourselves enough to remove ourselves from further harm and pain, which enables us to love the other more unconditionally from a distance.

Letting Go

Personally, I see the final challenge as our decision to commit to creating wholeness within, regardless of the relationship outcome. This commitment to self-growth is the foundation for sacred union. The final letting go of a karmic tie is the ultimate test of our commitment to self-love, which indicates total responsibility for our self-actualization. Since we choose partners who we've often been involved with in past-lives as lovers, spouses, parents or siblings, this also plays a role in the underlying dynamics and makes this a very challenging connection to release. So, one's self-love must be strong enough to withstand the pull to continue a dance of intimacy, which ultimately must be relinquished.

Hopelessly Devoted to You

Personally, I had to psychologically die and grieve every time I ended each subsequent dance round with my karmic ties. That is, until the maiden aspect within me had given up all hope. It is interesting to note that 'hope' was included in Pandora's glory box, which was gifted to her by the patriarchs. This is because hope will keep a maiden in a hopeless situation, as she clings to the hope that things will change. So too, hope springs eternal within our psyche, as our 'inner teenager' focuses upon the future rather than the present. Subsequently, our inner maiden must completely give up, by seeing a situation as truly hopeless, for us to accept responsibility as the inner parent and get us out of a harmful situation.

When I released all hope, I experienced an emotional pain so intense that I was wracked with acute physical pain in every cell during my menses (which is the letting go phase of a woman's lunar cycle). This was akin to a labor, as I was birthing a completely new identity through this soul transition. As with any birth, it is important to afford yourself support on all levels, to midwife you through such a death and rebirth process. I recommend having energy healings and asking your friends to help you with the mundane responsibilities, like picking kids up from school or making a pot of stew, during the final release of such a karmic tie, just as one would accept additional support during the grief of a physical death or birth.

Death of the Maiden and the Knight

When the hope of our inner maiden dies completely and we accept that we cannot wait around anymore, hoping for things to change, we completely let go. Ironically, this is the greatest catalyst for both partners in a karmic union to transform. This is because they are so energetically enmeshed, that when one partner makes this shift, it often catalyzes a psychological death within the other. The vacuum created by this loss also creates the space for each to embody their inner lover. (Which is why the self-pleasuring practices of a holy hermaphrodite in volume one are an essential part of the journey.)

Soul Love and Karmic Ties

It is possible to love those who are karmic ties very deeply on a soul level. This is because, at a soul level, a deep love is shared, regardless of the wounding that takes place at a personality level. These connections challenge our ego, so we may operate more from our true self or soul consciousness. This is the sacred contract we make with them prior to incarnating. As such, we agree to meet them at a set time and place, although we have free will to change the course of our lives as we choose. For a beautiful understanding of the nature of this connection, I recommend reading, '*The Story of Little Soul and the Sun*' by Neale Donald Walsch. It's a children's picture book written for adults, which I can never read aloud without breaking down, as he so touchingly explains the nature of forgiveness as child's play.

The nature of such a soul contract is that each will illuminate the other's shadow, to literally burn away their ego illusions about themselves. This obviously makes for a rocky ride because the soul connection is so strong, so no matter how many times we want to run from them because of the unresolved painful wounds they activate in us, we often get drawn back to them, as our love for them is so unconditional. This is ultimately the greatest teaching they impart...to love the soul, regardless of their ego's behavior - although this does not mean bearing the brunt of it. In fact, the contrary - we are called to step up and set appropriate boundaries that honor our deepest soul values. Once we set a boundary, it will be tested, so maintaining a boundary requires complete conviction to not compromise one's truth. Eventually, we may develop enough self-love to walk away from the karmic dance of re-wounding, while continuing to love them unconditionally, with eternal gratitude and reverence for the role they played and the lessons they came to teach us. It just means on a personal level, we recognize it is not honoring for either to persist in the old dance of relating.

Cord Cutting and Sacral Clearing

Once we've made the decision to end a relationship and take space to heal, we need to clear our energetic ties with them so we don't get pulled back into the old way of relating.

Cord Cutting Exercise

Find somewhere where you won't be disturbed, light a candle and put on some meditation music. Sit with your spine straight so the energy can flow unimpeded from the base to the crown. Next, take a few deep inhalations calling your energy back from wherever it may have been scattered. Now visualize yourself walking up an inner spiral staircase, up out of your crown. As you continue walking up this spiral staircase into the cosmos of stars, you see yourself becoming your higher self. This may be as an angel with huge white feather wings or a being of translucent light. At the top of your staircase surrounded by stars is a mediation table. You call in the higher self of the person who you need to let go of. You see them join you as their higher self, one who only vibrates to the frequency of love, light and understanding.

In your mind's eye, you now say whatever you have been unable to say to their lower self and they respond to what you have said. You then see yourselves exchanging scrolls, which you unravel, revealing the lessons you both agreed to teach each other during this lifetime. You thank them for being a mirror and a teacher on your path and send a pale blue ray of peace and forgiveness from your throat to theirs. You then invoke the presence of Saint Germaine (the Merlin) and together you use the violet flame of transmutation to burn away all psychic cords, hooks and webs that have bound you to each other in the old pattern of relating. You then say good-bye and watch them leave, retracing your steps back down your celestial staircase into your body.

(See the Resources page for an MP3 download of this meditation.)

Calling Back Your Soul Fragments

When I split from my husband many years ago I knew that we needed a separation ceremony to revoke the vows and energetic intent we had set in our wedding ceremony. In our case it was particularly important, as we had sealed our vows with a blood libation. (We both had a drop of blood taken from a finger - amidst much laughter, as the needle was blunt, turning me into a very loud pincushion and our ceremony into a comedy of errors! This libation was originally meant to contain the mixing of semen with menstrual blood into the Earth, but due to falling pregnant two months after our engagement, we created a libation by putting a drop of our mixed blood into a chalice of wine. As we poured it into the Earth, we affirmed our intertwining of DNA and family bloodlines.) Regardless of whether you have incorporated such alchemical devices, I strongly suggest recounting any vows you have made to each other, should you choose to end a marriage, be it legal or otherwise. Likewise, always call back your sexual energy from a lover once you have parted ways. You can do this simply, by visualizing the retraction of energetic cords that you may sense between your sexual organs, while stating you are each sovereign and free.

Establishing a Circle of Trust

When we end a significant relationship, we create a new chapter, so it is an ideal time to stop and reassess our lives. To apply the lessons we have learned, it is a good idea to reflect upon our needs and the boundaries required to honor those needs.

In my first book, 'The Inner Goddess Makeover' I created a process called, 'The Circle of Trust'. This process serves as a helpful boundary-setting exercise where one acts upon the authentic truth of one's soul, rather than over-riding one's true feelings according to a sense of duty or obligation.

To do this, draw three concentric circles and label them, 'Intimate, Friendship and Acquaintance' (starting from the inner circle).

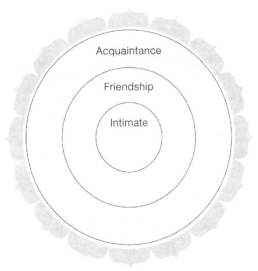

Next, attune to your inner self and write the names of those in the 'Intimate' circle, who you trust won't ever shame your vulnerability. Then in the 'Friendship' circle, write the names of those you trust you can share some of your insecurities with, and finally, in the 'Acquaintance' circle, write those who you don't feel comfortable exposing any of your human frailties to.

What it often reveals, is that those we feel we ought to be able to trust, because of their relationship to us, such as 'Mother, Father or spouse' aren't necessarily worthy of our trust, in actuality. When I've conducted this process with students, many place their family members in the 'Acquaintance' circle.

If we give our trust freely, like a child, to those who have not shown they are worthy of our trust, we betray ourselves. Just because we can trust them emotionally, does not mean we can trust them financially. Trust must be earned through demonstration of personal integrity and mastery in each area of our lives, or we only have ourselves to blame for any subsequent loss or pain.

Sacral Clearing

Given how we merge energetically when we engage in sexual union or sexual fantasy with someone, it is part of our essential self-care to clear the etheric cords of our physical, emotional and mental bonding in the lower three chakras, to reclaim our sovereignty and reconsecrate our temple when a liaison ends. This makes it easier for us to move on, less prone to addictive behavior and free to enter a new partnership without bringing old energetic cords and attachments into our next union.

This second exercise (which feels like a natural progression of the 'Circle of Trust') I was blessed to learn within our Red Tent circle. I then led more women through my own version in Red Tent gatherings, before finding the original creatress of this process, Anaiya Sophia, who has granted permission for me to share it here. Here is a link to view Anaiya's original version:

http://anaiyasophia.com/articles/how-to-create-your-womb-mandala

My Version of Womb Clearing

To begin, place your hands over your womb (or tummy for men), with your fingers pointing down so your thumbs and index fingers are touching. Close your eyes and breathe into this center, attuning to its energy.

Now visualize within your womb (or belly) a white room. Notice who's standing in front of you, to your right, to your left and behind you. Open your eyes and write the names of those people on the diagram below. Then close your eyes with your hands back on your womb / belly and notice who is standing in front of the person who is directly in front of you. Now observe, 'Who is standing to the right of the person on your right?' 'Who is standing to the left of the person on your left?' and 'Who is standing behind the person who is directly behind you?' Again open your eyes and write the names of those people in the second circle, where you saw them placed. Now close your eyes, re-position your hands and notice who is standing beyond those four people and write their names on your diagram in the final circle.

If you haven't done the visualization part of this exercise, don't read ahead as this is where we interpret the results...

The First Circle

The first circle indicates your intimate relationships. So these are the energetic connections that you are still carrying deep within you. When we consider that this is the sacral chakra where we create what we want in our life, if you have any past relationship partners sitting here, it's a good idea to clear them out so you can clear your receptivity for a new partner.

The Second Circle

The second circle indicates your friendships. The same applies, if there is someone sitting in your womb / belly energetically that you no longer consider a true friend, then it's time to reclaim this center by clearing them out.

The Third Circle

The third circle indicates your acquaintances. So again, if there is someone in this outer circle who doesn't feel like they've earned the right to be there, it's time to move them on. When you consider that if our lovers have not done this process before lying with us, we can literally have hundreds of people attached, as they will have brought all their past sexual partners unwittingly into our inner sanctum!

The Four Directions

See the guide below for the significance of where to find people in your inner sanctum.

In Front: Guides / Mentors / Teachers / Inspiration
Behind: Protectors / Supporters
Right: Male Energies i.e. Husband / Soul Brothers
Left: Female Energies i.e. Wife / Soul Sisters

Note: if you are female but your masculine polarity is dominant, you may find your female energies on the right and your male energies on the left, and vice versa if you are a male with a dominant female polarity. If this is the case, I recommend swapping them over when you create your healing mandala (see below and Anaiya Sophia's website) as this will help you to operate more from your foundation gender.

Clearing and Re-consecrating Your Sacral

Close your eyes and place your hands back on your belly or womb and visualize those in your inner circle. If there is someone there, who you no longer want in your inner sanctum, then in your mind's eye, see yourself telling them they must now leave in the name of highest love and light. Then clap or use a rattle to clear the energy. Next, ask for any of their attachments to now leave in the name of highest love, light and truth. Then clap, or use a rattle to clear the energy. Repeat this for each person, checking in with your inner self as to whether it feels right to keep them there. (For instance, I had the Christ behind me, who I was happy to have at my back, so he stayed, but my past personal loves were asked to leave.) As you clear out those who have outstayed their welcome, you may become aware of less dominant energies who you didn't perceive before. Again, these may be guides, including loved ones who have crossed over, ascended masters and animal totems.

Next, visualize the violet flame of transmutation spiraling within your belly / womb. If any of the energies you encounter in there feel resistant, try to re-enter or use emotional guilt to stay, then visualize their emotional umbilical cord attaching up to their own higher self. This comforts their inner child so they no longer need to seek out a host for their emotional security. Now visualize an orange flame glowing in your sacral chakra, flooding this center with a sphere of orange light, with a golden web of light encasing your womb / belly.

To close, place the protective symbol of Wotan's Cross (the symbol of the Grail Mysteries) - an even cross within a circle, in gold at the entrance to your cervix and yoni (or front and back of your sacral if you're a man). I also recommend placing one at the chakra behind your neck where lost souls can attach.

It is advisable to check your sacral on a regular basis and clear accordingly, especially if you notice your energy levels have dropped or an ex-lover keeps popping into your thoughts. Visualize filling your womb with rose petals, which fill it with the vibration of love.

Most healers, readers and holistic counselors already do a version of this practice on a regular basis, so they don't become energetically overburdened by their clients. I would also strongly recommend this process on a regular basis for anyone working in a service profession, to help minimize the risk of 'burn out' - especially those working in the sex industry, regardless of whether you engage in physical sexual acts or not.

For example, after I spent ten months working as an exotic dancer in my twenties, I collapsed with exhaustion and retreated to live alone in the forest, where I intuitively did psychic surgery on myself, using my inner sight to attune to all the cords and attachments that were sucking energy from my sacral chakra. These were the emotional umbilical cords of the men I had danced for, as I had engaged in energetic sex with them by visualizing them penetrating me as a lap dancer. I was upfront with the men that this was how I worked, as I wanted them to understand the power of energy and intent. This energetic connection to so many men resulted in me becoming overwhelmed by attachments, which appeared as etheric worms, like intestinal parasites. I once contracted an intestinal parasite from a past lover, who had hundreds of women attached to him, who I saw, when I did this exercise. This illustrated the degree to which I had felt drained physically, emotionally and mentally!

If we don't clear our sacral when a relationship ends, we risk bringing the energy of our ex into our next intimate sexual communion. Those who are sensitive may feel the energetic presence of others, even to the point of being distracted by the image of their face popping into their mind, during lovemaking! Not clearing ourselves energetically is dishonoring to all, making this a vital practice to teach to our children when they become sexually active.

Creating a New Moon Sacral Mandala

When you have cleared your sacral, you can then reclaim your power to consciously create without your creative energy leaking out unconsciously. To do this, draw the three concentric circles on a black sheet of paper and draw and write (or glue pictures) of what you now choose to manifest in each area of your life. For example, in the outer circle in front of you is your future, so by meditating on this area, you may get a clear sense of what you need to do now to embody your future self's highest destiny.

The optimal time to seed your intentions via a mandala is within eight hours of the new moon. (To find out the exact time of the new moon, simply Google the new moon for your current month and year. Then visit a time zone conversion website for your local area time.) With any manifestation, one must always honor free will, so I recommend writing at the top of the page, 'In accordance with free will and for the highest good of all'. This ensures that your intent harms none.

114

☤ Soul Mates, Twin Flames
and the Beloved

The Purpose and Role of Our Intimate Connections

In our evolutionary journey, we experience different types of intimate connections, which afford our soul varying initiations. We may journey through all types with the one partner but more often than not, they come in the form of different people along our path. Each is equal, as we learn lessons of equal value, however the characteristics differ according to our own level of intimacy with our own soul. Before we attract a graceful and symbiotic dance partner, we must revisit the awkward dance of opposites and learn to transcend the karmic patterns that have kept us bound for lifetimes.

'Blessed are those who wound us,
for they reveal the beliefs that need healing.'

Tanishka

When we approach life from the perspective of our personality (or ego), we have rational expectations about what we need from a relationship in order to feel safe. This is because the ego is ruled by the rational mind. The lower mind is the self-appointed protector who recalls our past hurts, and then anticipates potential problems in an effort to keep us from harm. Whilst this is a helpful function, it can keep us in a hyper-vigilant state of anxiety if our mind dominates. If we make decisions solely to avoid the pain of our past, we will also limit our future.

In direct contrast, the soul is the deep inner part of our psyche, often referred to as the subconscious mind. It stores the emotional and energetic imprints of our past, manifesting our unconscious expectations as an opportunity to heal and grow beyond them. This means we are continuously attracting events to push our ego beyond its comfort zone, so we can fulfill our potential. Our soul does this by choosing people and situations that will trigger our wounds, so we have no choice but to acknowledge our issues and heal them. These beings, with whom we share a sacred contract, are our soul mates.

Soul Mates: Mutually Assist the Liberation of the Soul

Everyone we venture into an intimate relationship with is a soul mate, so we can and do usually have more than one. In the old relationship paradigm, where people were expected to find one partner while still in their teens, then marry them for life, people were encouraged to find their one and only soul mate. This is a limiting perspective.

A soul mate is simply someone who our soul recognizes as we have a sacred contract with. This means both have agreed, prior to incarnating, to assist each other with their respective life lessons. As well as lovers, they may also show up as pets, friends or family members. There is a sense of feeling 'at home' with them, or sensing you have a shared destiny - new friends who instantly feel like old friends. Even people who hurt us, are soul mates. Those who we have strong karmic ties with us are soul mates.

Relationships bring our wounds to the surface, as the unconscious thoughts and behaviors of others trigger reactions in our unhealed psyche, like putting salt in a wound. As we connect to our feeling of pain in a current situation, any similar hurts that have not been resolved also arise, which can feel overwhelming, as we react to both conscious and unconscious events. If we apply self-enquiry, to discern when we have felt that particular hurt before (such as in early childhood or even in an alternate lifetime), we can identify the pattern and embrace the lesson a wound can teach us. By consciously embracing our wounds in this way, we become grateful for the opportunity to heal and gain insight, rather than feeling victimized.

Often, one will need to express the emotion before gleaning the insight. If we don't feel the e-motion (energy in motion), we become stagnant emotionally and mentally. Whereas, when we honor emotion by releasing it with awareness, we clear our channel, which facilitates the ability to receive clear intuitive understanding. The more we can cultivate the 'inner witness' to observe a given situation and also our reaction, the less over-identified with the pain we become, making it easier to transcend our emotional state and identify our patterns. This soulful approach to relating heals our reactivity to old issues and beliefs.

Journal writing is a great process to lessen our reactivity, as it enables us to express all of our small self's hurt in a way that won't inflame an immediate situation and create further wounding all round. Journaling provides a safe space to express our fears and emotions, after which we feel calmer, clearer and better able to view them from the perspective of our higher mind.

So, if you feel discord escalating with your partner, housemates or kids, call a time-out and go and journal everything you're feeling and thinking, ensuring you focus on your lesson, before trying to resolve your differences with others.

You Spin Me Right Round, Baby, Right Round

As we make the shift from the previous two thousand year cycle, known as the astrological Age of Pisces into the new age of Aquarius, we have created accelerated opportunities to heal our wounds and transcend any limiting beliefs, which have kept us on the repetitious wheel of fate (learning through cause and effect). This is why life has felt so intense, as we have each confronted relentless personal challenges, causing us to question our view of self, others and the world around us. These challenges have been an opportunity for us to activate the 'inner witness', who can see our challenges for what they are - tests which enable us to respond with awareness. Without this perspective, we react unconsciously from our wounded child self, which draws us back into another round of 'karma drama'...the old 'he said, she said'!

When we change our response, we no longer attract the same lesson. The people who trigger us the most are the ones with whom we have the most unresolved life lessons. So, instead of blaming and shooting the messenger, which feeds the drama with more emotional energy, we must learn to stay centered within our own awareness by focusing on the lesson that each situation has to teach us.

'The path to true love never runs smooth.'

William Shakespeare

Twin Flames: The Polar Opposites Who Assist Us in Burning Our Karma

Another type of soul mate is the twin flame. There has been a lot of focus given to twin flame connections in recent times. Many differ on the nature and purpose of the connection. The term is one often associated with spiritual ascension. This can easily become more about reaching some concept of perfection, which is more of a puritanical head-trip than being about the evolution of the soul. As a result, many hope to find their twin flame as proof they are ready to leave their body. Given our challenge, while incarnated, is to transcend being ruled by the mind and embrace the inherent perfection in everything, one must exercise caution when entertaining the concept of twin flames. My intuitive knowing is we are each here to anchor Heaven on Earth, so if your motivation is to 'get off the Mothership' you may need to re-examine your motives.

Author's Note: Like many, I experienced a very intense relationship in the lead up to the 11:11:11 gateway. (That being the 11th of November, 2011, a date which ushered us into the consciousness of oneness, as the pillars of the Aquarian Age.) This partner was my twin flame, a truth I became aware of as I noticed the effect he had on my energy field.

Whenever he walked into a room I would spontaneously experience a kundalini kriya. A kriya, is a surge of electrical energy which moves up one's spine, along the central nervous cord. Known as 'Shakti' in Tantra, it is the awakened essence of the sacred feminine. (This would happen even when I was asleep!) He also awakened the medicine of jaguar within me, as I saw cat's eyes with my inner sight whenever I experienced a kriya or climax (and have done ever since). The lesson of jaguar is to be able to see clearly in the dark. He was one of my greatest teachers as he came to show me all that I had disowned in myself. He was my polar opposite.

Dancing with Your Polar Opposite

The meeting with one's twin flame is intense, as nothing magnetizes like the meeting of two who are completely polarized. In fact, together, they generate a force field that is palpable. This is because we feel so complete in their force field. It is also what makes the sexual coupling so dynamic, so we can become hooked on chasing the erotic high, rather than doing the inner work to embody our disowned aspects - a process which is necessary if we are to complete our mission as star-seeded beings, remembering our totality.

Twin flames are, however, our greatest challenge. Our interaction with them often takes on mythic proportions, as the challenge they present us with is larger than life. It is akin to the duel a hero has at the end of his quest with his greatest adversary. A showdown, which tests him to his limits, almost costing him his life and everything he has set out to achieve.

Whilst we may have fallen in love many times with various soul mates, who our inner self recognized as having a shared history in other dimensions or incarnations, the twin flame is a soul mate who is encountered when one has actively begun to seek out and embrace unifying and balancing their internal polarities. This evolutionary lesson is known as '*The Holy Hermaphrodite.*' It is the final card depicted in the Major Arcana of the Tarot. It is the stage of personal integration, intended by an initiate on the path of Mysticism. (This does not mean one aspires to have the genitalia of both physical genders, but rather an internal balance of one's masculine and feminine polarities.)

To accelerate this process, our soul calls in one who is our polar opposite to confront us with everything we have rejected in ourselves, so we may reclaim our disowned aspects and become whole. This results in unions with lovers who challenge us to grow more than any other soul we've encountered to date. Often it will feel as if we've taken a huge step backwards, as these partners take us right into our dark side, demanding we revisit old addictions, values and patterns so we may review them from a place of increased awareness. This understandably creates feelings of concern amongst family members and friends, as one learns to dig deep into one's years of self-growth, to access the inner strength to resurrect from the ashes like a phoenix, transcending the pull of lower selves, jubilant in their quest for self-love.

Despite needing to end these torrid love affairs in the name of self-preservation, the eternal love shared goes well beyond this realm. For these are the beings who agree to play the role of 'the good enemy', so we can awaken the savior within and commit to our self-actualization above all bonds. 'The good enemy' is a Native American teaching. It refers to one who plays the opposing role to us, testing our commitment to our highest truth and growth, so we may strengthen our resolve, taking action on what is right and just. For example, when the Australian Prime Minister, John Howard, refused during parliamentary question time, to apologize to the Australian Aborigines for their genocide, he inadvertently drew attention to the issue. This refusal became the catalyst for a national debate, with the entire country saying, 'Sorry', creating a legacy of educational programs and a national 'Sorry Day'. In this instance, the publicly-expressed bigotry of our head of state, acted as a valve to question the bigotry of the collective. As such, John Howard played the role of 'The Good Enemy' - one who acts as a grain of sand, catalyzing the emergence of a pearl of wisdom. (For more about the teaching of 'The Good Enemy', I recommend the oracle, *'The Sacred Path'* by Jamie Sams.)

Our twin flame or polar opposite is the soul who appears to assist us in raising our frequency to that of an 11 master being. They do this by acting as a catalyst for the awakening of our twin serpents within. The twin serpents are the energy meridians known in Tantra as 'Ida', the feminine essence, and 'Pingala', the masculine essence. When awakened, they flow up through our major chakras, along our central nervous cord. For specific teachings and practices on how to awaken and balance these meridians, read volume one.

Twin flame relationships are about our journey of self-discovery, rather than the goal of building a relationship. Their role is to initiate us alchemically, by igniting our passion through the union of opposites. This passion fuels the transmutational fire which burns away all of our illusions, especially in the lower three chakras, where the energy is most dense and patterns are often most ingrained. These include our limiting beliefs, stories and expectations, which have run us physically, emotionally and mentally.

The ancients acknowledged the power of the serpentine currents of energy within us, which, when awakened, accelerate and expand our consciousness. This is why Royals wore the insignia of the serpent on their headdresses, indicating they had activated the essence of the God / Goddess within.

'Alchemy is associated with the quest to turn base metals such as lead into perfect metals such as silver and gold. The heart of alchemy, however, is spiritual: a means of personal transformation, purification, and perfection into a state of prolonged life or immortality. Alchemy was practiced by the ancient Egyptians, Greeks, Arabs, Indians, and Chinese. ... The entire alchemical process was based on the assumption that all things in nature evolve into their purest and highest form. Thus imperfect base metals eventually become gold on their own. Alchemy merely speeds up the process... The Egyptians developed one of the basic fundamentals of alchemy, that of 'first matter', that is that the world was created by divine force out of a chaotic mass. All things can be reduced to first matter through dissolving and combining, and transmuted to something more desirable. This transmutation was accomplished through the joining of opposites... Paracelus coined the term spagyric art, from the Greek terms for 'to tear' and 'to bring together,' to describe alchemy.' 'The Encyclopedia of Magic and Alchemy' by Rosemary Ellen Guiley.

Piercing the Illusion at The Seven Gates

So what does this alchemical process look like?

After a short honeymoon period, and a great deal of sexual fire stimulating the base chakra, the inner serpents awaken. As a result, both parties become more aware of the qualities they had denied, which are reflected in their opposite. They respond by externally judging their opposite with barbed words of condemnation, which pierce their lover's ego with their serpentine fangs of truth.

This process illuminates the polarization, illusions and unconscious behavior at the first gate (base chakra). After which, one or both parties reject the other and pull apart to transmute and integrate the poison of their unresolved wound, which has been re-opened. So they fight or break-up, rejecting their partner's inner Pan or Lilith (the base chakra archetypes) as unacceptable. Often, they will scapegoat their shadow onto the other, but if self-aware, they will embrace the intense pain their partner has brought to the surface to be healed, while retreating to reflect upon their self-healing and growth.

Due to the intense magnetism of their connection, and to their sacred contract to pierce each other's illusions at the seven gates, they will find it near impossible to stay away from each other. So after they've licked their wounds and shared their learned lessons, they'll re-unite to go another round and repeat the same process at the second gate (the sacral chakra). The more intense the connection, the more likely they will return to face their polar opposite seven times - to see and integrate their shadow self at all seven gates. Pictorially this process looks like the healing symbol known as the caduceus. (Pictured below.)

Author's Note: The more polarized we are individually, the more intensely this conflict will unfold externally. When journeying this dynamic in my own relationship, I was shown the image of two serpents, one black and one white which literally symbolized the light (conscious) and dark (unconscious) forces, as the ways in which we use our energy. My relationship with my polar opposite was one of my greatest spiritual tests, as it demanded I was honest with myself in every moment, so I could communicate my authentic truth to my partner. This required constantly risking conflict, in order to be true to my own soul values.

We Must Be Naked to Enter Eden

With the rising kundalini of the Earth activating 'Lilith, the Wild Woman' within us, it has become virtually impossible to lie to ourselves or another, regardless of our gender. This level of authenticity is understandably making this a very tumultuous time in relationships, especially if we persist in scapegoating our shadow onto each other, rather than taking responsibility for our own imbalance. Twin flames demand we are emotionally and psychologically naked, as souls. If polar opposites continue to operate out of the facade of ego, they will literally destroy each other, as their job is to tear apart each other's false personas. When we are able to be transparent and vulnerable as our soul selves, our union will be harmonious, as the energy will flow unimpeded.

Another hallmark of this kind of relationship is the sex between these couples is usually electric. This is because they charge each other's respective voltage at each of the seven gates. If the sex wasn't so electrifying, there would not be such a strong incentive to return for another helping of ego-to-ego combat.

The Showdown of Godzilla and King Kong

The challenge here is to transcend the old reptilian brain's way of ego dominance, which is 'survival of the fittest' into one of soul-centered trust and co-operation. Often it will feel like a showdown between the primal Godzilla and King Kong, as both partner's egos go 'head to head' rather than relinquish their sense of external power. The more they develop inner power through self-understanding, this tendency will diminish. If this Neanderthal unconscious belief of 'survival of the fittest' isn't identified, both parties will unwittingly compete with each other until they destroy their loving bond.

When one considers how the capitalist culture is built upon the premise of 'eat or be eaten', it is easy to see how ingrained this unconscious belief is, and how it can undermine our conscious effort to truly love one another. On the upside, the more incarnated beings who deconstruct this archaic way of operating, the faster this fear-based attitude of greed and power over another will become extinct. The reptilian brain is the part of us that acts instinctually but unconsciously. It is when the lower self reacts with aggression, rather than remaining centered in the soul self. The soul self witnesses the external dynamics and examines their own response and lesson, applying reason and intuition to create a win / win solution. Whereas the reptilian self has the attitude of 'me first', which is based on the fear it will miss out, if it isn't self-serving, like a small child. When interacting with a partner who is operating at this level of consciousness, it is an energetic, emotional and psychological challenge not to be drawn into a mindset of competition, which escalates drama. Energetically, this spirals both partners into a vortex of entropy (downward motion) where they can find it hard to rise above the lower, denser emotions and thought forms.

Author's Note: The more people transcend being dominated by their reptilian brain, the more conscious the frequency will be on Earth. This internal shift, made by the critical mass will end the manipulation of our group mind via the media, as the manufacturing of compliance based on the exacerbation of fear will no longer work on an awakened populace. So, rather than allow the mind to get caught up in a distraction about external conflicts, a Rainbow warrior takes up the fight within to heal their inner conflict. This means we rise above a mindset of 'us and them' - worrying about Reptilian beings versus human survival as this viewpoint only serves to anchor the lower mind's perspective of duality and separation. When we acknowledge all is within us, all is the divine plan and all is playing a role in our evolution, we can remain in our hearts, accepting of, 'what is' rather than operating from our minds, fighting 'what is'.

The War of Opposites

Similarly, it is duality and polarization that creates conflict in our relationships. The more unconscious both partners are, the more they will each deny their unconscious behavior and scapegoat all blame onto the other. Similarly, the more their ego yearns to possess the other, in order to feel whole, rather than focus on their own journey of healing, the more they will get re-wounded. Without undertaking conscious steps to heal destructive bonding patterns, it is only a matter of time before they leave, like a child who learns not to put their hand in a flame after being burnt.

'During incubation, the two principles within the materia prima, usually referred to as 'sulphur' (red, male, solar, hot energy) and 'mercury' (white, female, lunar, cold energy) are said to fight venomously, each eventually slaying the other and producing a black putrefaction, the nigredo, 'the black of blacks'. This completes the first stage of the Great Work. In the second stage, the blackness becomes overlaid with rainbow colors (sometimes depicted as a peacock tail or pearl), which are in turn covered by a whiteness, the albedo. At this point, the two principles of the materia prima reappear in a new form, as the 'red king' (sulphur of the wise) emerges from the womb of the 'white queen' (mercury, or the white rose). The king and queen are united in the fire of love, and from their union comes perfection, the philosopher's stone, the catalyst capable of transmuting base metals into gold and the key to enlightenment.' The Secret Language of Symbols by David Fontana.

So, the role of the twin flame is to bring out the worst in us - show us our 'blackest of black' dark side, that which we have denied, suppressed or rejected within ourselves and judged externally in others. This connection is often fiery, as both ignite other's passion, which also ignites their anger, should their ego feel challenged. This is necessary if we are to awaken the third eye of Isis, (depicted in the peacock feather) which is the gate where the two inner serpents meet. As illustrated by this quote, our opalescent auric field, emitting our full spectrum of light - the rainbow, cannot shine without first detoxifying.

The good news is, the more each partner is able to own their shadow at each of the seven gates, the more ecstatic the sex between them, as they unleash more of their Shakti / Shiva energy - their God / Goddess divine essence! Then are they ready to apply the lessons of the rainbow, the hieros gamos courtship through the chakras. (I share the basic practice later in the book to accelerate your inner transformation from base urges to the pure expression of your soul essence. For a more comprehensive journey I also offer an online course. For info see the resources page.)

As stated in volume one, without a structure the inner serpents of energy attack their opposite. However, when a staff is offered, they each coil their bodies around the staff in an upward motion, which is depicted by the image of the caduceus. So it stands to reason that couples who agree to a practice, which focuses their energies upwards, evolve together rather than spiral down into entropy, which is caused by the feuding of their lower natures.

Climbing the Tree of Knowledge with Your Polar Opposite

If both parties are willing to consciously look at their wounds and take responsibility for owning and healing them, these relationships accelerate their ascension process toward enlightenment. That being a state of self-awareness, rather than achieving some idea of perfection!

> *'An enlightened person is still a human*
> *with flaws, they just know who they are.'*

Darpan

Similarly, just because one has entered into a conscious level of partnership, does not mean there won't be disagreements or issues to resolve. However, with sacred practices to acknowledge and heal their wounds, they will lessen the degree to which they project their crap onto each other. Without this process, they will exist in a state of co-dependence, cyclically fighting about the same issues and never really resolving their individual wounds.

Over time this dynamic creates a silent divide of unspoken resentments, making physical intimacy impossible. One only needs to watch old sitcoms from the 1950s to see how interaction between the genders has progressed. Whilst it was once publicly acceptable for couples to put each other down with thinly veiled derogatory remarks about their partners, as well as direct verbal abuse, now couples file for divorce rather than stay in such a dysfunctional relationship. The challenge is to return to intimacy with a template for mutual growth.

The Beloved

This level of partnership is a mature love, entered into by those who have made the commitment to self-growth as their highest priority. It is a meeting of souls, rather than ego projections. This is only possible when both have invested considerable time, reflecting upon their journey to identify and master a number of significant personal lessons. This is the meeting of the 'High Priest King' and 'High Priestess Queen', regardless of their external professions. They are respectively a king and queen, not because they are heads of state but because they have embraced the strengths of their foundation gender by attuning to the solar or lunar cycle. They are respectively priest / priestess because they have devoted themselves as vessels to serve the divine plan. They have also developed the humility and discipline to submit to the wisdom of the natural cycles, ensuring they grow, both individually and as a couple.

'The beloved' is a term used to describe the divine in devotional scripture and verse. The beloved is therefore one who sees and honors themselves as a vessel for the divine. This is a meeting of the God and Goddess in form. Spirits in form, who have embraced the journey to unveil the seven faces of the feminine and masculine at their seven chakras, activating the rainbow bridge within so they become a clear channel for anchoring Heaven on Earth. Everything they do is part of their commitment to serve this intent, including the expression of their earthly love for themselves and each other. This is a path of devotion, to the divine potential and inherent perfection in all.

The beloved is one we love easily and effortlessly. Their presence has a calming effect on us, as we feel comfortable with them from the moment of meeting. This is because their heart is completely 'in tune' with ours, signified by effortless telepathic communication and the ability to intuit each other's needs, while being able to truly see, sense and relate to each other's authentic soul self. We feel a complete resonance with their values and philosophical outlook.

Often they are someone we have shared many incarnations with, so they feel like an old friend upon our first meeting. They are our greatest ally on our path who will support us to keep moving through our issues to fulfill our highest destiny. We will share similar issues and passions with them, as they are working through similar core wounds pertaining to the same chakra as we are. We will feel as if they really 'get' us, with a shared sense of humor and similar taste in music, food and authors. The beloveds often feel an intuitive knowing about each other straight away and feel compelled to trust the other completely, relating to them with the intimate bond one would share with a close friend.

Upon meeting them, we are struck by their beauty. Not their physical beauty, but the beauty of their soul. Often their physical appearance or what they do for a living is the opposite of what our ego would expect or choose. This signifies we have made the shift to being soul-directed otherwise we wouldn't have developed the ability to really 'see' and recognize them. What strikes us is how much we genuinely 'like' them, for who they are as a person, which is due to their ability to relate from the heart, with generosity of Spirit, displaying genuine humility and a strong commitment to serve, along with personal integrity. They have the ability to truly co-operate, giving and receiving from an open heart.

They are someone we feel proud to have beside us, because their soul beauty touches everyone they meet.

This union is one characterized by grace. Their energy is very complementary, which is often reflected in their natal chart being that of 'the divine complement'. (For example, having their sun signs in opposite signs and their rising signs in opposite signs - signifying they will help provide the balance needed to fertilize 'The Great Work'.) There is not the intensity of the twin flame connection, so there is not the drama or sense of need or longing if separated. One does not have to be perfect in order to meet with the beloved. One must only be operating in the paradigm of 5D Eden, which is the ability to be naked in oneself, willing to share all of who they are, including their vulnerabilities. We will feel 'at home' with this person, not in a way that feels familiar to our wounded child, triggering our wounds, but in a deep, serene way where one's soul feels at home because their heart is truly met.

Both will equally hold a space for the other to be completely vulnerable and instinctually know how to midwife each other through their personal processes. There is an understanding that this is their most important work together - to assist the other to heal into wholeness. As such, wounds will surface - not because they are re-wounding us, but because there is such a level of safety, so all that is not in the vibration of love, shows itself to be seen, acknowledged and released.

Lovemaking is soulful artistic expression from the first encounter, since art is the language of the soul. Heart centered communion is their natural state, with a safe space for all archetypal selves to be shared, both in and out of the bedroom, since all their gates are open. This allows for multi-dimensional and multi-orgasmic lovemaking, resulting in a deep sense of being met on a soul level.

Interdependence comes easily, as both have survived many descents, so both individually trust the process of life, surrendering to the flow of what is. They share a destiny to serve together, so they come together to birth a vision for the greater good which utilizes their inherent gifts.

They will often meet after they have undergone a huge personal shift, shedding their previous identity and taking a risk into the unknown towards their highest calling. If this doesn't occur prior to the meeting, it will happen shortly afterwards. Neither will be actively looking for a partner, as they will be so focused on their mission to serve all. Like the old adage, 'when the student is ready, the teacher appears' the same is true for our beloved, as they are our greatest teacher. Their role is to initiate us into the upper levels of our being through the internal alchemy of sacred sexuality.

The beloved wholeheartedly embraces the concept of relationship as a path for spiritual growth. They also understand the need for acknowledging the shadow, both personally and in relationship to others.

Author's Note: The symbolism of both the film, 'Avatar' and the children's animation film, 'Rio' have both played a role in awakening the role of 'The beloveds' on our planet, as we remember the power of love as our greatest strength in our return to Eden. Both films depict blue couples who find their wings to save the world. This signifies those who have awakened their higher heart, the turquoise colored chakra which is situated between the heart and the throat and activates the empathic heart of compassion for self and others. This is the resonance of one who has attuned to the 'World Soul' and so acts on behalf of the greater good.

Those who have opened this energy center have an innate sense of brother / sister, the lesson of the Aquarian Age. It is through this center that 'the beloveds' meet, so there is no seductive energy present, creating a very innocent exchange of heart intent. Due to their time spent alone, processing their life lessons, they have found the ability to transcend their human hurts by seeing them from a soul perspective.

In both films, the female protagonist is attuned to the untamed wildness and beauty of Mother Nature and the male protagonist is a aligned with civilized world of men and its inventions which illustrate the power of the mind. The female lead shows him the impact of the unconscious masculine upon nature, which threatens all life. He is then compelled to act, alongside her for the good of all. Both have a deep soul response to do their part to restore the balance, to honor the tree of life, which sustains all. They commit to working together to bring about the bridging of opposites.

When I was three, my parents took me to see 'Michael Edgeley's International Spectacular'. I have two memories about that production. One was the swirling black and red carpet in the foyer, the second was an act called, 'The Bluebirds'. A ballet pas de deux.

of a man and a woman dressed as bluebirds in blue light with blue feathered wings, who danced so lovingly in perfect union and grace. The year I met my beloved, my father sent down a 'Pandora's Box' full of my memories from childhood, including the program with a photo of 'The Bluebirds'.

In Russian fairy tales, the blue bird is a symbol of hope. The Navajo people honor the mountain bluebird as a messenger from Great Spirit who reminds them to rise with the dawn and honor the gift of light from the sun. In ancient China, there is an inscription on an oracle bone, from the Shang dynasty (1766-1122 BC) explaining that the bluebird was a messenger of the Queen Mother Goddess, Xi Wangmu, who was the protector of priestess girls and women who had taken vows to serve the light.

When I went to North America for the first time this year, on my second day I rose with the dawn and was greeted by a bluebird. This was within a year of meeting my beloved who was accompanying me on my tour to disseminate the teachings of sacred union and the Holy Grail. We met on my inaugural Australian tour, when he came to assist as a volunteer the week of the spring equinox, whereupon he offered his services to assist me in spreading my message further. The following spring equinox we began teaching our online Sacred Union course.

☤ Words Of Wisdom
from the Holy Couple

Riddles to Ask a Prospective
Lover to Ensure a Sacred Union

One of the most famous love stories is that of the Queen of Sheba and King Solomon. This is because they were a physical embodiment of beloveds, also known as, 'the holy couple' This term similarly describes a couple who have respectively awakened their higher selves so they come together to serve the divine as conduits of the sacred feminine and masculine.

Other 'holy couples' include Isis and Osiris, Jesus and Mari, Shiva and Shakti. (I would also include John and Yoko as modern day examples of a couple committed to serving the greater good through their union of opposites.) Just like Sheba and Solomon, these awakened couples had each respectively 'subsumed all of the lesser deities', meaning they sought to embody all of the divine masculine and feminine aspects consciously, making their loving exchange truly transcendent, as they expressed the full spectrum of their inner light.

So too, we can follow their example to create love matches that surpass our wildest dreams rather than settling for partnerships which are formed through the bonding of our lower selves, out of a fear of being alone.

'Being single doesn't mean you don't know anything about love. It just means you know enough to wait for it.'

http://www.facebook.com/pages/Running-to-nowhere/212683182110883

Sheba's Meeting with Solomon

The Queen of Sheba was well renowned in the ancient world. Her lands were vast throughout Africa and she traded extensively in essential oils and incense. She was said to value peace and was renowned for her wisdom. News of this exotic queen spread to King Solomon in the Middle East, who expressed he would like to meet her. When Sheba discovered he had a harem of five thousand concubines, she dismissed his request. Undeterred, he responded by writing her many letters which revealed the depth of his wisdom. ('Song of Songs' - a gospel in the Bible, is the retelling of their courtship which took place via the written word.) After this exchange of souls, he invited her to visit. For Sheba, this involved a six month journey with her royal entourage, crossing the Arabian desert.

Both prepared for this long-awaited meeting. Sheba put together various riddles to challenge Solomon's famous mind and Solomon built a temple to honor the 'Shekinah', the sacred feminine principle known as the' tree of life'. The temple was created out of crystal so it shone like glass. The floors in the foyer were also made of crystal, but beneath them were waters containing darting fish. When Sheba arrived and entered the temple, she noted there was a ramp at one end, made out of the sacred tree of life. So instead of using the ramp, she chose to hoist her robes as if to cross, only to laugh when she realized the optical illusion.

Meanwhile, Solomon stood behind a curtain eagerly watching and anticipating what she would do. He was impressed that she recognized the sacredness of the wood, used for the ramp and had instead, chosen to bare her lower nature by wading through what she thought was water. Solomon thereupon greeted her and commended her on her efforts. He confessed he had designed the foyer as a riddle and in her preparedness to wade through the water rather than using the ramp, she had demonstrated that she was a woman who would journey through the depths rather than settle for a shallow exchange. Secondly, by revealing her hairy legs as she hoisted her skirt, she indicated that she was true to her real nature and therefore a truly empowered woman.

Sheba counteracted, that he too, must complete a riddle. She had devised three questions which he would need to answer correctly if she were to consummate the sacred marriage after their long courtship. The questions she asked of him were:

'How do you see yourself?'

'How do you see me?'

'What do you want from me?'

Whilst there were many other mind games and riddles they reputedly shared amidst their lengthy discussions on sex, death, philosophy and astrology, it has been highlighted that each spoke their heart's truth freely.

So too, Solomon answered the questions she asked of him, from his soul...

'I see myself as a divine being, having a human experience.'

'I see you, as a realized being who emanates the diamond facets of the Goddess.'

'I wish to enter into the hieros gamos practice of love with you.'

With these answers, he passed her test. As rather than merely saying what his ego thought she wanted to hear, he spoke from his soul, acknowledging both their celestial and human natures. As an enlightened man, he was both appreciative of his gifts and humble in equal measure,

137

whereas an unenlightened man would dwell upon his attributes, as he saw them, hoping to impress his consort. For example, the kind of answers one might see on TV dating shows: *'I see me as a nice guy with wealth, looks and land and I see you as a gorgeous looking woman who's smart with a nice personality'*. If Solomon had replied in this manner, focusing on the values of the bottom three chakras: sex, power and wealth, Sheba would've ditched him. Equally those who are incapable of naming what they want, are incapable of creating or achieving it, so it is imperative for a conscious partner to comprehend what constitutes a sacred union in order to enter into one. (Hence the template I have been asked as a representative to share with you, as it is time for all unions to be elevated into their fullest potential!)

Below is another favorite story of mine, which illustrates the qualities of the holy couple...

The Tale of Sir Gawain and the Lady Ragnell

The legendary King Arthur was once hunting in Inglewood Forest when a deer stepped into view, which he slay single-handedly with one of his arrows. As the deer fell, a large knight, Sir Gromer stepped out from the shadows and threatened to take his life for a transgression upon that which was dear to him.

Arthur quickly offered the knight gold, land and anything he desired in exchange for sparing his life. Sir Gromer declined his offer, saying these things held no value for him. Instead, he insisted Arthur would have to meet him in exactly one year and a day with the answer to a riddle. *'You must tell me what it is that women desire most, above all else.'* said the knight.

When Arthur's friends discovered him ashen faced, they enquired as to the cause. he responded by shrugging them off, only later sharing his quandary with Gawain, his nephew, privately upon their return. Gawain suggested they ride into neighboring villages and towns and ask both men and women the answer to the riddle. So they set off on their quest to find the answer to the question men still ask today, *'What do women want?'*

Some said women longed to be adorned with jewels and finery, others said they wanted a husband who was handsome and strong, while others claimed it was a man who would never scorn them or seek to prove them wrong. Every answer was different and yet every person was convinced their answer was right.

With only a month to go, Arthur found himself back in Inglewood Forest, where he was approached by a woman who, while coveted in jewels and fine clothes was hideous to behold. She spoke the words, *'Of all the answers you have been told, none of them will help to save your life. Only I know the correct answer - grant me but one thing and I shall gift it to you.'* *'Name your price,'* said Arthur relieved to have a glimmer of light at the eleventh hour.

'You must grant me the hand of Sir Gawain, your nephew, as my betrothed. Either I marry him or you lose your head.' Unable to inflict such sufferance on his kind-hearted nephew, Arthur declined the lady's offer of assistance, but did enquire as to the woman's name. *'King Arthur, I am the Lady Ragnell'* she said.

Upon news of this fateful meeting, Gawain agreed to marry the woman in exchange for Arthur's life, saying anything less would be cowardly. And so Arthur sought out Lady Ragnell to tell him of Gawain's consent to wed, in exchange for the secret. *'Sir,'* said Lady Ragnell, *'the answer is simple, women want the same as men - to have sovereignty over their own lives.'*

The day arrived and upon hearing of the right answer to this riddle, Arthur was granted his life and freedom. True to his honor, Gawain married Lady Ragnell to repay the debt, affording her the dignity and courtesy, as if he had chosen her himself. Later that night in their bedchamber, he was shocked to see his bride appear in her nightgown looking ravishingly beautiful. She explained that a curse had been placed upon her by her brother, Sir Gromer. The curse meant she could either appear beautiful in the daylight on his arm for all to see, and like a hag in the evening when they were alone or beautiful in the evening for him in private and like a hag during daylight for everyone else. She then enquired as to his preference.

'Alas,' said Gawain, 'the choice is hard and either would grieve my heart, so I must place it in your hands. As whatever you choose I will support as your husband.' With that, he released her from the enchantment. For she had indeed found a man who could not just answer the riddle, but act upon it, ensuring she would always be beautiful in his eyes.

Meaning of the Parable

This tale, made popular by the film, 'Shrek' illustrates that when a man truly honors a woman's free will, that being, her right to choose what is best for her, he honors her as an equal, which engenders mutual respect. He doesn't see her as his possession, which is a patriarchal concept. This means she is free to choose him, rather than feel honor bound to serve him in accordance with societal expectations of her role as wife.

This parable illustrates how Gawain accepts the cyclic nature of life and the many, varied faces of the Goddess. This is a key feature of the practice of hieros gamos, 'the holy marriage'. This story also portrays a man who sees and values the beauty of his partner's soul, which is eternal more than her physical appearance, which is temporary. It also indicates that he will not reject her, even when she ages or shows her different facets, which make up the psyche or soul.

This is a parable of mature love which honors the cyclic nature of life.

This story also shows the archetype of the good king (played by Arthur) as a man who is guided by his heart to do what is right and honorable. He displays a willingness to seek 'the Grail', that being the wisdom of the dark feminine, that which is hidden, but essential if one is to mature. She is represented by the archetypal wise woman who resides in the forest during the darkest month of winter and demands the ego death of every questing hero - another key feature of the hieros gamos.

It is also significant that Arthur journeys for a year and a day to find the answer to the riddle. So too, in the ancient world, initiates of the hieros gamos married for a year and a day, renewing their vows each year in the spring. This allowed them to cyclically review their commitment, honoring their free will rather than staying together out of expectation. This feature of the story illustrates the degree to which they observed the ancient mysteries with the understanding of the role the seasonal wheel played in their interaction with their beloved.

This story heralds the Grail mysteries, where true gentlemen were expected to wed the dark feminine in themselves, to embody the wisdom of the sacred feminine as a precursor to marriage. Without this rite of passage, they would continue to unconsciously slay the innocent, symbolized by the deer. A pattern of behavior, which eventually costs a man his health, wealth and happiness, if not his physical life - if he doesn't stop to ponder the effect of his actions and learn to honor the teachings of death and decay afforded to us in the circle of life. One needs only see how much innocence is aggrieved in our modern day culture to see the omission of our sacred knowledge and rites...we need the good king to return in all men, if life on our planet is to survive and thrive.

Reclaiming the Hieros Gamos

The Sacred Wedding Between the God and Goddess

The hieros gamos was the Greek term for the holy marriage between two deities, traditionally, a God and a Goddess.

The holy marriage was publicly celebrated through the re-enactment of the holy couple. This took place between a 'High Priestess Queen' and a 'High Priest King'. Both were worldly, spiritual and sovereign. They were awakened beings who were individually wedded to serve and honor the Earth and her people, so each honored the circle of life through the wisdom of the ever-changing seasons.

The reigning worldly leader, the king was, 'A man for all seasons' - a man who honored all the aspects of himself; the knight, the king, the magician and the sage. Equally, the reigning spiritual leader, the 'High Priestess' was a 'A woman for all seasons' who honored all aspects of herself; the maiden, the queen, the enchantress and the mystic.

By accepting all these aspects in themselves, they could then appreciate and value them in each other. It is this perspective which nurtures the growth of a mature love. That is, one where neither rejects the other for doing what is natural - aging! This is only possible when one has made their peace with the inevitability of death. If we consider one can only honor life, when in right relationship with death, perhaps we can also concede we have a thing or two to learn from these ancient civilizations. When we consider our collective fear and popular culture's preoccupation with death in prime time entertainment, we can see in equal measure the general lack of reverence for all life. It is long overdue that we question the arrogant misconception that ancient cultures were less advanced in all things and consider now what they have to teach us.

The ancients were constantly humbled by the elemental forces of the seasons. This is because their lives depended on them as they lived close to the Earth and relied on their ability to harness the elemental forces to survive.

At each seasonal gate they bowed to the Season, embracing the psycho-emotional lesson to which they humbly submitted, if they were to personally thrive, sustain growth and age gracefully. They acknowledged the effect that each seasonal turning of the wheel had on every aspect of their lives. This included their personal relationships. For each element which governs the reigning season, demanded another aspect of their relationship had to grow or they would experience greater challenges.

How Mother Nature Initiates Relationship Growth in Every Season

Spring is governed by the element of Air: so during this phase we are called upon to question thoughts which may limit our growth. Failure to do this may result in arguments, stemming from one feeling held back by the other.

Summer is governed by the element of Fire: so during this phase we are called upon to express our passion that stokes our heart's fire. If we don't express our own creative ideas, we will criticize the efforts of others, creating resentment and inhibiting sharing.

Autumn is governed by the element of Water: so during this phase we are called upon to reflect upon our past actions and share our wisdom with humility. If we don't reflect, we will repeat past mistakes, escalating frustration in relationships.

Winter is governed by the element of Earth: so during this phase we are called upon to enter into stillness with reverence for what it takes to sustain physical life. If we don't come home to ourselves, we will have no center from which to make decisions. That uncertainty will translate as lack of commitment, undermining all efforts to relate to others.

Each season also calls forth another aspect of our selves.

Spring evokes the inner maiden and knight who help us to lighten up after the short days and long nights of winter, so we can take chances on sharing our ideas and talents with those around us. If we don't embrace opportunities to play and have fun, we will resent our responsibilities and others won't want to be around us.

Summer evokes the inner king and queen who ask that we take responsibility for tending what we have birthed, started or seeded so through the application of consistent effort it can fruit. If we fail to back our words and promises up with action, those close to us will lose trust in our word and over time, this will manifest as a lack of respect.

Autumn evokes the inner enchantress and magi who encourage us to consider how our harvest in every part of our lives is the direct result of our actions. If we fail to be personally responsible for the outcome of everything in our waking world, tracing it back to the origins of our beliefs, expectations and actions (or inaction), we look for someone to blame as a scapegoat, a pattern which is a real relationship liability.

Winter evokes the inner mystic and sage who invite us to lie fallow, so we may become completely receptive to insights from the superconsciousness, the universal collective mind of God. if we neglect this personal relationship between ourselves and the Divine, we become addictive and dependent, looking for someone or something to fill the void within us, which can only be filled by the infinite essence of Source.

Mother Nature: The Universal Spiritual Teacher

We have been taught to fear nature, in both subtle and overt ways over time, just as religious doctrines taught the masses to fear their own nature as demonic, impure or sinful. Like the saying, 'where there's fear, there's power'. If we befriend nature, we befriend ourselves, since we are 'of nature'. Our relating then becomes more harmonious, when we come from a place of self-acceptance. It is time for us as a species to seek to understand nature, both our own and that of the greater cycles, so we can better comprehend the effect of nature upon us...again, our survival depends upon it.

'Christianity's loss of its esoteric dimension has been one of tragic cultural consequence that is still casting its long shadow over the Western world. We are really only just emerging from a protracted dark age. This has meant the loss of those luminous mythic images that lead into the heart of philosophy and the art, the loss of the very archetypes wherein are found the higher energies that give life, intellectual power, and healing to a civilization.'

Victoria LePage 'Mysteries of the Bridechamber'

The Wheel of Eight - Consciously Journeying the Seasonal Mandala

The ancients paid particular attention to the zenith points of each seasonal shift, these are known as the 'wheel of eight' - comprised of the solstices, equinoxes and cross-quarter festivals situated half-way between each of these energy polarities.

These 'high energy' three day vortices are seasonal chakra points, offering an intensification of accelerated consciousness, for those willing to embrace the lesson of each gate. (More info about this in volume three with specific practices to journey the hieros gamos in my sacred union online course. For more info the resources page in the back of this book.)

Ishtar's symbol, the eight pointed star indicates that the eight seasonal 'holi-days' were an intrinsic part of her ceremonial rites. Her body, is depicted as the curvaceous figure eight, denoting her as a conduit for life force. In numerology '8' is the number of abundance and power. This is because 'eight' is the infinity sign, a symbol of eternal energy, flowing between opposite poles to generate life.

Sacred Union

Marriage to Self / Marriage to Spirit

The wheel of eight (later referred to as the Pagan Sabbats*) were the holy days sacred to the Babylonian Goddess of Love, Ishtar. This was because they provided a template to ensure sustainable unions, which honored one's Soul self, the Soul in all other life and the natural cycles.

*Author's Note: *The term, 'sabbat' comes from the 'Sabbatu' - the holy day of 'heart rest' honored by the ancient world, including the ancient Greek and Babylonians. This is where the Jewish religion derived the term, 'the sabbath'. Pagans, though portrayed as 'devil worshippers' by theologians to their parishioners, were simply nature worshippers.*

Ishtar's symbol was the eight pointed star, as she lived in communion with the eight seasonal star-gates. Her teachings were a pathway to awaken one's divine potential, through the observances around the seasonal wheel. The name Ishtar, also means 'Star'. She is the feminine aspect who, when unveiled, anchors our stellar nature, enabling us to activate the eighth chakra, known as the Godhead. One can only open this star-gate when they ascend to remember their true soul self, after surviving a descent to unveil their shadow at each of the seven gates (chakras). This understanding was key to making the commitment to be an initiate of the hieros gamos. As an inherent part of the journey was one's willingness to descend to face their most rejected and denied aspects. A process, which was catalyzed by the lessening solar light over the course of autumn / winter, accelerating one's inner dance with the shadow. Only through embracing these disowned traits, could one heal and find enough self-acceptance to experience both giving and receiving love in union.

Ishtar's priestesses, would therefore prepare for sacred union with their beloved by willingly descending each autumn / winter to unveil more of their shadow aspects to become wise. This is why the High Priestess would perform the, 'Dance of the Seven Veils' with her graduating priestesses, (those who had performed the series of initiations seven times) as part of a public demonstration upon their return at the spring equinox.

Author's Note: In 2007 I had experienced a flashback where I saw myself at Ishtar's Gate on the Day of the Great Rite. This occurred while I was waiting backstage to perform the 'Dance of the Seven Veils' at the national Goddess Conference in Australia. In the flashback, I was in ancient Babylon about to perform this dance for the king and the people. I was wearing kohl, veils and jewelry at each of the seven chakras, illustrating the seven divine gates of the resurrected Goddess who had cast off her illusions.

This Sumerian hymn sung by the resurrected High Priestess embodying the Goddess, Ishtar on the spring equinox, acknowledges all she has received from her journey to the Underworld and back. These qualities include all the opposite experiences and aspects she has seen in herself, through the reflection of her opposite, so she could truly know herself in truth.

> *'He gave me the art of forthright speech.*
> *He gave me the art of slanderous speech.*
> *He gave me the art of adorning speech....'*

Translated Sumerian hymn

Spring equinox was the most celebrated of all the eight holy days, as it marked the commitment of the God to the Goddess after they had witnessed the shadow in each other during the darker months of autumn / winter. Less mature unions would oftentimes not survive the descent of winter as both parties would reject all they had not yet owned in themselves, in their opposite. This is why the myths of the lovers feature a separation during the six months of autumn / winter.

Sacred Union

A truly sacred union is therefore not possible without both initiates first journeying consciously around the 'wheel of eight' to create sacred union within. For example, at the spring equinox (the gate preceding the marriage gate) one must transcend any emotional attachments, hopes or desires by surrendering completely to highest will. For this is the gate where one takes vows to wed themselves to their spiritual path. In the Kabbalah, this path is known as Death and requires one to look only to themselves for emotional fulfillment. It is the path from Netsach, the Sephirot governed by Venus relating to our lower emotions to Tippareth The Sephirot of the heart, governed by the sun.

My Personal Spring Equinox Rite 2012

Author's Note: Having just journeyed through spring equinox over the past three days I wondered why in the preceding week I had been constantly bombarded with images of the skull and crossbones and news of people and pets crossing over. Wanting to understand what Death was trying to show me through such persistent symbology, I set the intention to dance with Death at a dance meditation event so I might become one with Death and understand what Death was trying to teach me.

After smudging myself with sage, I entered the hall of the dance meditation to see an altar draped with orange and crimson silks, denoting the two faces of Venus. (Orange is the color of the sacral chakra governed by Aphrodite, the maiden and crimson is the color of the soul star chakra governed by Ishtar, the Queen.) This affirmed the lesson of this gate after I had seen multiple images of skulls and a billboard the previous day that read, 'He is Arisen' on the highway while my iphone shuffle synchronistically played a track called, 'Arisen'. (Ego death happens to be my ultimate life lesson, as my life path in the Kabbalah is the 'Death' path. This is in addition to my five planets in Scorpio, the sign of death and rebirth). So as I danced I shook out all my preconceived ideas about what I wanted or thought should be unfolding in my life. I activated the twin serpents energetically within using creative visualization, and saw myself as the Cretan snake Goddess, dancing with both of my inner energy serpents, Ida and Pingala in each hand.

I was filled with the beauty I saw in every face and body freely moving in communion with their souls and the energy of the dawning spring. I then saw with my inner sight, the floor blooming with a carpet of flowers. Faeries entered, forming a ring around me on the floor and crowning me as a fey Queen. Rainbow light started streaming out of my fingertips as I moved throughout the hall, spreading rainbow light amongst the other dancers. I was overflowing with joy, silliness and play, causing many to spontaneously laugh when I interacted with them.

*My Aphrodite cup was full and overflowing, despite not being met at that time by my Beloved. I then received the insight that by wedding myself to Death, I allowed myself to be born anew in every moment. In other words, by allowing all expectations to die in every moment, I would be eternally in the present, truly **with** Spirit and open to what Spirit wanted to gift me in each moment, rather than being limited by my own preconceived ideas.*

Given that death and birth are two sides of the one coin, it seemed fitting that to midwife myself through this gateway of birth, I first needed to understand the lesson of death. For the more I could release, the more I could open to receive and become. I felt as if I'd just been let out of the jail of my mind. (No wonder my niece had asked me to read, 'Rapunzel' the previous day and then two hours later I had opened a book at the airport on a chapter titled, 'Rapunzel.)

The Big Day!

The pomp and pageantry that was afforded this celebration was akin to that of a modern royal wedding, except the ancient Babylonians were far less backward in expressing their erotic desires via the ancient love art of poetry. So unlike the dour ceremonies enacted by the clergy in our modern day 'royal weddings', these titillating passages were re-enacted by the High Priestess and the reigning King. Here's a sample of what the Goddess, Ishtar has to say during the scene that depicts the royal courtship between her and Tammuz. (Ishtar and her beloved, Dumuzi, were known as Inanna and Tammuz in other parts of Mesopotamia - same archetypes, different names.)

> *'What I tell you*
> *Let the singer weave into song.*
> *What I tell you,*
> *Let it flow from ear to mouth,*
> *Let it pass from old to young:*
>
> *My vulva, the horn,*
> *The boat of Heaven,*
> *Is full of eagerness like the young Moon.*
> *My untilled land lies fallow.*
>
> *As for me, Inanna,*
> *Who will plow my vulva?*
> *Who will plow my high field?*
> *Who will plow my wet ground?*
>
> *'As for me, the young woman,*
> *Who will plow my vulva?*
> *Who will station the ox there?*
> *Who will plow my vulva?*

Translated Sumerian hymn

Not sure if that would get an arts grant today but certainly sounds like a chorus of wailing women I have been party to!

What I like about this excerpt is that she asks both, for herself as a woman and as a conduit for the Goddess, acknowledging that the Priestess Queen is both, mortal and immortal.

Here is a poem I channeled when I too, was calling out to the universe for my beloved, a la Ishtar! May this inspire you to pen your own calling from your soul to theirs and then share it with them when they return after the long winter.

To He Who Would Be King

by Tanishka

I have been entered
By the Great Divine
The Sky Father hath descended
into my flower of Creation
with an open heart
and I have met him
full and radiant
enamored of my own beauty
I am whole, complete
Fragrant woman
surrounded by the enigma of love
pure and sweet
I am she
woman
Goddess
Chalice of the Great Beyond

I open the petals of my delicate temple
revealing
the temple to the stars
Be not afraid
for what awaits is a homecoming
to your own presence
All omnipotent
Expansive Totality

Be the journeyman
Leave the rugged torment of your mind
and enter...into ecstasy
the star-gate to the Great Beyond
for the treasure is yours
awaiting...
beckoning...
be not afraid
for it is the inevitable truth
to which all travelers must return

Tarry not long
for your burden is great
and becomes heavier as you approach the light
drop your pretense
for it becomes you not
I see the greatness
emanating from the folds of your robe
and invite you to join me
forever in ecstatic embrace
our playground
eternal bliss.

And so it is!

The Great Rite

This sacred wedding known as the 'Great Rite' was celebrated throughout the ancient world on New Year's day, the spring equinox. The women would dress in their finery and dance through the streets heralding the arrival of the King to the Gate of Ishtar. (pictured below)

Built in the 6th century under the patronage of King Nebuchadnezzar II, Ishtar's Gate was decorated with dragons (denoting the sacred feminine) and lions (representing the sacred masculine) in gold and lapis lazuli, a crystal which the ancient Egyptians used to anchor the higher self. This ornate gate highlighted their deep reverence for the divine feminine as it symbolized the gateway to sacred union. The entire city of Babylon was designed using sacred geometry to anchor the intent of 'as above, so below' which means, 'on Earth as it is in Heaven'. This makes sense when we understand that they worshipped Ishtar as the Queen of Heaven.

There were eight gates in total throughout the city. The one pictured was the main entrance to the city of Babylon, whose name translated means, 'Gateway to the Gods'. Each gate represented each of the seven major chakras on the inner Tree of Life with the eighth being the Godhead - the place of the awakened one who had transcended the seven veils of illusion. To honor this, the city featured bountiful orchards, groves of trees and plentiful gardens irrigated by their canals. The processional way to the temple, once inside the main gate also featured the Hanging Gardens of Babylon, an act of beauty created by the King for his Queen, which became legendary as one of the seven wonders of the world.

> *'... and then there came a new image, the last vision. I walked up a wide valley to the end ... a classical amphitheater ... magnificently situated in the green landscape. And there, in this theater, the hieros gamos was being celebrated. Men and women dancers came on stage, and upon a flower-decked couch All-father Zeus and Hera consummated the mystic marriage, as it is described in the Illiad.'*

Claire Dunne, 'Carl Jung: Wounded Healer of the Soul'.

Author's Note: Synchronistically, while writing this book my local museum recreated Ishtar's Gate as part of an exhibition on Mesopotamia. I was very curious to go and see if I would receive any more intuitive downloads. What occurred to me upon seeing the Gate of Ishtar was that spring equinox was 'the return of the King' to Ishtar's temple gates. This was a celebration of their commitment to union after the tests of autumn / winter. This gate marked the annual royal engagement; the betrothal and consent of the annual Sacred Marriage which took place on the equinox, the day of perfect balance of light and dark, feminine and masculine polarities. Their union was not consummated sexually until the next seasonal gate of Beltane.

'The Babylonians would assemble in front of it and march through the triumphal arch and proceed along the Sacred Way to the seven-story Ziggurat, which was crowned near the temple of Marduk.'

http://www.bible-history.com/babylonia/BabyloniaThe_Ishtar_Gate.htm

The Magical Number Seven

This theme of seven steps was recurrent in Babylonian society; evident in the seven steps of the Ziggurat and the seven tiers of Ishtar's skirt, suggesting one had to pass a riddle at the seven gates to gain entry to her temple.

The processional leading to the Ziggurat featured other Gods. This inclusion suggests the acknowledgement of the other deities who govern the chakras as the pathway to wholeness.

As the sun descended, the royal couple were said to ascend the Ziggurat (a stepped pyramid), to the eighth level, which was decorated as an ornate bedchamber. It was reserved for the sacred sexual coupling of the High Priestess and the King of the land, who submitted themselves as vessels for the celestial energies of the universal God and Goddess. Patriarchal historians have interpreted this event as a superstitious ritual enacted to please the Gods. This says more about our modern day ignorance of sacred alchemy than it does about the practices of the ancients.

In this act of Tantric high magic, the role of the High Priestess Queen and High Priest King, was to open their energetic star-gates (dimensional vortices) simultaneously, unifying all aspects of the God and Goddess. They did this by anointing their crowns with spikenard oil. (This is also why Mari, the Magdalene (a High Priestess of Ishtar) anointed Yeshua, the Christ's feet with spikenard oil during The Last Supper.) Spikenard oil assists the simultaneous opening and spin rate of all the chakras. This assists the activation of the inner Twin Serpents, Ida and Pingala, (the major yin / yang energy meridians), up through the seven major chakras. This activates the multi-dimensional communion of all seven faces of the God / Goddess who govern the chakras. When these chakras open, all seven color rays, comprising the full spectrum of light, the rainbow bridge within our light bodies, emits all healing frequencies, creating a potent anchoring of harmony of all opposite polarities on all dimensions throughout eternity as a gift to all of creation.

'The transmission of energies by such a sexual method as the hieros gamos, undertaken by an adept, had the effective power of a genetic science and was capable of creating deep physiological and psychological changes in the royal line. What is hinted at here, of course, is the science of spinal energy centers in which the later Solar temples excelled, and which involved the Gnosis of the heart practiced by Christians of a later age. The same science that Jesus introduced to his inner circle of disciples was key to the forest rites that had long ago raised the consciousness and indeed changed DNA.'

Victoria LePage. Mysteries of the Bridechamber

The Rainmaker

'The Rainmaker' is an ancient parable which beautifully illustrates the philosophy behind the practice of the hieros gamos. The story goes...

There was once a drought stricken village. It had experienced no rain for five consecutive years. Many rainmakers had come and gone, each had tried their best to make it rain - but none had been successful, despite their many and varied attempts. Desperate and facing starvation, the villagers summoned a well renowned rainmaker from a distant province.

When he arrived at the village he performed no ceremony, no dance or special incantation, he simply asked to be left alone, whereupon he entered a small hut and spoke to no one for four days. On the fifth day, the heavens opened and it rained for four days straight.

The people asked him, 'How did you do it? How did you make it rain?'

He replied, '*When I came to your village I noticed everything was out of order. So if I wanted to play a part in restoring order in your village, I first needed to create order within myself. So I turned my attention toward restoring my inner balance so I was in right relation with Heaven.*'

Heaven on Earth

This is the ultimate inspiration and motivation for embracing the practice of sacred union. It is based on the understanding that we are each custodians of Eden. We are each vessels for restoring the sacred balance on our planet. When we return to living in a state of reverence for every experience as our teacher, including every moment of the greater cycles, the macrocosm will reflect the shift in the microcosm. We will have fulfilled our destiny and played our part in anchoring Heaven on Earth.

Embodying the Sun and Moon

Both the High Priestess and the King prepared energetically for this occasion, with particular emphasis being placed upon the observance of the first day of each lunar cycle and each monthly solar cycle, when the sun transited into a new sign.

> '*In order to care for the life of the lands,*
> *The exact first day of the month is closely examined,*
> *And on the day of the disappearance of the moon,*
> *On the day of the sleeping of the moon,*
> *The me are perfectly carried out*

So that the New Year's Day, the day of rites,
May be properly determined'

Translated Sumerian hymn

The recording of the importance of these esoteric practices in the Sumerian annual enactment of the hieros gamos signifies they were diligent in their devotional practice and receptive to divine wisdom. This enabled them to open up their energetic, mental, emotional and physical bodies as channels for the essence of the universal God / Goddess energies to anchor the frequency of a harmonic union of opposites. By creating divine balance in the microcosm, they acted as custodians, ensuring balance and harmony for the land and her people. So too, if we want our lives to be fertile and abundant, we can attune to the lessons of the sun and moon each month.

Author's Note: The observance of the solar and lunar cycles and not just the seasonal wheel makes perfect sense. I had felt this intuitively when I instructed couples as a private couples coach, initiating them through the seven meetings of sun and moon as part of the hieros gamos. So I was delighted to find this passage which affirmed my intuition. Before we can dance in an empowered way with our opposite, we must first empower our foundation gender. We do this by embodying the qualities of the sun if we are male, or the moon if we are female. So queenship is attained through women attuning to the lunar wheel and kingship is attained through men aligning with the solar wheel. This is why the holy couple were often depicted with her, standing with the moon under her feet and he, with the solar disc under his.

Activating the Solar King

The aforementioned excerpt also indicates that the Babylonians studied the astrological transits of the coming month, so they could honor the lessons being presented.

So too, modern men can empower their masculine self-expression by gathering with men on the day the sun moves into a new astrological sign each month, specifically to consider the ramifications of the approaching lesson in their own lives. This is the premise of the online course I created for men to structured template of discipleship for men's circles. Just as women have a moon lodge, it is equally important for men to have a sun lodge. A place where they can pause, reflect and regroup, without feeling any threat, should they show any sign of weakness. The power of such a monthly gathering also lies in men of all ages sitting in counsel together, for this is a space where men learn about all facets of being a man, just through honest, heart-centered sharing.

Young men from the age of fifteen are welcomed, giving them a safe place to confide all their life lessons and be mentored by a circle of men who have their best interests at heart. When men have this level of support, they are less inclined to indulge in reckless or addictive behaviors.

One of the shadow traits of the unconscious masculine is acting without thinking. So by gathering to reflect upon how they fared with their previous challenges each month, they learn to identify self-sabotaging patterns. This concludes with a briefing of the next month's lesson, based on the sign the sun is moving into. This spark of inspiration was lit twenty years before when I came across the work of Alice Bailey. Her book, 'The Labors of Hercules' uses the myth of the hero, Hercules to illustrate the archetypal challenges faced by the initiates ego as he journeys around the astrological mandala. (For more info about my Brotherhood Lodge online course see the resources page in the back of the book.)

Ultimately we are all affected by the sun sign each month, regardless of our physical gender. However, men will feel the Solar transits more as the sun rules the masculine. It is therefore as prudent for both men, especially to check the astro forecast at the commencement of each solar month, which is as practical as checking the tides before heading out on a fishing trip.

Awakening the Lunar Queen

Similarly, the lunar cycles affects us all, however women will feel the effects of lunar transits and phases more than men, since the moon rules the feminine. So while it is important for men to be mindful of the lunar cycle, if they want to balance their emotion wellbeing - it is especially important for women, given the effect it has on our psyche and hormones.

New moon is the beginning of the lunar month. Also referred to as 'dark' moon, it occurs two weeks after full moon, when the moon appears dark in the sky. Traditionally women gathered in moon lodges (also known as red tents) at the start of the lunar cycle. It was here they would reflect upon the qualities they had seen in themselves in the previous month. By gathering together, they would increase their ability to intuit insights into their personal challenges.

This is the forum where young women learn about all facets of being a woman, such as learning domestic crafts, healing, divination, sacred sexuality and all facets of child rearing. Having a circle of mentors ensured young women could individuate from their mothers with ongoing support from women of all ages. This is especially important through ones maiden years when we experience some of our biggest lessons and have little experiential wisdom of our own to draw upon.

For twenty years I have facilitated Red Tent circles and initiated girls into their womanhood. It was seeing the profound impact of these circles upon modern women's lives of all ages that inspired me to create an equivalent template for men! (If you'd like to know more about my Red Tent online course visit the resources page in the back of this book.)

This practice of monthly men's circles and women's circles, provides a societal structure to support both men and women of all ages to continue growing beyond their challenges with the support of their community. This takes a lot of pressure off intimate unions, as such a regular opportunity to process unresolved issues, minimizes the chance of conflict on the home front.

 **Becoming a Sexual Activist**

How Sexuality Holds the Key
to Our Liberation and Evolution

The Deliberate Misrepresentation of the Hieros Gamos

It is specifically because of the power generated by the alchemical sacred sex practice of the hieros gamos, which included the Holy Grail, that all knowledge of it was suppressed.

Those who practiced and taught these ancient teachings were hunted down and killed to prevent the practices being disseminated. This is why Jesus was killed. As were all the Cathars who hid Jesus and Mari after his resurrection. All the followers of the Cathar religion were completely wiped out between 1208 - 1244 in France when the Dark Ages church murdered hundreds of thousands of them. These teachings were the hidden gospel of Mari, 'the Magdalene' (the title of a High Priestess of Ishtar) - based on her initiation into this ancient practice that was conducted throughout ancient Mesopotamia.

'Mary offered a real challenge to male dominance. She made no pretense of fading into the background, nor was her role a lowly domestic one. The Apocrypha make it clear that she was the leader among the women disciples and at all times made her presence known, giving dissertations to the other disciples that explained the master's teachings.'

Victoria LePage, Mysteries of the Bridechamber.

Then there were the witch hunts during the Middle Ages, when again the practice resurfaced. A strategy instigated by the Illuminati, fronted by the Catholic church and medical fraternities to stamp out the rising of kundalini which would result in the power of the people rising to challenge those who dominated the economic landscape.

Those who sought to suppress the consciousness of the populace, (so they were easier to manipulate and control) then orchestrated a distorted view of it, so people would look no further. So rather than acknowledge, understand and revere the power of our sexual energy to awaken our consciousness, when raised with intent, people were taught to suppress and fear their human sexuality.

In addition, dark associations were propagated about the hieros gamos to skew public perception, such as linking the hieros gamos to fetish sex, group sex, voyeurism and domination fantasies. These have nothing to do with the hieros gamos. However, just as all the sacred observances were hijacked by the monotheistic religious cults, practices like the hieros gamos were intentionally inverted by the shadow elite in their secret society gatherings to deliberately anchor their agenda of total domination.

Become a Sexual Activist!

When we comprehend the ramifications of this, we also understand that to reclaim this practice is an act of power, accessible to every adult woman and man, willing to play a part in restoring the balance of power on our planet, back into the hands of the people.

The more people awaken the inner serpents of light, (the channels for raising kundalini) the more they will stand in their personal power by living their truth and making choices that reflect the authenticity of their Soul. For when the serpents awaken, so do the people. You cannot oppress people who have liberated themselves from the illusion they are less than divine.

> *'The most powerful thing in the hands of the oppressor are the minds of the oppressed.'*

> Steve Biko

When we remember ourselves as divine beings and honor ourselves and all life accordingly, we will create Heaven on Earth in every choice we make, as all permanent change starts with a spark of awareness, which ripples outward into our words and deeds.

> *Life's design is meant to be erotic, not neurotic!'*

> Jun Po Denis Kelly Roshi

When the critical mass is reconnecting to the natural forces, attuning to their cyclic rhythms, it creates a groundswell that is powerful enough to transform our entire soul sick culture. Yes, the days of angry picket marches are over, now is a time to truly 'make love, not war'! For when we remember our true power as creative beings, powered by the eternal essence of life - which is LOVE, we can harness and direct our potential using energy raising techniques and creative visualizations in conjunction with an understanding of the alchemy of the natural cycles.

The Art of Sex Magic

Sex magic is one aspect of the hieros gamos, just as it is one aspect of Tantra. Sex magic involves the raising of energy which one then uses to intention an outcome.

If we consider that 'energy raising techniques' are anything natural that assists us to feel joyful, happy, ecstatic, connected and playful, we can see that saving the planet doesn't have to be all doom and gloom!

'Participation is bliss because the whole universe is celebrating. Every moment it is celebrating. It is a great celebration, a constant celebration. Only we are not part of it. We have detached ourselves and are in misery. Man is in misery because of the mind. The flowers are participating in the celebration, the moon is participating, the stars are participating, the Earth is participating, the oceans are participating, the air and the clouds – everything is participating in that continuous, eternal celebration.

"Only man has become an outsider – and because of his own efforts. On his own, he has separated himself from existence.'

Osho, The New Alchemy

The hieros gamos teaches us the power of using our own bodies as wands of light to consciously manifest our intent into form: magic! We do this by becoming crystal clear vessels. To become clear, we simply commit to cyclically process our unresolved experiences, enabling us to bring more of our unconscious patterns of behavior into the light of understanding so we can take full responsibility for what we create, both consciously and unconsciously.

Sex magic is an ancient art. It is an art form we have been taught to fear as anti-life when in fact it is working with 'the force' - our life force! Suppressing this knowledge of responsible energy usage, one could argue is anti-life - evil, which is live spelled backwards. (Spelling is exactly that, using words to cast intent and so much of our language origins need to be understood and reclaimed.)

In sex magic, one simply uses the energy they raise during the art of lovemaking to focus on a positive and loving intent for the good of all. If we view sexuality as dirty, chances are we'll perceive sex magic as evil. Whereas, if we see our sexuality as a sacred expression of love, we'll equate sex magic as a healing art.

This starts with creating a sacred space, such as creating an altar upon which you place a symbol of the sacred feminine and masculine, in acknowledgement that all life is created through the ecstatic union of these polar opposites. I also recommend using the elements to create a space that is charged with loving anticipation. For example:

Air: Scent the air with spicy warm essential oils in an oil burner to arouse passion, such as clove, cinnamon, patchouli, cardamom, black pepper and ginger.

Fire: light lots of candles in your boudoir, (making sure no billowing candles are going to catch alight).

Water: Bathe beforehand so that you feel soft, receptive and reborn.

Earth: Put on some sensual music with sultry rhythms.

Next, sit opposite each other and anoint each other with spikenard oil to open your chakras. Speak a blessing as you do this to honor your beloved as a vessel for the God / Goddess.

Then share what intention you would like to charge through your lovemaking and agree to both visualize your shared intent as you climax.

Note: This can also be done as a practice when one climaxes during self-pleasuring.

The Power of Creative Visualization

Creative visualization is a proven tool for success used by elite athletes. It is a simple process which involves seeing in your mind's eye a desired outcome, then charging that intention with intense feelings - literally giving it energy!

"Over two hundred studies prove the nervous system cannot tell the difference between what's real and what you vividly

imagine. Journals like Psycho Neuro Endocrinology report creative visualization results in 'specific molecular changes'...and 'positively impacts' your genes."

Lisa Nichols

Creative visualization has been around a long time, however it has only been in the last few decades that science has validated its effectiveness. The key to its success lies in two ingredients.

First, one must choose a highly specific goal, then see it as already being achieved, seeing it in as much detail as possible. The degree to which one activates that vision by engaging the five senses, the more real it becomes as it is charged as a multi-sensory experience.

Second, ensure after your visualization that all your spoken words and actions affirm that which you have already set in motion. For it is in the process of being manifested by your sub-conscious in conjunction with the superconsciousness - the collective unconscious or 'mind of God' and you don't want negate your invocation.

This is a technique which was brought to the awareness of the mass consciousness through the film, 'The Secret' but had been pioneered in the West decades before by writers like Shakti Gawain. It is also interesting to note that blockbuster films about magic such as 'Harry Potter' are also appealing to the group mind.

Traditionally, practitioners of magic would raise energy to cast their spell using a 'cone of fire'. This involves wearing conical clothing, such as long skirts, robes or conical hats so the energy raised along the central nervous cord, (the central channel for kundalini known as Sushumna in Tantra) spirals upwards, creating a vortex that harnesses and directs the energy. This is also why people, 'cast a circle' and stand in circles, to create a vortex of power. (Churches adopted this concept when they built steeples on their rooftops.)

That is not to say all magic uses sexual energy to raise power. Non-sexual magical practices raise energy using a 'breath of fire'. Yogis also use the 'breath of fire' to heal energy blockages and raise kundalini to expand consciousness. The 'breath of fire' is simply done by breathing in and out rapidly through the nose.

Despite classical Tantra being full of various breathing practices, personally I don't find it necessary to focus on a breathing technique when doing sex magic. The reason for this s that love is the most potent energy there is. So if we're in our heads, trying to maintain a specific breathing rhythm, we are not going to be as potent as if we were to completely surrender to the energies raised, when we allow the serpentine energies within us to writhe and express their divine ecstasy in union with our beloved. When we consider the combination of masculine / feminine energies can create new life, we can appreciate just how powerful sex is as a force for creation of any intent.

Author's Note: I am not advocating that every time you make love, should you focus on healing the world. As a general rule, I recommend dedicating your full moon once a month to a Tantric practice which includes sex magic in service to the greater good.

Fear Not, Gelfling!

It is however, important to not affirm fear through our magical workings. By that I mean, be sure to not focus on your fears of what could happen but instead your joy at what you are taking part in co-creating. For everything we have created unconsciously in this realm, is merely a catalyst to awaken our true power and purpose as creative vessels. It is only when we forget this truth, we feel powerless. When we remember the truth of who we really are, we are unstoppable. The fine print on this contract is that this does, however, mean taking full responsibility for ourselves, such as our well-being - emotionally, physically, mentally and energetically.

We Are the Ones We Have Been Waiting For

Through the suppression of kundalini raising practices and understanding their significance, we have come to see wealth and power as indicating one's right to rule, based on an individual's bloodline. Similarly our political leaders are sponsored by corrupt corporations which has led to tyrants ruling the people and destroying the land. So too, we have been taught to fear our own power as alchemists - sacred magicians. This was specifically so we would be too ignorant to notice the dark occultist techniques being employed against us, by those who sought to oppress the Earth and her people for their own personal gain.

We are living in exciting times. Where once it was dangerous to practice the healing arts for fear of losing one's life, now the mass raising of kundalini is making it such an unstoppable force as the light increases in our realm, aided by our shift into the band of particles known as the Photon Belt or 'Rings of Alcyon' which is the Great Central Sun around which our planet is now spiraling. The more one aligns to the natural cycles and practices kundalini raising techniques, the more empowered, aware, creative and vital they become. In addition, life becomes more graceful as we live in the flow of natural rhythms rather than against them. To practice this with your beloved is a sure fire way to raise the vibration of your bodies, your relationship, your home and all reverberating aspects of your life and our planet.

♆ The Seven Stages of the Conscious Courtship

'Surrendering to' Rather Than 'Falling in' Love

In our modern wedding tradition, the bride wears a white veil as she walks toward her beloved to take her vows. This is not merely a standardized fashion accessory for the occasion. It signifies we must unveil our true self (our soul) for our beloved if we are to enter a sacred union of souls. Without this understanding and personal preparation, our modern day marriages have focused more upon the parading of one's assets, both physical and financial, with brides dieting and grooms going into debt to prove their love by creating the ego's idea of the 'perfect wedding'. In the extreme, this 'bridezilla / groomzilla scenario' has led to more attention being paid to the pre-nup than the vows.

Alternatively, conscious courtship, does not mean both parties are sober. Nor is it about chocolates, flowers and expensive dates. It simply redirects one's focus on developing the tools for intimacy, so an authentic and deeply truthful exchange can occur. Since the sexual revolution, the notion of a courtship has been viewed as old fashioned, with most modern couples sharing a meal or two, then road-testing each other's bodies. This bonds lovers in their base chakras, fusing their lower selves together in a bond of 'wedlock'. So shackles made of fear, dependency and need become the foundation of the relationship!

It is little wonder that once this sexual bonding has occurred, there is less time made for the sharing of inner selves, as

173

animal instincts derail soul connection with lusty desires. A little known fact, is that this feast of lusty lovemaking at the onset of a relationship, actually unleashes large amounts of kundalini into the nervous system. This awakens suppressed fears which have lain dormant, so the newly-bonded couple are like a time bomb, ready to trigger and detonate all their unresolved issues, which will stop the honeymoon phase faster than a bout of bridal cystitis!

So if we want a soul mate relationship, it makes sense we start by connecting soul to soul. For a conscious courtship demands a meeting of equals. We can only discern this, if we take each step in the descent of intimacy with clear intent and a commitment of mutual honoring. This requires complete transparency, as both must risk being vulnerable, speaking their truth about everything, and taking the time to really get to know each other...not just fast tracking to knowing each other in the Biblical sense...then the divorce court.

So unlike the ego dating game of trying to dazzle with one's persona, charisma and perceived best assets, this path reveals our willingness to truly share our inner selves, which is the greatest aphrodisiac. Without this willingness we unconsciously try to compensate, by gifting expensive dinners, wearing seductive clothes and trying to impress by 'being something or someone' other than our naked, humble and human selves, all to win the love and affection of another.

So Who Is This Sacred Union Dating Road Map Intended For?

- for singles wanting a dating strategy to create a truly honoring and intimate relationship.

- for teenagers wishing to transcend the conditioning they should barter their sexuality for love.

- for existing couples, as an annual practice to reconsecrate their union prior to renewing their vows and commitment.

The Seven Dates at the Seven Gates
(That is my favorite title yet!)

Below is a map for sharing yourself step-by-step with someone who resonates with your soul. It may be that this person turns out to be a great friend, as they are someone who attracts you at some gates but not at others. Alternatively, you may discover this person, despite an initial attraction, repels you the deeper you delve or they may turn out to resonate with you at every gate and become the love of your life. Regardless of the outcome, it is a model for connecting at every level, a great foundation for any partnership, regardless of whether it's a new connection or a marriage where intimacy has become a distant memory.

Date One: Crown Chakra - Sharing Your Connection with Spirit

Share your earliest memories of connecting to a omnipotent presence or higher force. Discuss your spiritual journey; what you have done in your search to find that sense of soul connection and meaning. Share your preferred paths to ecstasy, the pastimes you enjoy so much, that you could literally lose yourself for hours being 'at one' with the present moment. You might like to follow up by taking each other on your respective activities to experientially share them with each other. For example, a fishing trip (if, like my Dad fishing is your religion) or something active and experiential like dance mediation or kirtan chanting (two of my faves). Spirituality is different for everyone, so this is not about finding someone who is a carbon copy of you. Rather it is about sharing an appreciation for each other's natural highs.

Date Two: Brow Chakra - Sharing Your Wisdom

On this date, I recommend discussing some of the greatest challenges you've had to face and what you've learnt about yourselves as a result. You may wish to do a bit of journal writing before this one in preparation, to assist your memory recall. As always, intimacy with the self precedes intimacy with another. Sharing what you have learnt from the down times, such as illness, depression and relationship breakdown all reveal your maturity and understanding. Sharing these pearl of wisdom ensures we don't make the same mistakes, rather than the old paradigm of trying to hide your dark episodes or blaming others to win sympathy as the victim. At this gate you may wish to also share titles of books or teachers you found helpful as signposts on your journey of self-understanding.

Date Three: Throat Chakra - Sharing Your Vulnerability

On this date, it's time to risk going a bit deeper by sharing your wounds and vulnerabilities. You may also share healing methods you've developed or adopted. Disclose how your family and friends responded to your willingness to reveal who you truly are inside. Such as how those around you reacted to your unconventional assertions of selfhood. Including changing your name, country of residence or career. You may also wish to share your favorite music, be it your own compositions or music that really resonated with your inner self or helped you to heal, as the throat chakra is best healed through tenderness which soul sounds evoke.

Date Four: Heart Chakra - Sharing Your True Heart

On this date, try sharing what you have learnt to accept and love. For example, what traits you once rejected in yourself and others, but now have come to accept as part of yourself. Consider sharing where your heart is happiest, such as what landscapes and home environments truly resonate with your heart. As well as what you like doing most when you spend time at home. This will give you both an indication as to whether you are compatible domestic partners. I also feel it's nice at this gate to share what has truly touched your heart in the past. This gives insight into what is important to you and what touches your heart, which can serve as a source of inspiration for future acts of love.

Date Five: Solar Plexus Chakra - Sharing Your Purpose

This chakra is about the meeting of minds, so this would be a great opportunity to share a playful game of strategy, such as Chinese Checkers on a picnic rug in the park during spring or Backgammon in a cafe with an open fire in winter, giving you the chance to test your wits against each other and enjoy the tension and tease of brain sex! I also recommend sharing what you have come to see and value as your soul gifts; the talents you have uncovered in yourself. Dare to 'show and tell' an example of what you've created, constructed, written, invented or theorized and share what you see as your life's purpose. Discuss how you see your role in helping to make a better world and those who have inspired you with their service to others.

Date Six: Sacral Chakra - Sharing Your Creativity and Joy

For this date, you want to let loose and let your inner child out to have some fun. You may want to surprise each other with an activity that is guaranteed to get you laughing. From hired pogo boots to laser gun wars wearing homemade tin foil space cossies. This date is where you risk looking like a fool to enjoy a shared experience between your magical inner children. Go out for ice cream afterwards and share your happiest memories from childhood and even a few handpicked photos from the family album! Find out what each other's ultimate idea of fun is and how you lighten up by doing that which truly brings you joy. The sacral is also the place of beauty, sensuality and romance, so you may also wish to discuss the most romantic gesture ever done for you, or that which you have done for another to give them an idea of what truly melts your inner lover's heart. Try playing a fun game where you each have six minutes to say what you love about both your inner and outer self.

Date Seven: Base Chakra - Sharing Your Passion

It's time to get naked - in every sense! This is where you share your naked ego by revealing your lower nature's flaws and primal desires. If all is going well in your conscious courtship, this final date is going to have you both purring with anticipation! So savor the moment, rather than pouncing on each other. I recommend doing something quite primal like eating a meal on a fur rug in front of a fire or feeding each other with your hands. You may even like to go away camping and cook on an open fire as you share what has 'got your goat' and peaked your anger and how you tend to express your anger. You may also wish to discuss what you love about nature and the elements, how comfortable you are with your natural self, including nudity and body functions, and your favorite foods. Finish by sharing your sexual turn-ons and fantasies...

So there it is, how to court like a Love God or Love Goddess...Eden style!

Clarke's Notes

Below is a quick recap for those wanting to assess whether their prospective mate is able to really meet and honor them at the seven gates.

The Seven Soul Love Tests

Crown: Do they have their own spiritual connection and honor mine?

Third Eye: Have they transmuted a lot of their past pain into wisdom and do they understand and value my insights and perceptions?

Throat: Can they speak their truth and intention to me clearly, exposing their vulnerability and equally honoring mine?

Heart: Are their actions gentle, tender and considerate and do they equally value this trait in me? Do their actions cause me to feel safe and expanded or hurt and contracted?

Solar Plexus: Do they see their own gifts and are they cultivating those gifts to be of service? Do they value and honor mine equally?

Sacral: Do they take responsibility for their own inner child and their emotional needs or do they rely solely on nurturing themselves with sensate gluttony such as beer, food or sex which distends their sacral? Do they also honor my practices for balancing my emotional needs?

Base: Do they honor their sexual energy by engaging only in sacred sexual practices or do they unconsciously seek to engage their sexual energy with others to bolster their vitality or ego? Are they comfortable with their body's natural functions and erotic nature?

Reviving the Spark

As mentioned in the previous chapter, I received an intuitive download about the ancient rites of hieros gamos when I looked upon the recreation of the 'Gate of Ishtar' at an exhibition about ancient Mesopotamia. At the next Red Tent circle I conducted after visiting this exhibition for new moon in Virgo, (the sign of the priestess) I was spontaneously directed to lead the women through a re-consecration ceremony to reclaim their temple and honor their divine spark. This felt like something we had done before, in a time long ago. Here is an account of what unfolded.

Author's Note: On the day of the Red Tent we had a very deep and emotional sharing circle processing the previous lunar cycle of full moon in Pisces. A cycle, which had catalyzed karmic and emotional endings as preparation for our renewal. We then did 'Nia', a sacred dance art form where we caressed our bodies and enacted our dance with the Earth and Moon. This was followed by 'Ayurvedic' teachings, where we learnt to honor our body temples through a greater understanding of our elemental constitutions.

Then as part of our lunar manifestation, I asked the women to write down three things they would do in the coming month to honor their bodies as sacred temples. I spontaneously was guided to suggest they each reconsecrate their partnerships by doing the seven step conscious courtship with their partner while abstaining from sex until the final week. this would reclaim their sovereignty and elevate the frequency of their interaction. For the women who were single, I suggested they journal the seven questions to create greater intimacy with their soul self.

During this period of time, I suggested they might also wish to reconsecrate their boudoir with flowers, oils, fabrics and cushions, seeing this as an opportunity to explore the full spectrum of love arts to ensure they and their partner appreciate each other as a whole person and not take each other for granted, as can easily happen with the familiarity of co-habitation. It also struck me how many of the women had turned up coincidentally wearing tiered skirts and dresses, looking like the statues of Ishtar, the Snake Goddess dressed for this Consecration of the Bride Rite.

To then anchor the aspect of Ishtar within us, (the ascended Aphrodite who has learnt the lessons of self-love) we then blessed ourselves with spring water, infused with spring blossoms, my 'Sacred Union' crystal essence and the liquid crystals: moonstone, silver and diamond (Ishtar's crystal). We then anointed our crowns with spikenard oil to open our seven gates and took it in turns to say, 'My name is .... and I am divine' to which everyone responded as a ring of reflection by saying one positive quality they saw in us.

Earlier that day I had expressed tears bemoaning my fate that there was still no sign of a King in my midst. To which one wise elder woman channeled the message that when I found my temple, he would be there. Later in the day when I brought this practice through, I figured this was the temple they were speaking of. In other words when I could love myself in the physical realm (by doing regular yoga and exercise and staying off wheat and gluten) I would be met in the physical by a man who could honor both himself and myself at the seven gates. Exactly one year later I met him a week before spring equinox, the day that marks the return of the King, in the hieros gamos cycle of mysteries.

I recommend this practice of abstaining sexually between the gates of spring equinox (Sept 21-23 Southern hemisphere / March 21-23 Northern hemisphere) to Beltane (Oct 1st Southern hemisphere / May 1st Northern hemisphere) to renew one's commitment to self and Spirit as preparation for renewing one's vows with one's beloved each Beltane.

☤ Lovemaking with a Woman's Cycle

Understanding the Phases of Feminine Sexuality

Before a woman's moon time (menstruation), the archetype of the wild woman, Lilith, surfaces within her psyche as her kundalini rises. The raising of her base chakra 'inner fire' brings her instinctual self up to frontal lobe! So it is at this time of the month that fertile women yearn to be taken sexually by their mate. Importante! Don't tell her she just needs a good shag or you may end up sleeping on the couch. This urge is often not a conscious feeling of arousal, more than it is a state of being completely stressed, bordering on hysteria. This is because just prior to bleeding is when she feels more tension than at any other time of the month. Pre-menstrual tension is a state of everything feeling physically contracted, which contributes to contracted thinking, such as fear based thoughts of separation resulting in feelings of overwhelm. This leads women to look for external validation for their state of mind, seeking signs of proof that they are in fact, alone and unsupported as what their inner feminine is most desperately in need of is additional support and deep union.

During PMS (pre-menstrual syndrome) women often experience contracted muscles, resulting in secondary aches and pains, such as tension headaches. Emotionally they can feel uptight, leading to angry outbursts and tears of overwhelm. Mentally, they can feel impatient. In addition to their hormones, this is because Lilith's emergence demands facing the shadow truth. So whatever has been suppressed throughout the past month surfaces to be acknowledged, expressed and ideally, resolved. This enables a woman to start her next lunar cycle, clear of unresolved issues, which keeps her well on all levels. This is why a woman may be misinterpreted as 'picking an argument', when she is needing to get to the bottom of all that is causing her tension, so she can put it to bed once and for all - rather than sweep it under the rug and then trip over it again in a couple of weeks.

Lilith is the archetype of death and rebirth. So at this time of the month, women benefit from a complete letting go on all levels, which sexual release can offer. Not surprisingly, this is often followed by a huge outpouring of emotion!

Author's Note: Loving partners, this is not a sign that anything is wrong. In fact the opposite. Should your partner dissolve into tear during lovemaking, chance are she feels safe enough to let it all go. So just midwife her through her catharsis, encouraging and supporting her to release everything she's been holding on to.

How to Approach a Pre-Menstrual Woman for Sex: The Taming of the Shrew

Allow me to share what I know so you don't end up with a frying pan to the back of the head. I'll be honest and say this is a maneuver that requires more courage and skill than you'll see enacted by Van Damme in an action flick. (Lesbians, please accept my humble apologies for the passage below using gender specific language. This does apply to same sex couples as well.)

Step One: Identify PMS. It's a no brainer - your female partner is noticeably tense. Examples include:

1. She's finding fault with everything you do.

2. She's being a martyr by trying to do everything herself and sighing a lot.

3. She's manically multi-tasking like the Duracell Bunny on amphetamines.

Much easier to get to know her cycle, by making a note in your smartphone or Google calendar on the first day or her period so you've got an idea what date in the next month the storm approacheth!

Step Two: Help. (Not you, her!) If she's running a story that she has to do everything then the fastest way to thaw her armor of ice is to show her, through action that she was just entertaining hormonal illusions. Show initiative and help **without being asked**. See something that needs doing on the domestic front and do it. This will win you more brownie points now than at any other time of the month, as it's really when she is at her most vulnerable, so trying to keep it all together is costing her more that it usually would.

Step Three: Be Available to Listen. Given this is when she most needs to vent, let her unload without interrupting, fixing or reacting. Just let her get it all out. The more calm and centered you are in your heart, regardless of all the fear-based accusations she throws in your direction, the more reassured and held she will feel by your complete loving acceptance of her. Ensure your attitude is co-operative and all will be well. Encourage her to identify her underlying fears rather than focusing on all the symptoms and she will feel heard and understood. Meet her by agreeing to look at your own behavior then she will be more willing to look at her own. This final point is most important - you must be 100% sincere in your intent or she'll have your balls on a platter and rightfully so, if she feels she's being played.

Step Four: Touch Her. Put your hand on her back and rub her in a nurturing way that reassures her you've got her back. (Warning: Do not then try and slip your tongue in...or anything else.) You might massage her shoulders a bit, kiss her on the back of the neck in a tender way, with no hint of foreplay. If she responds sexually then you've got a green light to proceed, easing more of her tension. If she responds with gratitude, then be happy that you won't all have to walk around on eggshells and don't push for sex or you'll undo all your good work. It is so important for a woman to receive regular loving touch, **without the expectation of sex** as otherwise all touch becomes a turn-off if she feels like it's only ever to get something rather than being a true expression of loving affection. The more you gift her sincere loving touch throughout the day, and show her acts of kindness, the more you will be met with sexual responsiveness at the end of the day, should you make your advance in the boudoir.

Cat on a Hot Tin Roof - When a Woman Can't Get No Satisfaction

When a woman's unconscious desire is not consummated, her fire rages on as her Lilith feels unmet and unclaimed. She copes with her feelings of sadness and perceived rejection by internally rejecting him through finding fault with her partner. This can often emasculate him in the process, as she names his shadow in an effort to poke him into stepping up and being a man for her. A woman needs a man who can be strong for her when she is feeling acutely vulnerable. (This is also true during the act of giving birth.)

Unfortunately, this can lead women to choose men who can assert their strength, especially sexually, even if this means they dominate them. For the primal part of a woman wants to be with someone who is confident enough to really claim them. If they feel they are stronger than their mate, they will lose respect for them. This is especially so during PMT (pre-menstrual tension). Ideally her mate will demonstrate both tenderness for her increased vulnerability and strength to hold her. If her partner is only capable of domination, she will eventually tire of them and leave.

Author's Note: If your female partner no longer menstruates, then use the moon cycles of new moon as her 'moon time' and full moon as her, 'ovulation'. Women cycle energetically after their physical cycle stops, regardless of the reason.

When Her Moon Comes In - Honoring the Wisdom of the Crone

As her moon waters flow, a woman softens from a state of hypertension into the deep abyss of her inner feminine. This occurs on every level as the blood spirals in her belly, taking her consciousness down deep into the trance state of menstruation. During this time in her cycle, she is still, quiet, inward - at one with Great Mystery. This is her most meditative time. In traditional wisdom she was said to be 'closest to God'. To lie with a woman sexually during this time of a woman's cycle was considered the greatest honor as this was her most sacred time.

It is also when a woman's psychic powers are at their strongest, so it takes a man who is sure of his own heart and their bond to even dare to navigate this deep sacred space of the feminine. This is a woman's 'death phase' when she is drawing back from giving to everyone else and focusing on the replenishment of her own energy and psyche. She will probably let her appearance go and her lack of energy will make her appear pale or haggard.

A mature man honors this time as her sanctuary, ensuring the household is as least reliant on her as possible. This honors she is losing her life force, and so needs to receive the nurturing she gives to everyone else the rest of the month. A mature man understands she is shedding her old skin on all levels (including her uterine lining like Lilith, the serpent) so she is temporarily unavailable to give energy, which includes any expectation of sex. Ideally, he will demonstrate reverence for her Red Tent time each month, supporting her to take time to fill herself anew with feminine energy, by returning to the void to contemplate the mystery of life.

The Re-Emergence of the Maiden

When she re-emerges from her menstrual cocoon, if a man has been loving and supportive during her 'hag' phase, Aphrodite will greet him with such adoration for loving her completely, it is as if the courtship can begin anew. This is the time to really enjoy each other's company and show your affection through romantic gestures. Spend time away from mundane chores, sharing ideas, pastimes and nurturing your friendship if you want your love to thrive.

Long Live the Queen!

A woman's estrogen spikes before ovulation. This is the phase when she is most fertile as she releases an egg from her ovaries. Her yoni juices become slippery and wet as if she were putting out a welcome mat! She smells enticing and has a glow of feminine charm. Emotionally she feels increasingly close to her partner and yearns to join with them - heart, mind, body and soul. This is when a conscious couple acknowledges the high tide of 'lurve' and creates the time and space to connect in a sacred and loving way.

This is the ideal time for a shared bath, sensual pleasure and honoring of all that they are to each other. Ovulation is an ideal time for sex magic. Full moon is also the most common time for women to ovulate. Lovemaking with the full moon is an opportunity to create union on all levels, knowing it will transform them both through the internal alchemy of opposite poles in harmonic union. Couples who do this practice will be more inclined to solve differences easily and amicably. For touching upon the very core of each other's essence, is the cyclic strengthening of the bond between them, which enables them to endure any external pressures the rest of the month. After this coupling of the God and Goddess at the height of emotional fullness, both feel truly met, seen and reassured.

To Recap...

- Simple random acts of kindness and gratitude keep a woman open, flowing, juicy and succulent like a flower in blossom, so she is available to regular sensual touch which can deepen into sexual desire easily.

- Be willing to discuss the hard questions when she is pre-menstrual and your willingness, humility and truth will be rewarded with trust and intimacy, without inhibition.

- As her period approaches her estrogen wanes, and her wild woman comes to the fore. She may come across as brazen, base and dirty in her humor and self-expression. If she is up for sex, she may prefer vaginal entry from behind. Sex may include earthy, guttural sounds, with intense and passionate encounters that release pent up frustrations as her fire increases. This is the best time for a man to take the risk of seducing her with great daring, as he is most likely to be well received - if he has shown earlier in the month that he is capable of honoring the changing face of the Goddess. For then she knows she is safe to completely surrender, knowing he sees and acknowledges her totality. This trust frees her to express her full erotic power with complete lack of inhibition, knowing he will never judge or condemn her wild self.

The darker aspects of the Goddess, Lilith, the wild woman who surfaces within a woman's psyche just prior to bleeding and Hecate, the crone who surfaces during her bleeding time are two of the most vulnerable aspects of a woman in relationship. As these are the two that have been most misunderstood, shamed, rejected and dishonored. So when a man seeks to understand and honor these aspects in a woman, she feels truly free to be herself, rather than just play a role to be acceptable. Let it be emphasized, however that unless a woman has first sought to understand and accept these aspects within herself, she won't be comfortable with expressing them or having others see these aspects within her.

In the ancient world, this understanding formed the basis of the custom of the honeymoon, where a newlywed couple was granted seclusion so the groom could lie with his bride for a full cycle of twenty-eight days. This was so he could meet her many faces, hence the unveiling of the Goddess in the ceremony where he agrees to leave his boyhood behind to journey with the greater cycles through the conscious coupling of sacred union. Loving a woman is a practice, just as nature storms, rains and erupts with fire - so too, does his bride, if he will grant her the sovereignty to be her true nature. If he can endure this organic unfoldment of life itself, rather than seek to tame his Shrew he will know riches beyond any he could possess.

Lovemaking with a Man's Cycle

Understanding the Phases of Masculine Sexuality

Because men are ruled by the sun, their waxing and waning energy cycle is seasonal rather than a monthly lunar tide to be observed. For men, their virility, power and strength increases as the solar light increases. Because this occurs over a more lengthy cycle, the changes are not as easily observed or considered as erratic as those of women.

For men, their psycho-emotional death happens at winter Solstice, the longest night. A time, when men of old took their sons on retreat to be initiated into the ways of men, such as hunting, acts of bravery, charting of the stars, sacred numerology, purification rituals to clear the mind and body and contemplation of the inner self.

This was then replaced with acts of war, as the conquering tribes rose up to form armies and empires that demanded men leave their homes during the darker months of autumn and winter to fight for new power and territories, at a time when they weren't needed to plant and harvest their crops. Had it not been during the dark months that men were asked to submit to the will of the dark lords in power or risk the might of their wrath, many may perhaps have felt more brave in the light of the sun, to question why they should honor the gift of life with acts of cruelty, when it simply made more sense to be with the ones they love, making hay while the sun shines.

Given that autumn / winter is the time when the male psyche is more prone to an annual descent of depression to face the small (ego) self, naked and alone, one can only imagine what mental and emotional torture they endured as they faced their inner selves, enacting barbaric acts in the name of manhood. Is it any wonder drinking became the acceptable coping mechanism for men not permitted to truly be authentic with themselves and each other?

Collectively, since we have all been both genders, many carry the soul imprint of these winter battles, so on top of their inward descent to question themselves and their lives, is a soul torment that senses the crimes against humanity and the suffering endured at this time of the seasonal wheel. I suspect this would be more acute in the Northern hemisphere, given that this is where more of these empiric battles were fought. If we have participated in war campaigns during these months, this is when inner conflict would surface, seeking resolution. For those who doubt this phenomenon, consider if you struggle with negative feelings just prior to your birthday each year. This is not, as we've been conditioned to believe, just a fear of aging but part of an annual death of the ego. This occurs as we approach the same position, in relation to the sun when we were born, each year in our annual Solar return. Each birthday is therefore an opportunity for rebirth. So what precedes is a process of letting go, identifying what we have outgrown, if we are to grow into a greater self. Those who have birthed children will also find this occurs before the birth dates of their children each year, as they revisit the energetic reverberations of their birthing journey prior to the act of birth each year. This can therefore be a powerful time to launch new projects, as one has already anchored successful birth in their somatic body.

S.A.D. (seasonal affective disorder), is a term coined by the medical community, which describes those who experience depressive symptoms during winter, attributing the cause as being an extra sensitivity to light. Sensitivity is a sign of evolution - the more evolved we become, the more aware we become of our subtle sensations. We will therefore see more people acknowledging the affect the seasons have on them and accepting it as natural, rather than labeling it a disorder. Such a rational perspective implies we should operate like machines, with no fluctuation of energy or mood, in response to natural cycles. Animals hibernate in winter and so should we, as natural beings. The expectation we should 'soldier on' when there is scant light or warmth elicits a soul response which is a natural and healthy response to an unnatural societal expectation.

To make matter worse, it is mainly men (and those operating out of their masculine) that are expected to rise early, even when it is dark in the colder months and journey to jobs that are far away from home, returning after dark. This is because most high paying jobs are centralized in cities, attracting the primary earners. Where as those in the more feminine role of primary care givers, often work from home or flexi-hours near home, so they can help children get ready for school.

For men, winter is akin to their annual menstruation! It is their death and rebirth, as the sun, which governs them, wanes down to the shortest day, which is the winter solstice. This is why men would traditionally go on retreat to support and midwife each other during their psycho-emotional descent. Without any understanding or validation for the effect this seasonal cycle has on their psyche, many men struggle with stress, anxiety, depression, anger, lethargy and often an increased dependence on substances to suppress and mask these symptoms. This is also when men are most prone to experiencing physical ailments, not just because there is less energy but because their bodies are expressing their unexpressed emotions and vulnerabilities.

How to Love Our Men in Winter

For relationships, this means that autumn / winter is a time when men are not as open and loving with themselves, let alone their partners and children. So women (and same sex men in partnerships), you would do well to exercise more patience during these darker months and assist your partner to weather the dark by granting them more headspace and freedom to attend to their inner process.

Winter is the time of the sage, the elder who is deep within his cave - contemplating, growing his wisdom. (Or at least he would be, if he didn't just 'flick on the tube' and become more pessimistic and cynical with the distraction of politics, and prime time murder shows.) This is also the football season, which is a ritualistic war game, which keeps me in a mindset of 'us and them' which entrenches separation rather than union during a time of the year, when it's already a challenge. Men who lose themselves in these pursuits engage in an outer battle rather than an inner one so miss the opportunity each winter to contemplate life and become wise.

The more we honor the cyclic masculine and the needs of our partners over winter, the more our lack of pressure will be well rewarded as the solar light returns. (So best to refrain from nagging your man to fix everything around the house over winter if he takes time to rest.) Men have enough pressure placed on them by society to always be productive, so home needs to be a place where they can also be encouraged to just 'be', especially during the darker months. (This doesn't mean returning to the 1950's, where men were not expected to lift a finger around the home.) It simply means, making allowances for their cyclic nature, especially if you want them to honor yours. The more a man feels his partner loves him for who he is and not just for what he does or provides, the more generous his response with outward affection and tenderness.

If a woman is not comfortable with her darker aspects and need for introspection, her immature maiden will become increasingly neurotic and clingy as her man withdraws to his winter cave. Such demanding behavior will only push him further away as he has less capacity to deal with anyone else's dark side except his own, during this window.

Alternatively, a psychologically and emotionally mature woman will make allowances for this cyclic descent, knowing that she can use the time to gestate her own insights, gestate creative ideas and focus on her own healing rather than needing regular updates on his process. For women who smother and mother their men, only do so for fear that their inner maiden will be unsafe or abandoned, should she not micromanage and/or manipulate his feelings to her ends. None of this is done consciously - for who would choose to live in that kind of mindset and dynamic? The shift comes with understanding and compassion when we learn to identify and observe the patterns which opens a new way of relating.

So for men while their pseudo period comes but once a year, they experience a more drawn out version of PMT. So while spring is when their inner knight will happily take an adventure with you and try new things and summer is a time when he will want to enjoy the good life with you, relishing the fruits of his harvest...autumn is a time of the magi. One who seeks the mysteries to gain a deeper perspective, which will support him in his soul-searching questions mid-winter when he faces his human frailty, and ultimately his mortality. This is therefore a time when men also confront their legacy and their sense of self-worth, so be sure to affirm his gifts rather than knock his attempts to share his inner gold.

Summer is alternatively the time when men are solar powered sex machines. Yes! Just as the sap rises in the trees as the thermometer rises, so too does men's libido, along with their mood. So do not fear you are no longer lovable in his eyes if he stops wanting to ravish you when the thermometer drops, trust if you love him in his frailty, the king will return stronger and more virile than before.

The True Power of Oral Sex

Worshipping the Temple Gates

In the West many view oral sex as a perfunctory favor which must be exchanged before the real act of intercourse can begin. Some feel uncomfortable receiving oral pleasure due to deep shame about their own sexual organs. Whilst others feel repulsed at the idea of giving oral pleasure, seeing it as dirty or beneath them. Both of these inhibitions illustrate our societal denial of our primal archetypes, Lilith and Pan - the psychological aspects who govern the base chakra.

Our genitals are their voice, their expression. So when we feel unable to access and express our inner wild man or wild woman without inhibition or shame, we feel squeamish about genitals, be they ours or someone else's.

When gifting oral pleasure, one cannot avoid a confrontation with these archetypes, as the act is so primal and literally 'in one's face.' So to heal one's revulsion towards either fellatio (licking and sucking the male phallus) or cunnilingus (licking and sucking the female vulva), one first needs to befriend their own genitals. I cover how to do this in volume one.

As mentioned earlier, Lilith is the primal feminine aspect who points out a man's shadow when she surfaces within the psyche each month before a woman menstruates. If a man runs from facing his disowned aspects, the sex will die shortly thereafter, as she will lose respect for her psychologically immature lover. If, on the other hand, a man is receptive to her insights or actively seeks to uncover his denied aspects, he will be repaid with full erotic worship. Not as some sort of

197

strategic manipulation on her part, but because his willingness to mature is her ultimate turn-on! Just as she confronts her shadow each month to become wise, as part of her monthly cycle, so must he or she will outgrow him.

For it is a man's willingness to acknowledge and grow beyond his perceived limitations that enables him to step more fully into his male power. Authentic male power is Lilith's ultimate arousal and will make a pussy of any lioness! So if he's able to stand his ground and face the dark feminine aspect of his partner as his mirror, without running away in fear, she will be moved by his genuine love for her and devour him with an unsurpassed erotic fervor.

Author's Note: This is the erotic worship men fantasize about and have tried to imitate with porn. A recreation which makes any Lilith activated woman sigh because it's inauthentic and therefore lacking any real erotic power.

A Lilith activated woman when truly aroused is a power that is exhilarating to behold and experience. The complete liberation of feminine kundalini is electrifying for any man, including those who were under the illusion they suffered from erectile dysfunction. Shakti is life force, so her spontaneous, wild and free sexual expression, instantly heals and arouses the wild man who has been shut down, shamed, rejected or judged. A Lilith woman has no shame, whatsoever. Just like an animal, she'll explore every lusty desire instinctually, comfortable in her own skin and with her primal urges. She is in total oneness with her body, so submits completely to the will of the body, without any interruption from the mind. To experience this is literally mind blowing for a man. It will, however, call him to stand in his full primal power as a man to meet her! This is how Lilith activated women initiate men to experience their inner Pan in a way that is more empowering and life changing than any porn experience could ever be.

Let Me Hear You ROAR!

Lilith activated women are often very vocal during lovemaking. For when the cervix is relaxed, so too, is the jaw and each sound of pleasure she emits, helps her to open deeper to be a receptacle for more energy, so she can ride the waves of ecstasy without being dumped by a wave - i.e. prematurely peaking and collapsing energetically. The more pleasure she is able to charge her cells with before climaxing, the more intense her orgasm and the more life force she will generate, as a vessel for Gaia's essence and then bestow upon her mate. (This more than compensates for any life force lost through the emission of semen!)

Bow Before the Queen!

A conscious man will instinctually honor the primal feminine aspect of Lilith by worshipping and kissing her mouth, which is the vulva. This symbolically entails bowing so that his forehead, including his third eye (the seat of his soul) honors the entry gate to his lover's temple. This act acknowledges the power her doorway of death and rebirth holds. For once he enters this gateway of psychological death and rebirth, his consciousness will be altered thereafter. He will be stripped of his persona and boyish notions about women. If he enters into sacred union as a practice with an initiated priestess, his illusions will be shattered at each of chakras as he climbs her staircase to experience complete dissolution of his mind in ecstatic communion with existence.

If a man has no understanding or regard for this psychological aspect of Lilith, he will view the primal dark feminine with suspicion, fear or repulsion. This will cause him to view the naturally hairy and engorged vulva as ugly, smelly and confronting. This is why, sadly today, so many young boys ridicule natural girls who have kept their pubic hair. They have been initiated into their sexuality by the fantasy of Eve, the living doll portrayed by the porn industry. Whereas a man who really understands the role of the dark feminine, appreciating she is necessary for his evolution, will lose himself in deep reverence and worship Lilith by kissing her mouth passionately. This is why a man's willingness to truly worship the vulva with his face (the mask of his ego) is a good indication of his ability to honor the feminine. In other words, *'Ladies, if your man does not worship your yoni (vulva) before lovemaking, by kissing the temple gates passionately and with true reverence, he hasn't earned the right to go marching in with his battering ram!'* If one wants to gauge a man's receptivity to cunnilingus, try serving him some yoni treats such as oysters, figs or mussels as an appetizer!

Similarly, women who banish Lilith by 'waxxxing' their pubic hair completely off so they look like an eight year old Eve, have unwittingly put out a welcome mat for boys to desecrate their temple. Strong words I know, but Lilith ain't no girl, she's a 'Superpussy' who demands respect in and out of the bedroom. So guys, if you do honor her, by owning your shadow and honoring this gate of raw feminine power, you will awaken an erotic passion like none you have ever known, so the pay off is truly worth it!

Marvel at the Power of Excalibur!

Equally, the same can be said of women who purse their lips at the thought of bowing down and orally worshipping their lover's phallic wand of light! This magic staff is the key that ignites your light body - the rocket fuel that charges your flight! So sisters, when we can genuinely lose ourselves in devotional worship of the divine masculine in this way, we can experience ecstatic climaxes while giving oral pleasure. For sadly, just as many women are not comfortable with the raw primal male power of Pan, the beast inside every man who incites the razor's edge of excitement and panic as he is overtaken with lust in the last stages of his chase to consume his prey.

Should a woman still be nursing some distorted view of the primal masculine as 'the devil man' thanks to early conditioning, she will shame his lust rather than look at her own inhibition and judgement. Whereas, the more a woman can see the 'beauty in the beast' and truly adore and delight in her wild man's fur, smells, phallus, power and lust, the more he will respond with the boundless devotion of 'The Lion King' himself, connecting with her passionately and instinctually in each unfolding moment without mental chatter or shame.

Should a woman remain in her head, unwilling to submit to the beast, she will not generate enough energy in her base chakra to open any subsequent star gates. As a result, her lovemaking will feel completely passive, as she is unable to connect to the source of her primal feminine, the Earth. So she will not be amped by the pulse of the elements surging through the thousands of energetic meridians throughout her body. This means, lovemaking will not revitalize her on every level, charging her cells with life force and she'll be less inclined to want to do it. So try as he might, it may be 'mission impossible' for a man to turn a woman 'on' when her main switch is permanently shut down.

Author's Note: Such a shut down base chakra in a woman may be due to early indoctrination about sex being dirty or unholy or due to sexual abuse, leaving an imprint in the body that sex is painful, disempowering or shameful. In either case, there is no overnight cure. However, reclaiming one's body / heart / mind connection as sacred and sovereign is the first step, so do have a look at my chapter on the art of self pleasure as a powerful sacred practice in volume one.

Blessed Are the Genitals

Personally I am saddened that our unconscious lack of reverence for our bodies has diminished oral worshipping of our sex organs to that of a lesser preparatory act to thaw our lover's icy exterior before the main event. (The original 'warm-up guy').

When we truly understand and honor each other's sacredness, inner alchemy and power, we open to experiencing a deep love for these magical organs which gift us life. Then oral lovemaking takes on a whole new perspective.

Barbie Doesn't Grovel For Anyone / GI Joe Only Goes Down When He's Shot

I suspect that men (and women) who fear or dislike meeting this gate of death and rebirth at close range are afraid of having an ego death. In other words, they are operating out of the persona they have manufactured, based on the cultural programming sold to them. Icons repeatedly enforced during one's formative years, such as Barbie, the perfectly manicured girl or GI Joe, the jock with swag. This leads people to construct a persona, with an array of inner and outer qualities in the hope that will make them popular, acceptable, successful, rich and loved. This often means imitating conventional looks, celebs, fads and even socially acceptable career choices, (like the Ikea catalogue lifestyle realization awakened to by the protagonist in the film, *'Fight Club'*).

To truly humbly worship our most base selves, which are often rejected or suppressed, requires a complete embracing of one's own animal self. To do this, we must forgo our social mask. As you can't worry about what you look like when giving oral pleasure and why would you want to? In addition, the degree to which we genuinely relish the act of oral copulation is in direct relation to the degree to which our partner will feel aroused by it. This energetic transmission cannot be faked. Which is why sex with an 'Eve' girl or 'Peter Pan' boy 'performing' rather than 'relishing' is so empty and unfulfilling.

Why Faking It Isn't an Option

Despite well-rehearsed moans, our energy body cannot lie. You are either genuinely lit up inside or you're not. It is this energetic activation that generates increased volts of wattage in your partner. If you think it's your looks that gets your partner off, think again. If they are simply focusing on your body parts, without feeling your every nuance and responding, then sadly yes, they are simply bolstering their ego by possessing the features the magazine told them was fashionable. They are simply trying to prove their own value to themselves as they have no clue about who they really are. These are the one night stand folk who are not making love to you. They are 'getting off' on having the idea of someone like you. Trust me, if someone is truly attuned to you, they will know in an instant if you fake a moan. They will also know in a millisecond if emotion is brewing for you, even before you do. They will intuit your every desire!

If you lie with someone who really isn't into you personally, it is perfectly understandable you feel would self-conscious about giving or receiving oral pleasure in your most intimate place from a total stranger. In this instance, I would not try to force this level of intimacy...on any level.

Sometimes we can feel self-conscious about receiving oral pleasure if our partner is self-conscious about giving it, as it can feel like our desires are an imposition. This lack of genuine excitement is evident if they seldom initiate giving oral sex and say they enjoy it, but their energy levels of arousal do not match their words. In such a circumstance, do dare to talk about this openly. If you don't feel comfortable enough with someone to speak up on your own behalf to honor your authentic feelings, they shouldn't be allowed to touch you!

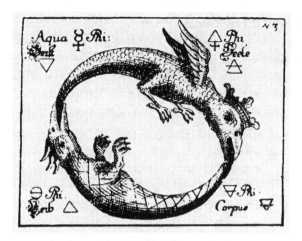

(Pictured above.) Ouroboros, 1760. Ouroboros as a crowned double-dragon, symbolizing the four elements. Line engraving from Abraham Eleazar's 'Uraltes Chymisches Werk,' Leipzig, Germany, 1760.

I find it interesting that oral pleasure mimics the sacred symbol of the ouroboros, the double-headed dragon who eats his own tail, particularly when both are engaged in oral worship simultaneously (known colloquially as a '69-er'). This is synonymous with the Chinese yin / yang symbol, signifying the balance of opposites. Equally, by orally ingesting the sexual juices of our opposite, we actively balance our own inner feminine / masculine polarities, which helps us to shed our conditioning of what a traditional man or woman should be and assists with our alchemical transformation to become the 'Holy Hermaphrodite.'

Awakening the Ability to Receive Ecstasy

If you are repulsed at the thought of someone licking and sucking your genitals and tasting your sexual juices, chances are you'll have trouble fully relaxing and receiving, when a lover gifts you with this adoration. For women, this stigma and shame can be attributed to the cultural misogyny which likens one's ambrosia (sexual fluids) to that of old fish.

Similarly when mother's talk about the funk of old semen in their teenage son's bedroom, the same negative association is anchored. To transcend these negative associations, take back your power. Know Thyself: taste yourself - your sexual fluids, your menstrual blood, your semen. You are not repulsive, dirty or sinful. You are natural. If you eat a natural diet and regularly bathe and exercise, your intimate taste will be pleasing to the palette. We feel empowered when we get the facts direct from the source rather than filtered through someone else's issues, conditioning and dogma.

That said, if your partner does not taste pleasing to your tongue, do not suffer in silence as this is not self-honoring. The more toxic someone is physically, emotionally, mentally and energetically, the more they will taste sour, salty or bitter rather than sweet. So while pineapple juice can help a little in improving the taste of semen, ultimately the more alkaline one's diet and loving their thoughts and daily intent, the more they will be a joy to devour. (Best ad for a yoga practice and whole food diet ever.) Yes! We are what we eat, so if you live on beer and fast food, don't expect your partner to be in a hurry to eat you!

Awakening the Ecstasy of Giving

I feel one of the greatest pleasures of oral sex is that it enables us to attune completely to our lover, before diving completely into each other's energy field. Allow me to explain. I recently saw a documentary film called 'I Am' which illustrated why flocks of birds, schools of fish and herds of gazelle can move simultaneously as the one entity, without needing any sole agent to lead the group. It is because their degree of empathy is so highly developed that they can sense what another is feeling and respond instantaneously. Developing this ability is what ensured their survival.

I then coincidentally saw a re-run of the film, 'ET' which again highlighted how the loving extraterrestrial communicated with

Eliot, his human friend. Again, it was through the attuning of their hearts they could sense how each other was feeling without words.

It struck me that this is what I had experienced in lovemaking. By opening my heart so completely I had felt every sensation my partner felt. This was most noticeable during oral lovemaking as I became multi-orgasmic during the act of giving fellatio. I literally became one with his phallus, owning it as mine, so I could feel the sensations he was feeling, while I was giving him pleasure. This meant I intuitively knew what he wanted in every moment and was truly satiated by the experience of giving. In addition to my own multi-orgasms I would climax when he came, as his energy would set me off, which was lovely to experience simultaneously, riding those waves of ecstasy together. More about developing one's ability to be an empathic lover in the chapter on the lovemaking languages.

Oral Sexual Healing

When we apply this concept of applied empathy to the art of oral lovemaking, we can appreciate how opening our heart in true devotion when caressing our lover's genitals is profoundly helpful in dissolving any feelings of shame they may be holding. Not just shame which may've resulted from their personal experiences but collective, cultural shame. When we consider how we unconsciously use our genitals to abuse each other, we reveal how we subconsciously scapegoat these magical organs with our darkest emotions. For example, when someone cuts you off in traffic and you yell, 'You arsehole, cunt* or dickhead' - how do you think your body consciousness responds to that? Every part of our body has an awareness within its cells, so when we abuse someone by screaming out the name of our genitals, we are also directing that rage into those cells. When we really understand our energetic power to harm with unconscious intent or heal with conscious intent, we can appreciate how deeply healing oral sex can be, restoring reverence for these most maligned organs. (*I am aware the word, cunt was once considered a term of reverence but when it is used as a curse, the intent is far from honoring.)

Another consideration is that in the ancient Taoist tradition of sacred sexuality, the genitals contain energy meridians which correspond to various internal organs. For example, the head of the penis relates to kidney chi (fear) then as one moves further up the shaft it is followed by liver chi (anger), lung chi (grief) and heart chi (love) at the base where it joins the perineum. Similarly, the inside of the female labia relates to kidney chi (fear) then as one moves inside the vaginal walls, liver chi (anger), lung chi (grief) and heart chi (love) at the entrance to the cervix. When we have this awareness we can approach each part of our genitals and those of our lover's with deep sensitivity to the emotions that massaging and kissing them may provoke. Encouraging our lover to connect with their feelings by placing a hand on their heart while giving them oral pleasure can further help to bring these sensitivities to the surface. The more pain they can release the more alive and orgasmic they will become. (For more info about Taoist Sacred Sexuality see the resources page.)

In addition, the tongue connects to the heart according to traditional Chinese medicine, making oral sex the most profound way to touch your lover's genitals with your heart energy. This is why kissing with both tongues connecting is so deeply intimate. In addition, if we place one hand on our lover's heart while embracing their genitals with our tongue, we create a circuit connecting both hearts with their genitals. A connection which helps our lover to open their empathic heart, enhancing the quality of lovemaking.

As with self-pleasuring, I recommend while giving oral pleasure you use deliberate hand strokes to disperse generated energy from the genitals down the legs and into other parts of your beloved's body. Massaging your partner's feet while devouring their genitals with your mouth is another great way to help ground their orgasmic energy and delay orgasm, giving them more time to build more pleasure and store energy within their body temple. Directing energy down into the feet also strengthens their immune system by charging up their earth element.

Awakening Empathy: The One Heart

Again, in the film 'I Am', the director Tom Shadyac visits the Heartmath Institute where they conduct an experiment where electrodes are placed in a Petri dish of yoghurt and hooked up to a monitor to record sensations being felt by the bacteria contained within the yoghurt. When Tom is sitting a foot away from the dish and is asked to think about something that will produce heightened emotions, the needle on the monitor spikes as the yoghurt feels the emotional intensity of him thinking about calling his agent. Every time he says the word 'agent', the needle spikes showing how the magnetic field we project affects everything around us. This simple process effectively demonstrates how two neurons even when physically apart remain connected energetically. In the film, they spoke about this phenomenon is evident amongst twins. However, it is possible between any two people if they attune to each other's heart, such as friends and lovers. This is why our telepathy is increased with a lover. We can feel if a text message is from them before we look at it, or the phone rings and we just know it's them. This is because in opening our heart to them we have merged energy fields, making us ultra-sensitive to whatever emotional state they're in. This is why our partner knows if we are not being completely honest with them and why they can feel our mood before we open our mouth to speak. Just as body language is said to account for 70% of our communication (according to a Marquette University study) I would dare to say, it is our energetic transmission more than our physical gesturing that is most perceived subconsciously and responded to. So it is the energy behind our words and actions that is more powerful than what we say and do. Like the old saying, 'Intent is everything.' This also emphasizes how changing our intent affects the energy field of our beloved more than our verbal requests. Similarly, the more you consciously connect in your heart energetically with your lover, the more profound the energy generated for personal transformation and healing is.

Empathic communication is therefore an essential language for lovers to develop, as it generates deep reverence for the effect their magnetic field has on the other. Just as most partners will be able to recall how uncomfortable it was to be in close proximity when they were in a black mood or hyper-tense. So too, we can harness this shared energetic communion to assist each other to heal and experience greater states of ecstasy. Now that our cognitive mind is assured with the physical evidence to validate this phenomenon, we can become more energetically responsible and aware as a species.

The Seven Languages of Lovemaking

Expressing the Archetypal Light Body

Have you ever wondered why some lovers you are more compatible with in bed than others? Or why it is that you can have a wonderful connection with someone and then get to the bedroom and find that it feels awkward and unfulfilling? For those who don't have sex before marriage, the unanswered question of sexual compatibility can create understandable anxiety. So what is it that makes us compatible with some partners sexually and not with others? Two words: archetypes and chakras.

As explained in volume one, we have seven feminine and seven masculine psychological aspects which make up the feminine and masculine spectrum of our psyche. These aspects are referred to as 'archetypes'. Archetypes are universal energies, which are within us, since we are each the microcosm of existence. They also exist externally as planetary energies (in the macrocosm). The ancients acknowledged them as the Gods and Goddesses in their myths and legends.

When we understand they are not merely forces outside of us but also aspects within us, we dissolve our sense of separateness and feel at one with existence. Religious doctrines stressed it was arrogant to see the divine within us. They taught it was blasphemous to see ourselves as 'learner driver' Gods and Goddesses, an ideology which perpetuated our sense of separation. Fortunately, many are now questioning the doctrines they were raised with and are instead using their own conscience as their spiritual compass. This means many souls are now transcending the illusions which kept them blind from the truth of their nature as divine beings. This is inevitable as we evolve into more loving, self-aware and empowered beings who question all that is based in fear and separation.

So How Does That Relate to Sex?

When we consciously understand and express each archetypal energy within us, we clear each of our major energy centers which they govern. For example, if we express our inner Aphrodite, (the maiden Goddess of love, beauty, joy and play), in a positive way, the feminine energy meridian, Ida can then flow unimpeded into our sacral chakra, which is our emotional center. This creates emotional intelligence and emotional balance, which promotes healthy emotional interaction in our relationships. (See diagram below.)

Each chakra is a vortex. the word 'chakra, means wheel of light. They are vortices - portals to perceive another dimension of life. As we learn to give and receive energy at each gate we experience more light and greater connection with others. So instead of our relating being limited to one dimension, we experience the full spectrum of each other as souls.

Sexually this means we are able to explore each other's energy field at each dimension. For example, if their sacral chakra is open, they are someone we can enjoy sensual, playful and emotive lovemaking, which is the sexual signature of the sacral chakra.

Whereas, if we only ever operate out of one or two archetypes, our energy can only flow at those two gates. This makes us a 'two dimensional person', meaning we have only developed a couple of aspects of ourselves. For example, if a woman has only developed two of the most socially acceptable feminine aspects: 'Aphrodite, the beautiful maiden' and 'Demeter, the inner mother' who nurtures, supports and listens, she will only be able to connect with her partner through those two energy gates.

Sexually, this means she will enjoy cuddles and kisses, spooning and the missionary position, but may never have explored sexual expression through her other archetypal gates. This would enable her to experience wild sex, kinky sex, healing of trauma through deep healing sex, spiritually ecstatic sex or deep Zen states through sexual intercourse. (Kind of like only eating meat and potatoes then discovering other cuisines!)

The Secret of What Makes a Good Lover

Soulful sex is the communion of two light bodies, connecting through the nuances, perceptions and interplay of their subtle energy fields. It is the unspoken expression of our multifaceted inner selves, who, through this dance of light, feeling, touch, emotion, sound, taste, smell, thought and intent meet each other, through the giving and receiving of energy. It is the dance of the inner serpents of light, Ida and Pingala, spiraling up the nervous system of each partner, turning them on by lighting up their lotuses of light, one at a time as their inner archetypes feel the excitement of meeting their divine mirror at each of the seven gates. So if a chakra is blocked because an archetype is undeveloped, dysfunctional or dormant we are not able to perceive and respond energetically to our lover at this gate.

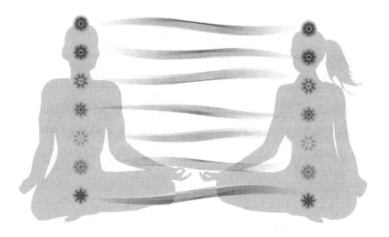

This is why being a great lover has nothing to do with the size of your breasts or appendage and everything to do with the levels of consciousness you have managed to access. In other words, the more effort you put into understanding yourself, the more of your true self you'll uncover and share. Evolution is what makes us sexy! (The ultimate revenge of the nerds - or more correctly, swamis. Yes, imagine 'Baywatch' with folks in saffron robes running on the sand as the cultural icons of sexual mastery!) Sounds ridiculous, but it's no more insane than the idea of worshipping those who focus on their external bodies, neglecting their light bodies. As this is what makes someone dull company and sexually bland.

That's not to say we should neglect our physical bodies, but in a culture that doesn't even acknowledge the inner energetic self, we certainly need to redress the balance. The focus on the external world is ego - the masculine unbalanced by the feminine. Which is why women and men with a developed feminine are more likely to pursue inner growth, by developing their emotional maturity, artistic expression and spiritual awareness, whereas men or women with a developed masculine are more likely to pursue outer growth, developing their physique, material wealth and assets. To be a great lover, we need to be fit and healthy enough to move with suppleness and strength, but we also need to be sensitive enough to perceive ourselves and our beloved so we can respond accordingly. So sisters, do exercise if you want to feel more sexually desirable and powerful. Equally, brothers, do read self-help books and learn Reiki if you want to become a more sensitive lover and vice versa!

A Seven Course Degustation Menu of Sex

The word, 'buffet' is amongst my favorite in the English language. The more highbrow version of this involves not even having to leave your table for minimal exercise between courses! It is the degustation meal, which is a sampling of high culinary art. It consists of many courses, small portions of a chef's signature dishes, designed to indulge all of the senses. This is a pleasure which is intended to be shared in good company. This is the best metaphor I have found to describe the art of lovemaking known in Tantra as 'High Sex', which features seven lovemaking languages.

Just as the more dishes a chef masters, the more mind-blowing the meal, so too, the more archetypes we develop, the more chakras we open, and the more mind-blowing our sexual artistry becomes. This is a love banquet that includes both sensate pleasure of the earthly senses and the transcendent ecstasy of our subtle senses. This is the type of sexual communion I recommend setting aside the time for at full moon, if one wants to exemplify this quote I heard spoken by a chef with a strong spiritual commitment who spoke of her relationship to sex:

'This happy disposition is not just because of the doughnuts.'

Julie Goodwin. Australian Masterchef winner.

Sexual Compatibility

As stated earlier, each set of chakra archetypes has their own lovemaking language. That includes arousal preferences and styles of physical and non-physical communication. For instance, if you have a big base chakra (like I do, symbolized by booty with 'tude) then your wild self is a strong archetype. So chances are, you like to be met by a partner who is not afraid of expressing their instinctual and primal nature in bed. If you have a big heart chakra (symbolized by a buxom bosom), you probably love lots of heart connecting cuddles and tender kisses.

This is why cosmetic surgery can muddy our search for a truly compatible partner. For example, if you get liposuction to reduce your ample bottom and a breast enlargement you are signaling to potential partners that you are a woman who prefers to mother and nurture partners, rather than get carried into the boudoir and shagged senseless.

Below I have outlined each of the seven lovemaking languages. You may recognize the ones you prefer, which indicate which archetypal selves you have most developed. I would encourage you to gently explore each at your own pace. The sexual cuisines you are least familiar with will expand the buffet of sensual and sexual pleasure available to you. If a particular lovemaking language feels confronting or fearful, do not persist to please your mate. Instead, work on developing the archetypes which govern that gate psychologically and emotionally.

How the Archetypes Affect Monogamy and Polyamory Sexual Lifestyles

I encourage deep exploration of all the inner aspects as a foundation for soulful lovemaking. For when the inner self is freed of conditioning it makes it much easier to trust oneself and express each aspect authentically in the bedroom. When we are more self-aware and empowered we will also be more allowing and encouraging of our partner's sexual expression at all seven gates. It is this inner work that makes monogamy so deeply rewarding on every level, as the more trust and openness we develop with someone, the more we feel safe to let each of our aspects to come out of the closet!

However, if we stay with a partner who refuses to grow, as their mirror, we will feel different parts of ourselves atrophying through neglect. This is why, without an understanding of archetypes, many people in monogamous unions fantasize about getting the needs of a particular aspect met outside the relationship, if it's not being met within the union. This can range from being infatuated with a screen idol to having an illicit affair.

Not surprisingly, polyamory has made a big return on the social scene now we're feeling the energies of the Aquarian Age kick in. The Aquarian energy frees us from social conventions, encourages multi-dimensional self-expression, energy connections and love of all humankind. In the shadow, Aquarius detaches from emotional expression and commitment and is idealistic, focusing on ideas without being grounded enough to work out the details. Put that together and you've got a fertile hotbed for what has been termed, 'free love'.

The last time 'free love' was socially hip was during the 1960s when the cusp energies of the Aquarian Age entered the planet. As a result the 1960s was an exciting time of social change and innovation which helped shift the conservatism of the previous era so real growth could occur. During this cusp period, however, the Aquarian values, were expressed in Piscean forms, as the new astrological age blended with the old. So people touted Aquarian ideals, while still perceiving through the Piscean filer of duality consciousness - seeing everything as 'black or white'. For instance, marriage was seen as 'old school' and 'bad' and 'free love' seen as 'evolved' and 'good'.

Well, the middle path is the road best taken since extremes that are good to explore but ultimately are not sustainable. For example, one or two dimensional marriages that limit one to only expressing part of who they are, are undoubtedly unhealthy but so are non-committal sexual liaisons with multiple partners, where lack of personal accountability and responsibility results in STD's, unwanted pregnancies, emotional insensitivity and detachment toward personal vulnerabilities along with an unwillingness to embrace the shadow.

So equally, without a comprehension of the framework of archetypes which make up our psyche and energy field, those in open relationships can unconsciously seek out different archetypes in different people, rather than journey to experience multi-dimensional communion with one person. When we have a map, we can identify which aspects aren't being met and discuss their need to be met at a certain gate.

If this is openly discussed, it can be ascertained whether both parties are willing to develop their other archetypes and if not, the union can be respectfully dissolved. If both are happy to only connect at a couple of gates and get their other aspects met elsewhere, that is up to the consenting adults involved, but at least the decision is well informed.

Archetypes as a Map For Sexual Healing

Whilst I do not advocate sex as the primary means to unveil a completely unconscious archetype, which could induce

218

trauma, it is a wonderful tool to further encourage the expression of an archetype, once it is semi-conscious. For example, if you find you are being drawn to buying and wearing a lot of the same color, this is a sign that you are working on clearing a particular this chakra. (Chakra colors are listed below.)

Furthermore, by having an awareness of the lovemaking languages for each chakra, you can discuss your observations with your partner and embrace your lovemaking sessions as another healing modality which supports the full reclamation and expression of your archetypal selves.

Author's Note: I encourage you to read volume one if you haven't, as this will provide you with the understanding to express all of the seven feminine and masculine archetypes which govern the major chakras, allowing for your full sexual expression at each of the seven gates.

The Seven Lovemaking Languages

I have listed each of the seven lovemaking languages below.

For Couples...

I recommend initially, you spend a month awakening each center with your partner if you are in an existing union. Once all gates are open, you can spontaneously move from one language to another in no particular sequence, which is akin to having the full spectrum on your palette of energetic paints to play with.

For Singles...

If you are currently single, consider exploring these lovemaking languages in your self-pleasuring or take a lover, specifically to explore a certain gate. If exploring soulful sex with someone who is not your beloved, be sure to state your boundaries clearly at the outset and be sure to honor both your own and theirs accordingly. This will ensure your interaction is deeply reverent and safe physically, emotionally, psychologically and energetically.

Incorporating Aromatherapy into Your Lovemaking

I have included the essential oils that stimulate the flow of energy in each of the chakras. You may like to anoint each other with a few drops of the recommended oil in a base oil, such as jojoba on the location of the chakra you are exploring together.

You may also like to incorporate Tantric Massage into your foreplay. To do this, apply some of the chakra indicated oil in a carrier oil onto your fingers, then rub the corresponding chakra in the shape of the infinity sign. (The figure eight on its side.) This helps to awaken the twin serpent at each gate and balance the energies at each gate.

Once all gates are open you may wish to anoint all seven gates with their chakra oils prior to lovemaking or anoint the crown with spikenard oil in jojoba, which opens all the gates simultaneously.

'The Tantrics will anoint their hands with jasmine, their cheeks and breasts with patchouli, their hair with spikenard, their vulva with musk, their thighs with sandalwood and their feet with saffron. This is a part of their body language, learnt in their temples or societies for their Maithuna or ceremonial sex union. Each part of the body has its language'

The Wise Wound by Penelope Shuttle and Peter Redgrove.

The First Lovemaking Language

Base Chakra: Red

Element: Fire / Earth (Volcanic)

Governs: Physical Body

Key words: vocal, uninhibited, instinctual, primal

Archetypes: Lilith, the Wild Woman and Pan, the Wild Man

Ideal Setting:

- Outside in nature on soft grasses or next to a camp fire.
- In a cave or tent.
- If at home, place faux fur on your bed or make love on a sheepskin rug in front of a fire.

Turn-Ons: Anything that appeals to your base desires, such as:

- Sexually explicit photography.
- Erotic art images, like those found in the many printed versions of the Kama Sutra.
- Leopard print or red lingerie.
- Vibrating sex toys like butt plugs, which sound horrendous, but aren't. They can be used to relax, energize and excite the perineum, anus, anal passage and prostate, which are great to use when self-pleasuring or with a partner. Great for dissolving tension, shame and trauma which is often held in these areas for years, which inhibits pleasure. Use with deep reverence and gentleness to heal sexual blocks in the base, so one can open to feeling more pleasurable sensations in these areas.

Essential Oils for Anointing: Black pepper, clary sage, clove, sandalwood and cinnamon. (Be sure to blend in a carrier oil as spicy oils if applied directly will burn the skin.)

Sense: Smell.

Every perfume counter will try and convince you that their commercially manufactured scent will enhance your attractiveness to the opposite sex, when in fact the opposite is true! Your natural scent is the first thing that attracts a prospective mate. So if we cover that up, we are impeding our instinctual attraction and arousal. Instead of buying each other scents at Christmas to mask your pheromones, explore each other with your olfactory sense to stimulate your endorphins. Notice the difference in your pheromone response as you smell different parts of their physique, such as their hair, neck, armpits, backs of the knees, under the scrotum, around the vulva and anus.

Base Music: You may like to just play some of these tracks to wake up your lover's base chakra or ask them to dance for you. Alternatively, fix them a drink and dance for them or dance for yourself before self-pleasuring! Perhaps, make a playlist of base chakra tracks and get down and funky!

To activate your base try electrifying rock like:
- *'Fire'* by Jimi Hendrix
- *'Mama Said'* *'Always On The Run'* and *'Are You Gonna Go My Way'* by Lenny Kravitz
- Deep rhythmic bass lines like *'What Does Your Soul Look Like'* by DJ Shadow
- Serpentine music like *'Awaken the Snake'* by Peruquois

Lovemaking Language: Animalistic Lust

Lovemaking Positions

Rear Entry: either with one partner kneeling on all fours, like an animal or bent over with your partner entering from behind, as this stimulates the perineum (the physical floor of the base chakra) or anal sex. Oral sex and orally worshipping your lover's sphincter are also base chakra expressions of loving the beastly selves.

On All Fours: This is the classic pose known in the animal kingdom as 'she's presenting' - when the feminine partner becomes so aroused that she backs up to her mate to offer herself for entry. (This is the position high heels mimic.) During lovemaking, when a woman is pre-menstrual she may 'present' by tilting her bottom flirtatiously, or she may break from a more submissive position and get on her knees, tilting her bottom high in the air like a wildcat presenting her engorged vulva as a sexual demand to her lover. This is when her primal self wants him to respond without hesitation by confidently taking her by the mane (without hurting her) and riding her so her perineum gets a good pounding, as this releases all the stored tension she has been holding. She will be further aroused by his audible lusty sounds and words (without putting her down). If a woman signals to you in this way, she wants to hear you assert your power, so she can submit 100% to your primal, physical dominance. (This, is equally applicable to women in same sex relationships using a strap-on, dildo or finger to penetrate their lover's vulva.)

Bent Standing Pose: This can be done by bending your lover over a piece of furniture, such as a couch, desk or kitchen sink or by bending them forwards, depending on their suppleness and balance. This is often easier for those with protruding discs in their back than the previous position. Back complaints aside, it is wise for the partner being entered to have something to hang onto to steady themselves, such as a bedside table, ottoman or chair so they aren't distracted by trying to stop themselves falling over. Ladies, wearing high heels and no underwear is a great invitation to your Pan to please his carnal urges. Great if you have a pool table!

Anal Entry: Warning - never thrust anything into someone's anus as you will tear their anal passage. Having said that, if you gain consent for anal play, first tease them by massaging their buttocks, stroking their inner thighs, stimulating their perineum or licking around their anus, if they've evacuated their bowels, have no intestinal parasites and have bathed or douched with an enema. You can then stimulate around their anus with a finger moistened with your saliva (and a shortly clipped fingernail), then venture in asking them every step of the way if that feels good.

Don't overstimulate the first few times, a little leaves a lot to the imagination and their sense of taboo will leave them thinking about this kinky pleasure between lovemaking sessions. When they're really comfortable with the sensation (which takes a little getting used to because it can feel similar to the urge to poo), tease them by taking your finger out and having them beg you to keep stimulating them.

When they're really begging you, you can introduce a phallus ever so gently, a millimeter at a time, which may produce very deep, guttural sounds as they release blocked energy from their most primal self. Deep respect is called for, as you are being gifted with their deepest trust and vulnerability.

Personally, I think if men are penetrated anally in some way, it helps them realize just how vulnerable a woman is when she is penetrated, in any way by a man. In addition, men get to experience the pleasure of their male G-spot being massaged and the thrill of being submissive, if they can allow themselves to experience being in the receptive polarity, without fearing that equates to homosexuality.

An awareness of basic hygiene is essential with anal love and play. Be sure to wash your hands and underneath your fingernails with a soapy nail brush before and after entering with your finger. Cover cuts with a latex glove and do not put a finger that's been into someone's anus anywhere near their vulva or mouth as this introduces anal flora into these areas which will cause a thrush infection.

Seven Ways to Explore Your Erotic Power

1. The Power of Primal Sound

The jaw and the anus are connected, as they correspond to the base and the throat chakras, which are known as the two 'power chakras'. When open, their free expression allows us to express our authentic truth. This is why birthing women are encouraged to keep their jaw loose and release on sound, as it helps their cervix to relax and open.

So too, when lovemaking, the more we are uninhibited about releasing our primal pleasure on sound, the more blood flows into our genitals and the more physical sensation we will feel in our body. Equally, if we can't let go and make some noise, we are more likely to stay in our heads and allow our physical sensations to lead. This is especially so for those who have experienced insensitive lovers or sexual abuse. (For more about the power of sound, read the chapter, 'How To Self Pleasure Like A Hermaphrodite' in volume one.)

2. Owning Your Sexuality

When we develop a really healthy and loving self-pleasuring practice, we make the shift from being a sexual performer, when being sexually intimate with a partner, to someone who is authentic in their sexual responses, without any shame or inhibition. This means we will speak up if something feels good or doesn't. Self-pleasure generates feeling of self-love and self-worth. The more we feel good about ourselves as sexual beings, the more confident we are in sharing our sexual appetites and self-expression with our lover. This means we can initiate sex when we feel aroused, as well as suggesting sexual experimentation with positions, fetishes, fantasies and inspirations as they occur.

Self-Pleasuring for each other is a great way of being truly seen as a sexual being, enabling you to really own your erotic nature. This is the ultimate pornography - to watch the person you love and adore, experience genuine waves of increasing ecstasy and divine rapture!

3. Claiming Your Partner Sexually

Women, in particular, have a fantasy of being taken. This is because the feminine polarity is receptive, so our deepest yearning is to experience complete trust, so we can submit and surrender 100% to our lover and the experience of pleasure. Women want a man to be strong enough in his masculine energy to lead, to take control - not 24/7, but in the boudoir, especially when we are pre-menstrual.

Men also have a subconscious fantasy to be taken and devoured by a wild woman. According to Jung, the Lilith aspect of a woman is every man's fantasy. Although there is also tremendous fear of this aspect (depicted by the portrayal of Glenn Close in the film, 'Fatal Attraction'.) However if a man understands and empowers his wild man aspect, he can also enjoy being sexually dominated by his wild woman at that time of the month, when her sexual appetite is intensified, as he knows and understands the nature of the beast - both his and hers!

So to assist your inner wild man or woman in claiming your mate sexually, I have included a sample below, of how one might go about doing this. Whilst I appreciate that we all have different tastes and what may be a turn-on for one, may be a turn-off for another, go with your intuition for you know best what will suit you and your partner better than anyone.

4. How to Take a Woman

A woman's vulva is like a flower, so you can't just fumble back the petals and pummel her raw and say, 'You were taking her like a wild man'. First, you have to get her out of her civilized mind and into an Earthy mood for sex. In fact, the more in her head she is, the more she probably needs a good shag, but the bigger the feat to make it happen!

Author's Note: To all Pan's seeking sexual admittance - read the chapter, titled, 'Seven Brides For Seven Brothers' in volume one. This will give you the low down on how to be 'all man' in her eyes, so you don't get kneed in the nuts trying to pull off this maneuver.

Importante! This approach is intended for lovers where trust and consent is already established. I am not advocating this approach with a woman you have just met in a bar!

First, approach from behind and go for an erogenous zone, like the nape of her neck. Nuzzle in and kiss her tenderly, then more erotically with your tongue and soft nibbling and mock biting with your teeth, indicating that you wish to devour her.

Next, use a very deliberate stroke on her opposite buttock that stakes your claim in no uncertain terms as to your intent. Don't wait for permission, as she'll probably remember her 'to do list' and fob you off. Instead, continue asserting your lead, by taking your finger (moistened with your saliva) and twist your way inside her knickers and start lovingly stroking her pussy while you continue to kiss her neck and tell her she needs some cock.

It is important that your touch is not too rough or impatient and that you genuinely enjoy opening her lotus of pleasure, rather than see it as a perfunctory deed to getting your end in. You can guarantee she will discern the difference and if you come across as selfish, that will be an instant turn-off.

You may also like to caress her breasts and stimulate her nipples, through her clothes, while you continue to stimulate her yoni and kiss her neck. When she's really good and wet and moaning, heaving and gasping with pleasure, wrench her underwear down deliberately, gently bend her forwards and with your cock in one hand, give her pussy a taste of what pleasure awaits, by moving the head of your cock back and forth at the entrance to her open, wet labia lips.

Don't waste too much time before giving it to her, holding her neck, pushing your fingers through her hair and thrusting. If there's a seat nearby, you might also like to shuffle back while still inside her and invite her to squat up and down while sitting on top of you. Make sure you give her a really good going before you swap to her controlling her satisfaction and don't be afraid to thrust while in the sitting position if she starts to tire, or change position.

The concept of 'grabbing' is classic 'cave man' behavior, which is common in male dominant cultures, such as modern gypsy communities, known as 'travelers'. As part of their mating ritual, the young males grab a young traveler girl off the dance floor and carry her out to the car park and snog her. Unfortunately, this alpha male gorilla type behavior often coincides with domestic violence, if not balanced by other archetypal awareness and maturity. Equally, if a man cannot take a woman she will fantasize about a man who can.

5. How to Take a Man

Start by putting on something erotic since men are visually aroused. I recommend wearing something with easy access to your erogenous zones, like a lace robe or bra and suspender belt, with heels or a corset with boots. Then come up behind him and place both hands on his hips and slide your hands down his thighs with a strong, deliberate motion. Next, embrace him, so he can feel your breasts pressing into his back and wrap one leg around him like a serpent, as you rub his pecs with hunger in your touch, through his clothes. Then suggestively fondle his nipples and say in a low whisper, gently in his ear, 'I need some cock.'

Then slide your arm down the front of him and start stroking his cock through his clothes, murmuring with pleasure as you continue to writhe against him from behind. Keep taking the initiative, so he has no alternative but to keep giving in to feeling more intense states of arousal.

Move around to his front, undoing his belt, unzipping his pants with no hesitation, then slide down to your knees and worship his cock with your mouth and your hands. Press firmly on his perineum to stop him from ejaculating as you work yourself into greater states of shared ecstasy and sexual anticipation.

Then tell him, 'I want to sit on your cock, Honey.' Lead him to a chair, couch or bed and tell him to sit or lie down, then straddle him and rub your wet pussy on his cock as your kiss him on the mouth, face and neck, until you guide his cock into your hot pussy and fill yourself with pleasure.

Author's Note: Given the majority of women don't have the developed quad muscles that men do, you may find it helpful to take hold of the bed head with your hands, while squatting with your weight on the balls of your feet or alternatively, your lover can help to support you by locking your fingers and pushing against each other's weight to help stabilize yourself.

6. Male Fertility Rite

When you make love at this gate, worship the power of the male phallus, of your man's virility, his ability to give you great pleasure with his rod and the potency of his seed which can fertilize new life.

A mantra is helpful to take you into an ecstatic trance state of devotional worship. In the ecstatic tradition of Tantra, mantra is used to invoke a state of awareness through the power of word. For example, when one chants the name of a deity or a quality, such as the word, 'love', they become one with the vibration of that being or quality. We can therefore apply mantra to oral lovemaking, with the intent of worshipping your lover's wild man. To do this you would repeat the same words over and over again in your thoughts, such as 'I worship your cock'. When one's intent is to worship, using the power of incantation to raise their energy, they will work themselves up into such a state of hyper anticipation, that they are ecstatic at the thought of tasting and drinking their partner's seed and then subsequently delirious at the point of release, resulting in a frenzy of passion, reveling in their partner's juices and smearing it all over themselves in complete adoration of their fertile male power. This is what porn tries to unconsciously recreate, but because it is not done with any genuine reverence or love, it ends up being the exact opposite - an insultingly fake representation, affirming how much they don't love their onscreen partner, which is a complete turn-off for anyone connected to their true erotic power.

7. Female Fertility Rite

Similarly, mantra can be applied to worshipping the vulva, which is the mouth of hairy wild woman, Lilith. It is not meant to be pretty, looking like a poodle that's been groomed at the vet. It is naturally designed to declare one's primal feminine power. She's meant to look fierce, potent and mysterious.

Now depending on the time of her cycle, her yoni juices may be clear and slippery or opaque and thick to touch. This is another good reason to get to know your woman's cycle. If still cycling physically, when she is ovulating, she will be clear and slippery. This is the preferable time to devour your woman's vulva, with the intent of worshipping her erotic female power, while repeating a mantra in your thoughts, such as, 'I worship your pussy'.

Some partners may enjoy devouring their partner when she is bleeding, which is a distinctly Earthly taste on the palette and a powerful act to revere the dark feminine gate of death and rebirth. Only if a man reveres the aspect of Lilith can he truly worship a woman sexually when she is menstruating. This was considered the ultimate honor and now, after 6000 years of patriarchy is considered the ultimate taboo.

The Second Lovemaking Language

Sacral Chakra: Orange

Element: Water

Governs: Emotional Body

Key words: Sensual, romantic, fluid, wet, emotive.

Archetypes: Aphrodite, the Beautiful Muse and Adonis, the Beautiful Greek God (this is the lover aspect of Ares, the Warrior / Dancer)

Ideal Setting:
- In a spa bath, surrounded by candles or an outside hot tub, surrounded by fire torches.
- On a secluded island or beach, preferably somewhere hot, wet and humid.
- On a daybed by a pool or on an inflatable airbed or rubber yoga mats, (cover with a plastic sheet if inside) and drizzle with warm sweet almond oil, so you can slide sensually upon each other's bodies.
- Consider buying an inflatable wading pool which you can fill with any of the following: warm water and flower petals, bubble bath or edible jelly.

Turn-Ons: Anything that appeals to our emotions and senses.

Essential Oils for Anointing: Bergamot, tangerine, rose geranium and sweet orange.

Sense: Taste

Use anything oral to arouse your lover's hunger for pleasure. Foods such as honey, chocolate sauce or whipped cream. Devour your lover's body, telling them how much you want to lap them up or suck them and how good they taste.

Music: Emotive music, like film soundtracks and sultry, rhythmic music, such as Latin or chill out music, such as drum and bass tracks augmented with watery sound effects like dolphin or whale sounds.

Lovemaking Language: Sensual and Romantic.

Lovemaking Positions: Missionary position and lying on one side facing each other.

Missionary Position: This allows for deep penetration, stimulating the cervix for maximum emotional release, especially if the woman's pelvis is elevated with a pillow. In this position, the woman lies on her back and the man kneels between her legs or lies on top of her, supporting his body weight with his arms, so he can control entry to her yoni (vulva) with his lingham (phallus). This position also allows for eye contact, heart contact and mouth contact. It also stimulates the conjunction of nadis in the sacral. These are the pathways in the light body also known as the pranic body, which extend four centimeters out from the physical body.

Lying On Side Facing Each Other: You can straddle and scissor your legs so your feet can caress each other, as you writhe your pelvis rhythmically with your beloved and passionately kiss and embrace.

Bathing Rite: Put on oceanic music, light candles, scent the air with orange blossom and take turns washing each other with a sea sponge, stimulating their skin and erogenous zones, such as their nipples, neck, inner thighs and genitals. Next, wash up the spine, drawing the energy up the chakras. Then, stimulate down the front of their body. You can do this sitting behind them in the bath.

Filling Your Cup: When we lose our libido it is often because our sacral chakra is blocked. In other words we have neglected our need for self-love so our inner cup of joy is empty. So when we feel we have nothing to give and no creative inspiration to make artful love, filling our senses with pleasure is the fastest way to fill our own cup. Here are a few suggestions to top up so your cup runneth over:

- Have a massage or have a spa treatment.
- Visit a hot spring.
- Go to a place of great beauty.
- Swim in the ocean.
- Go out for an exotic meal and a tropical mock tail or glass of nice wine with a great friend.
- Have a good belly laugh at one of your favorite comedy films.
- Go salsa dancing or do a Zumba class to shake out your pelvis.

How to Seduce Her: Striptease / Lap dance

Many guys and masculine dominant women love the concept of a woman dancing for them, but stop short at the idea of repaying the favor. Love is about willingness, sharing and risking being seen in your vulnerability so dare to do a mating dance...(if it wasn't a tried and true means of wooing, then 99% of the natural world wouldn't bother). Your mate will appreciate your efforts and you will reap the rewards to the moon and back!

Let your hair down and have fun role-playing your Adonis or butch buck, with show pony characters like the mechanic, the cop, the warrior or GI...(just work through the Village People options at your local costume hire shop!) Rip your shirt, pound your truncheon, thrust your pelvis, flex your muscles, show your buns and just enjoy moving about your lounge room to your fave dance music. If this thought fills you with terror and dread, consider taking some Latin dance classes or watch the Chippendales or Manpower troupes on DVD or You Tube for ideas. Gone are the days of men only nodding their head to music! Above all, just let go - have a laugh and enjoy yourself. Below are some specific suggestions:

- Put both hands behind your head (suggesting dominance), as you thrust your pelvis forward with your knees bent and legs apart. Then bring one hand down and play with your nipple while you continue to thrust.

- Place your partner's hands on your butt cheeks and move them from side to side to the rhythm of the music - you can do this while facing them and also with your back to them.

- Straddle them and thrust repeatedly while pulling at your pants or underwear.

- Wear Lycra leggings and pull at the waistband in anticipation at sharing your manly package to tease them with a wry smile, then turn around and pull them down with your legs together and straight to reveal your butt in your underwear.

- Try some floor work by lying on the floor, doing a few push-ups then rolling onto your side, relaxing on your right shoulder and drawing up your left leg and pretending to offer your package by pulling at your drawers.

- Wear a G-string under your underwear to draw out the tease and give them a thrill they won't expect.

Suggested Music tracks:
- *'Closer'* by Nine Inch Nails
- *'Dirty Old Man'* by Faithless
- *'Sex'* by George Michael

How to Seduce Him: Striptease / Lap dance

Ladies, you don't need to have double D breasts and a cellulite free derriere to dance for your lover, as ultimately it's not what you have, but how you use it that creates the allure. If you are having fun, playfully expressing your inner flirt or vamp - he will too. So role play by dressing up as different naughty sex sirens such as the school girl, nurse, baby doll, French maid, burlesque showgirl or cat woman. Using props is a great way to give yourself something to focus on if you feel self-conscious about how to move. So consider using saucy accouterments such as cigarette holders, long gloves, a feather duster, feather fans or a feather boa. Personally I like to use long gloves, as they frame whatever part of your body you are showcasing for your lover.

This makes for a great annual birthday or Valentine Day treat for your beau, which you will have as much fun planning as he will have receiving. It is actually harder to strip for your partner, than it is for a stranger, so consider wearing a wig or mask to help you move into your chosen alter ego or alternatively, give him a pair of sunglasses or a Zorro mask to wear.

I also recommend dimming the lights if you have a dimmer switch, or throwing scarves over lamps or lighting candles, so you don't feel like a deer in headlights! Don't stress about how to take your clothes off seductively to begin with, just wear something sexy and dance! As good eroticism always leaves something to the imagination, this enables you to focus on the tease rather than feel you need to do a XXX live sex show.

That said, you may like to give him just a taste by titillating your nipples with a moistened finger or brush your nipples and breasts with a feather fan or boa. Choose corsetry, push-up bras, fish-net suspender stockings and high-heeled boots that highlight your curvaceous form. Then just enjoy teasing him with your treats, while he sits in a chair, unable to touch. You may wish to tie his hands behind his back with a silk scarf before you begin. Below are a few more specific suggestions:

- If playing a naughty schoolgirl, twist your knickers and give him a glimpse of your yoni from behind as you pull at your underwear.

- Pull at your bra strap in anticipation, pulling it down over your shoulder and back.

- Lean over him and give him an extreme close up of your breasts.

- Sit on a chair opposite him and put a finger in your mouth then simulate self-pleasuring, by holding your finger millimeters away from your yoni and pretending to stroke your orchid. This can be done with your G-string or underwear on.

- Bend over in front of him with your legs straight and wiggle your bottom suggestively.

- Lean against a wall on tip toes with your knees together and bent, twisting to either side. Then stand with your weight on one straight leg, with the other bent and look back over your shoulder at him as you tear at your buttocks with black gloved hands. You may also like to circle around the entrance to your yoni with one gloved finger.

- Put the feather boa between your legs with your legs standing straight and apart.

Suggested Music Tracks:
- *'Need You Tonight'* by INXS
- *'Love To Love You'* by Donna Summer
- *'I Touch Myself'* by the Divinyls
- *'I Want A Sugar In My Bowl'* by Nina Simone
- *'Remember Me'* by Blueboy

The Third Lovemaking Language

Solar Plexus Chakra: Yellow

Element: Air

Governs: Mental Body

Key Words: Exploring Polarities and Opposites, Domination, Submission, Anticipation and Mind Games.

Essential Oils: lemon, grapefruit, basil, peppermint.

Archetypes: Athena, the Golden Heroine and Apollo, the Statesman.

Ideal Setting:

- Somewhere unfamiliar or unexpected, such as hiring a motel room.
- On a leather recliner in his or her office.
- Blindfold them and take them into the garage where you have an A frame artist easel which you tie them to.
- Hire a room at a brothel or from a local dominatrix.

Turn-Ons: Wearing dress-ups of subs and doms, such as:

- Latex fetish wear
- Leather wear
- PVC
- Kinky boots
- Spike heels
- Masques

Sense: Sight.

Visual Erotica: Since sight is the sense that governs this gate, another way to connect sexually at the level of mind is through fantasy erotica films. Rent titles like 'Sex and Zen', 'Quills' (about the Marquis De Sade), a French art film or download some vintage porn from the sixties, which is less offensive and very theatrical. Watching erotica can stimulate the expression of your own fantasies. Similarly, you might want to head to your nearest bookstore or library or search online for images of erotic art, like those of Eric Stanton which are very much in the 'S and M' vein.

Music: Classical music to heighten the senses, such as compositions by Bach or dramatic Neo Classical music such as Holst's 'The Planets' or 'Chariots of Fire'. Acid and cool Jazz featuring brass instruments, such as John Coltrane and Miles David or even the understated tension of the 'American Beauty' soundtrack.

Lovemaking Language: Mind Games Exploring Duality.

Lovemaking Positions: Male partner standing penetrating their partner lying on a bed, swing or table. Woman on top holding bed head for stability or squatting over her lover, holding his hands. Both positions allow for fast, dominating thrusting. Tying a partner with silk scarves to a chair or bed. One partner standing over the other during oral sex.

Sadomasochism: Otherwise known as 'S and M'. This can be done between consenting partners without it being humiliating, degrading or painful. Trust and safety are essential at all times or it stops being lovemaking and starts being abuse.

Mind Sex: Stimulate through the power of suggestion. For instance, if someone has a high-powered job with a lot of responsibility, complete loss of control may be their ultimate turn-on. So you could limit their freedom by tying them up, handcuffing them or wearing clothing that can only be laced from behind. This is equal to someone who has no responsibility having the thrill of absolute control, such as having their own sex slave for an hour. Consider playing with the possibility of each taking turns in the dominant / submissive roles.

Share your Fantasies: Recount your secret fantasies verbally or write them down and have your lover read them aloud. You might want to keep them in a silk bag in your nightstand, so either party can draw upon them for inspiration at a later date. Just talking about them will start you pondering upon the possibilities of enacting them. (Share even the ones you wouldn't enact, so your lover knows the dynamics of all your sexual desires, so they can recreate them in a way that doesn't compromise your health and well-being.)

Erotic Literature with a Twist: Read your lover erotic literature while dressed provocatively in fetish wear. Read books by Anais Ninn or '*Lady Chatterley's Lover*' or you can even pick up some Mills and Boon romance novellas from your nearest thrift shop. Articles of clothing to consider wearing, include boots, power dressing hats, jackets, corsets, things that take a long time to undo or have a peekaboo pockets for stimulation of one area. Erotica is when we adorn ourselves artfully, but leave something to the imagination to stimulate the mind's fantasies. Being completely naked is more the terrain of your inner wild selves at the base chakra.

'S and M' Love Rite: Ask your partner to sit on their hands and set some ground rules. You may find this easier wearing a costume that promotes role play. For example, they may not be allowed to make a sound, or show any sign of enjoying the pleasure you inflict on them, as a playful mock taboo. You might like to set the scene by leading them into an unfamiliar setting, wearing a blindfold, to accentuate their sense of vulnerability.

Whilst blindfolded, tie them to a bed, chair or A frame artist's easel. (Obviously check whether they're up for this sort of play first!) Make them beg for what they want or order them to perform sexual acts for rewards or punishments.

Try dripping hot wax on parts of their body, being sure to telegraph each sensation visually by showing them the intended sensation, milking their sense of anticipation. Try putting ice in your mouth, then sucking different parts of their body or rub the ice on different parts of their skin, such as their nipples or under their arms.

Experiment using soft then hard textures on their skin. For example:

- Feathers followed by the straps of a soft leather whip.
- Alternating hot then cold sensations, such as sucking their genitals with a hot mouth from sucking a 'Fisherman's Friend' hot mint lozenge then blowing cold air on them. It's all about the thrill of the unknown, the build of anticipation. Dramatic music will heighten the titillation.

Fetish Date: Go out wearing no underwear and fondle each other under the dinner table or give your partner the cordless remote to some vibrating love balls or similar sex toy.

The Fourth Lovemaking Language

Heart Chakra: Green / Pink

Element: Earth

Governs: Feeling Body

Key words: Closeness, Love, Communion, Tenderness, Nurturing.

Archetypes: Demeter, the Earth Empress and The Green Man.

Ideal Setting:
- At home, in the garden.
- On a picnic rug, in a park or on green rolling hills.

Turn-Ons: Acts of kindness, generosity of Spirit, sharing one's heart or gifting something made with love, such as a meal or a creating a flower bed for their favorite blooms. Either clothed or naked, rub the back and front of each other's heart. If not clothed, lubricate your hand with a natural oil such as almond oil for a wet touch, or corn flour or talcum powder for a dry touch.

Essential Oils for Anointing: Rose, vanilla, nutmeg and ginger.

Sense: Touch

Loving touch with no sexual agenda. The more non-sexual touch a woman receives, the more she opens sexually to a man. This would also apply to feminine dominant men. Non-sexual touch can include various types of touch on a regular basis, such as a reassuring stroking a cheek, hand in the small of a back, holding hands, caressing hair on their head or giving a foot rub.

Music: Schmaltzy, romantic big band music such as swing, Yanni, Cole Porter as well as soft gentle acoustic music, such as folk and stringed instruments including guitar, harp and cello. Heart centered bands like, 'Crowded House'.

Lovemaking Language: Cuddling and holding.

Lovemaking Positions:

Heart: Spooning with both lying down, one cuddling the other from behind as this allows one to receive love in through the back of the chakras. Can enter from behind in this position sending heart light into your lover's heart from behind. Women can spoon their partners and caress their nipples and pecs which opens the heart.

Kissing: Since the tip of the tongue connects to the heart, spend a long time just kissing and cuddling if you want to really find the door to your lover's deepest feelings for you.

> *'Awakening the empathic lover is experiencing*
> *yourself and your beloved as one sexual being.'*
> Tanishka

Empathic Lovemaking: As mentioned in the chapter on oral worshipping, opening the heart enables us to connect through our feeling body. We then sense what our lover is experiencing, so we feel equally aroused by giving as much as receiving. This ability to give and receive in equal measure is an indication of an open heart.

To promote this open-hearted connection in lovemaking, place one hand on your own heart and breathe into your heart center to connect with your true self. Next, place your hand on your lover's heart and look deep into each other's eyes (the windows to the Soul.) Where possible, keep one hand on your partner's heart when touching them on other parts of their body. (Don't take this suggestion to the point of a final round of Twister!)

I see this empathic activation of the higher heart (the turquoise chakra located between the heart center and the throat), as the new sacral (emotional center). In other words, when one has taken responsibility for their wounded inner child, whose unresolved issues sit as blockages in our emotional center, this counterpoint lotus of light opens. This occurs when we are able to experience true compassion for both ourselves and others, in equal measure, transcending all perception of victimhood. This is true emotional intelligence, which enables us to relate to others emotionally, without our projected wounds getting in the way.

Opening this energy center is the key to being a great lover, as it enables one to connect heart to heart with a lover in a completely vulnerable and unguarded way. Those who have developed this capability in esoteric circles are referred to as 'empaths' - folk whose heart is so open they feel what others around them are feeling. This ability, once developed means one can act as a spiritual midwife, assisting others with healing or guidance. This is done by completely attuning to their heart, so they can intuit what the other person needs to relieve their suffering. The awakening of this sensitivity also means one must be vigilant in cutting and clearing their energy field, once a session is complete so they aren't continually hooked in intimately to the energy field of others, or they will continue to surrogate their feelings and feel drained.

This phenomenon also explains why some clients develop a dependency on their psychologists, for when genuine empathy is shared in a private session, the heart opens causing them to bond energetically. Without understanding how establishing an energetic interaction can assist practitioners to go straight to the heart of the matter, mainstream counsellors have continued to dissect their client's conditions from a rational perspective.

This clinical model of detachment also stems from a fear of 'getting involved', a fear which is perpetuated in training institutions which advise counsellors to maintain a professional distance from their clients by shutting down their heart center. This impedes their ability to attune to the soul of each client and intuitively access words of guidance and processes that would help each individual patient to ease their suffering. This is how shamans have long assisted individuals to transform their wounds into wisdom. Fortunately, Scott Peck, psychiatrist and author of 'The Road Less Travelled' broke significant ground when he suggested that one could not truly assist another to heal without opening their heart to loving them, while maintaining professional and human ethics in 1978.

Author's Note: Self-Pleasuring with one hand on your heart chakra can be more effective to revive lagging energy levels than a nap. Particularly recommended for tired parents since the heart chakra is the archetypal gate of the inner mother and father. So when bub goes down for a nap, try spending a little quality time with yourself!

Heart Nurturing Love Rite

Wash your lover's hair, gently massaging their scalp or tend to them by tenderly shaving their whiskers or the hair on their legs. Alternatively, show them a little TLC by bringing them their favorite breakfast in bed. Then put on some Sunday morning music and have some cuddle time. Express your feelings and appreciation of all the little things you've noticed about your partner and what they've done for you, while touching them tenderly. This may or may not become sexual. It is important to remember that lovemaking is not limited to lusty fornication. It is literally any act that generates feelings of love and pleasure.

Author's Note: If you lover is Vege-quarian, try my personal favorite - Eggs Atlantic!!! Poached eggs on avocado and smoked salmon on sour dough toast with lemon juice, seasoning, capers, chives and Hollandaise sauce.)

The Fifth Lovemaking Language

Throat Chakra: Blue

Element: Ether

Governs: Etheric Body

Key words: Vulnerability, Healing, Gentleness, Compassion

Archetypes: Artemis, the Medicine Woman and Chiron, the Healer

Ideal Setting:
- In a mountain cabin.
- Camping under the stars or in a tent, in a teepee or yurt.
- Somewhere where you won't be disturbed.

Turn-Ons: Safety, trust, emotional honesty and intimacy, friendship and dependability.

Essential Oils for Anointing: lemongrass, eucalyptus, blue cypress and cedar wood.

Sense: Hearing

Mantra / Chanting Lovemaking: You may wish to go to an ashram or devotional chanting event to experience how the repetition of a sound opens the higher heart, again taking one into higher and higher states of transcendent bliss, without any physical touch or sexual heat. This is great to experience, either on your own or with a lover, as the group energy creates a vortex which amplifies the joy. Some chanting events go for 24 hours or longer, which I have been told is the most similar high to the drug ecstasy.

Music: Folk music, world music from mountainous regions like the Andes. For example, panpipes, flute, woodwind instruments and ambient trance. Traditionally, the flute sent forth a message that the one who approaches, comes in peace. 'Nakai' is one modern day Native American Kokopelli whose CD's are soothing for throat center soul connection.

Lovemaking Language: Energy healing and emotional release.

Lovemaking Positions: There is no one particular position which enables lovers to connect at the throat chakra. However, feeling each other and holding a space to allow vulnerabilities to surface is key. Rocking each other, stroking each other, touching each other with healing intent are all more important than being in a specific position.

Sexual Healing Rite

For communion of your etheric bodies, I suggest giving an energy healing. This allows you to attune to your partner's energy field, without any agenda of sex. If you end up having sex after the healing, it will have a very healing and tender quality to it, as a continuation of the session. Following an energy healing with a possible sexual communion is only something I advise for couples in an intimate relationship and not for Tantric practitioners. (I have heard of Tantric practitioners taking sexual advantage of clients in their vulnerability and so encourage discernment when choosing a healer, regardless of their years of experience or credentials.)

Preparation: First cleanse your own auric field before doing energy work on another person. You may wish to burn a smudge stick of bound dried white sage, fanning the sacred smoke tendrils through your energy field. Then put some soothing music on and ask your partner to lie on a mattress or cushions on the floor, and cover them with a cotton blanket. Next, place your hands on your higher heart (located between the heart and the throat) and draw energy up from the Earth Mother below your feet and down from the Sky Father above your head.

Accessing Stored Memories in the Cells: When you're ready, place your hands over the part of their body that you feel guided to channel healing energy into. Close your eyes and attune to that part of their body, asking what it wishes to show or communicate to you. Speak what you receive and use your intuition to move energy blocks using visualized color or toning whatever vowel sound and pitch you're directed to use to clear the old energies. When you feel guided, move to another part of their body and repeat. You may feel your hands get warmer as the energy flows through them and feel guided to fan old energies using your hands and creative visualization to cleanse their field.

Restoring the Sacredness of The Erogenous Zones: If it feels appropriate, you may then ask their consent to touch their erogenous zones, such as their breasts and genitals. As you tenderly massage and stroke each intimate part of their body, verbally offer an apology to those cells for anyone who every touched them in a way that was not with absolute reverence and love.

Encourage your lover to feel into where and how their body was dishonored and breathe into the memory of it and let it go. This may bring up tears. If so, encourage them to release the sadness out of their body, thanking their body for all that it has held. At the end of the session, you might offer to hold them, rock them and hold a safe container for them to release any old emotion. They don't need to know what it was about in order to let it go.

Author's Note: Since there is a connection between the base and the throat chakras, you may sometimes find when there's big sadness wanting to be released, it may surface in your lovemaking initially as really fiery primal sex. Primal grunting and moaning takes us deep into the base chakra, which can clear out a Pandora's Box of old suppressed traumas. So if a partner connects with deep guttural anger during sex, be aware you may need to midwife them through a big emotional release.

You can do this by encouraging them energetically to continue building the energetic intensity with a quickening of rhythm and breath. If they feel you are with them 100%, surrounding them energetically with your fierce love, they will feel safe to really let go. Chances are, if you hold the space for them, they will dissolve into a big outpouring of grief. Deep grief sits underneath anger, which we can use as a form of self-protection. So if your partner begins sobbing uncontrollably during sex, stopping abruptly and withdrawing isn't always the best thing. Stay with them in every sense, if you're inside them, stay inside them but just hold them strongly so they feel a strong container into which they can dissolve.

It may feel appropriate to reassure them through touch, words and shared eye contact and then every so gently use the rhythmic motion of gentle hip motion to continue moving the energy through. For if we stop suddenly and pull apart, demanding verbal answers by asking 'What's wrong?' repeatedly, we rob them of the opportunity to just feel and release due to our need to rationally understand. If big emotion surfaces during lovemaking this is a golden opportunity to help your partner release old pain.

The Sixth Lovemaking Language

Third Eye Chakra: Indigo

Element: Void

Governs: Cosmic Body

Key words: Visionary, stillness, receptivity, ritual, initiation.

Archetypes: Hecate, the Wise Mystic and Hermes, the Sage.

Ideal Setting: Somewhere quiet, candlelit room with an altar or in a cave.

Turn-Ons: Intent, wisdom, sensitivity, visionary herbs and invoking of the elements.

Essential Oils for Anointing: Lavender, chamomile, rosemary and sage.

Sense: Inner Sight and Inner Hearing

Music: Trance inducing music such as theta rhythms, meditation music and music embedded with subconscious healing.

Lovemaking Language: Meditation and shared inner visioning.

Lovemaking Positions: Again there is no specific position, however, sitting in lotus (cross-legged) opposite your partner, while bowing third eye to third eye before lovemaking will promote this connection, especially if you visualize an eye opening in the brow chakra and indigo energy flowing between you. Similarly, watching a video animation of mandalas, crop circles or kaleidoscopic patterns or looking through a kaleidoscope will promote the opening of this center. At the time of yang orgasm, if possible, try to clutch the back of your lover's neck and direct the energies upward with intent and motion. This will help energize the upper chakras.

Yin Orgasm: I speak about this in detail in volume one. Suffice to say, it is the cooling, descending energy which creates a deeply meditative and expansive state of consciousness after the yang orgasm, which is the ecstatic release of built up sexual heat that we recognize as an orgasm in Western culture.

To experience loving communion in this center, practice by doing meditation together on a regular basis. You can also agree to lie with each other in the stillness post-orgasm, with the intention of journeying the inner worlds together. If possible, without breaking your deep state, lay with your foreheads gently touching to enhance shared inner visions during your post coital yang orgasm. Bathing before lovemaking will assist in opening your receptivity to such a deep, shared meditative state.

You may also like to try drinking a visionary herbal tea or smoking the dried herbs of blue lotus (used by the ancient Egyptian royalty) or mugwort (used by druids and priestesses during Sabbats) prior to such a practice.

Those who have taken hallucinogens such as magic mushrooms, DMT or LSD or have done a lot of meditation may find this easier. If you find you can't move after sexual climax without breaking your state, stay where you are and just visualize with your inner sight, indigo light joining you and your partner in this energy center or visualize you both in the starry abyss together in the inner realms and see where the visions take you. Try not to second-guess your vision with you rational mind, discounting what you receive by dismissing it as imagination. As the creative center of the inner child, the sacral must be an open active component or one won't be able to get out of their head (rational mind). Afterwards you may like to share what you experienced and see which of your visions were shared.

Inner Vision Lovemaking Rite: This is great to do in the bath as the water acts as a conduit, while relaxing and putting you in a receptive state. You can accentuate this by putting essential oils, such as lavender, in the bath water and anointing each other's brow chakras before lovemaking. Take it in turns to be the giver and receiver. Next, stroke your partner slowly with a sea sponge or washcloth to coax them into a deeply relaxed state, using your voice and ask them to close their eyes. Alternatively, you may wish to do this after physical lovemaking which circulates a lot of energy. Taking the weight of your partner's head against your body, stroke the energy up the back of the neck and then gently using one finger in an upward motion along the third eye. This will promote light shows of color patterns in their brow center. Be sure to bring them out of this deep subtropic state very gently.

The Seventh Lovemaking Language

Crown Chakra: White

Element: Light

Governs: Galactic Body

Key words: Ecstasy, bliss, devotion, worship, union, cosmic.

Archetypes: Ishtar, the High Priestess and Dionysus, the Zen Buddha.

Ideal Setting:
- On cushions in a sacred circle of rose petals.
- On a daybed with satin sheets and cushions.
- In a four poster bed or bed with a canopy.
- In a honeymoon suite or private holiday resort room.

Turn-Ons: Shared sacred practice, anointing, blessing and dedicating energy raised, breath, sound, color, light, altered states of consciousness, sacred hedonism and mantras.

Essential Oils For Anointing: Spikenard, frankincense, Peru balsam, jasmine and rose.

Sense: Intuition (inner knowing) and channeling.

Music: Ecstatic music that builds specifically up the chakras, such as:

- *'Chakra Transcen-dance'* by Leyola Antara
- *'Good Morning Chakra Workout'* by Tanishka
- *'Chakra Dance'* by Jonathan Goldman
- *'Seven Chakras and Elements'* by Alan Roubik

I would also encourage you to play devotional albums like:

- 'Grace' by Snatam Kaur
- 'Love's Deepest Calling' by Peruquois
- 'Love Light' by Darpan

Lovemaking Language: Devotional Sex Magic.

Lovemaking Positions: When we connect in the crown, every gate is open, which enables all of our archetypal selves to express themselves spontaneously and be embraced by our beloved. This is when the inner twin serpents of light, Ida and Pingala flow effortlessly from one gate to another, depending on where the energy takes you both moment to moment.

Devotional Lovemaking Rite: Set up a beautiful altar for the act of sacred lovemaking. You may wish to create an altar with a symbolic representation of the union of opposites, such as the shiva lingam (phallus) and yoni (vulva). You may also like to use nature to create an act of beauty, such as a flower mandala or circle of rose petals around a cushions or a mattress on the floor, covered in beautiful sheets. I also recommend lighting candles and scenting the air with essential oils.

Next, take a ritual bath with mineral salts, infused with energetic intent (hold them up to your third eye to program them), with vibrational crystal essences and essential oils. Then anoint your crowns with spikenard oil diluted in a base oil to assist the simultaneous spinning of all of your star-gates.

Then offer a blessing honoring the Divinity you see in each other and start worshipping every aspect of them. As outlined in the third eye rite, do not break into social space once you orgasm, simply rest, still holding the energetic space of love and allow the energy to return to the base and build again. As the energy begins to rise, start worshipping each other again and repeat as many times as you feel.

Riding the Serpent to Enter a Multi-Orgasmic State

When you do this three or more times you will enter into an orgasmic state. This can last for up to a few hours afterwards, especially if you prepare by doing yogic practices such as the *'Tree of Life'* meditation, *'Twin Serpent'* meditation or *'Chakra Toning'* tracks which are on my *'Good Morning Chakra Workout'* CD. Activating our internal alchemy assists the flow of the masculine / feminine energies and their union at the seven gates.

This occurs when we allow ourselves to become completely receptive as a vessel for the ecstatic healing energies of all seven aspects of the divine to be expressed through us. By staying with the energy after orgasm, we allow our state of mind to deepen and expand through the yin orgasm, so the next time we raise the energies and experience the yang orgasm, we soar higher than the previous time, followed by another yin orgasm where we descend deeper than we did in the previous cycle. The more we breathe deeply into the energies that are circulating in our body, the more we open to deepening the experience in every cell. Again, moaning and releasing on sound helps to contain and prolong more pleasure in your vessel.

When one enters an orgasmic state, you don't have to 'snap out of it' in order to function. You can still walk, go to the toilet, make lunch etc. except you will continue to feel waves of deep pleasure moving throughout your body, catching your breath as you feel overcome by moments of ecstasy. You will find your senses are super-charged, so you perceive everything as deliriously pleasurable. For example, urinating feels orgasmic, showering or swimming feels so incredible, both inside and out as you experience the sensation of water on your skin, so you can't contain your moans and sighs of absolute exultation. When we are in this state, we charge everything we touch, like King Midas with the frequency of divine union. It is wonderful to cook in this state and share the food with friends and family or swim in a body of natural water, using your intent to charge the water molecules, so everyone who enters thereafter receives the healing gift of this activation.

If you want to stop the waves of orgasmic energy circling within you at any given time simply put your third eye on the ground and send any excess raised energy down into the earth. Kundalini is a natural electrical current within the body, so as with electricity, you can earth the energy to stop it moving in a chaotic way. This can be handy if you need to go out in public and don't wish to draw attention by moaning loudly.

This state is what the drug ecstasy mimics, and to a lesser degree marijuana. Whereas sacred sexuality offers a natural high with no negative side effects.

⚕ Sampling the Dark Fruits of Your Lover at the Seven Gates

Connecting Soul to Soul in the Shadowlands of Autumn / Winter

In our modern culture, psychologically trained relationship counsellors provide couples with coping strategies, support, compassion and guidance but don't complement their rational (yang) approach with esoteric (yin) practices, leaving couples feeling like they need to 'work' on their relationship rather than 'grow' as lovers.

As a Tantrika, I was led intuitively to devise a hieros gamos journey to support couples to see the light and dark in themselves and each other at each of the seven gates. As I complete the final draft of this book, I am about to teach my first global class of students in this ancient practice via an online course. My intuitive knowing was that the annual ceremony celebrated in the ancient world as the 'Great Rite' was merely the public celebration to mark the completion of this series of very private initiations.

Entering the Shadowlands

As stated earlier, each year, during the darker months of autumn and winter, due to the diminishing solar light, we experience our darker thoughts and emotions, making it the most challenging time for partnerships, as our wounds get triggered more easily and often.

Spring was therefore a time to celebrate that the holy couple had survived each other's dark side, and would again renew their commitment to willingly descend to face the shadow in themselves and their beloved. This commitment to journey the circle of life as a union of opposites, ensured life would continue to grow and prosper.

Owning the Shadow

To assist couples to own their shadow, without projecting it on to their partner, I created a deck of 'Light and Shadow Oracle Cards'. I would then ask them to sit in 'Yab Yum' (pictured left), a Tantric pose and lead them through a meditation to connect them energetically at all seven gates. They would then anoint each other to honor the God and Goddess within, then they would each pull a shadow and a light card.

They pulled the cards without looking at the fronts of the cards, as this ensured it was their subconscious, rather than their conscious mind which pulled the cards. They would then share with their partner, how they had seen that trait in themselves, and how that had impacted on their partner and loved ones.

Unveiling the Light

Bringing the light of awareness into one's disowned traits on a regular basis ensures transparency within a relationship, which is what maintains emotional and psychological intimacy and mutual honor and respect. This practice makes it possible for the sacred sexual coupling of the God and Goddess to occur each full moon. This is when the light of the moon reflects the most amount of light in the sun, promoting a powerful alchemy of opposites, both within and without. So, in addition to the shadow practice I was guided to give couples a sacred union ceremony to unveil the God and Goddess at each of the seven gates, which took place over seven full moons. This, I was told was the preparation undertaken before the Sacred Wedding ceremony took place. To restore the resonance of sacred union to the planet, I hope to initiate as many couples as possible to undertake this series of initiations to unveil the God and Goddess within. It is my pleasure to share that practice with you here. (To be facilitated through the full hieros gamos journey visit the resources page to find out about my online course.)

The Seven Gifts: Sacred Union Communion with Your Beloved

In the Tantric tradition, when couples meet to express their love, they customarily present each other with a gift. These gifts are not big, flashy expensive presents, but are rather gifts of one's divine inner self. So what follows is an outline of the seven gifts you can exchange with your beloved during the darker months at each full moon. It is an inspired structure to help you to share each of your divine aspects at each of the seven gates.

Unlike, the conscious courtship, this journey starts at the base, with Pan and Lilith who initiate us into deeper intimacy through owning our shadow. You will notice in preparation for each couple's conscious communion at full moon, there is a preparatory communion with oneself at new moon. It is structured this way, because we can't share deeper levels of ourselves with our partners, if we haven't first journeyed to explore deeper levels of intimacy with ourselves self at each gate. The new moon is therefore a time of seclusion and self-discovery which creates a yearning to come together and share discoveries at full moon.

The Gift of Passionate Truth: Base Chakra

The Challenge: To allow the other person to see your ego, completely naked by telling them what you see as your flaws and then allow them to see you physically naked and explore your primal instincts together.

Archetypes: Pan, the Wild Man and Lilith, the Wild Woman.

Best Time to Start: Autumn Equinox. The Black Wedding.

Key Words: Primordial, Animal Self, Blood, Sex, Power, Physical, Passion and Transformation.

New Moon Rite: Sacred Union Within

1. **Guided Meditation**: Listen to the guided meditation on my 'Sacred Union' meditation double CD to meet your inner Pan and Lilith, the God and Goddess who govern the base chakra. (See the resources page).

2. **Art Therapy**: Draw the aspects you saw or felt and write down any information you received so you can share this with your beloved at full moon.

3. **Journaling**: Take your awareness within and ask your wild self what it wishes to share at full moon with your beloved. This might be an aspect of your shadow or a poem or a picture, depicting your wild self to gift to their wild self. To access your wild self, go into nature and sit with your back against a tree and write in a journal at the top of the page: *'What Does My Wild Self Wish To Share With My Beloved?'* Then just start writing whatever comes without editing. For more ideas read the full moon rite. I also recommend reading about Pan and Lilith in volume one to get better acquainted with these aspects.

Creating Sacred Space: Create an altar for your inner wild man and wild woman and the base chakra which they govern. You may wish to decorate it with natural objects, a red altar cloth and red candles and a statuette of a symbolic yoni and lingam to honor the joining of opposites, (even if you are a same sex couple, these polarities are still ever present). You may also wish to up a crystal grid of the six-pointed star with base chakra stones like bloodstone, vajra lingums, garnet or serpentine in the center. For more info on setting up crystal grids read volume one.

Full Moon Rite: Sacred Union with Your Beloved

Full Moon Ceremony Prep: Find a cave or power place in nature to camp and spend the night. Consider taking fishing gear so you can cook what you catch for dinner (if you're not vegan). Alternatively, forage for 'bush tucker' or if you're a carnivore, take a BBQ chicken so you can gnaw bones together and plenty of water to drink. Might I recommend a decent mattress, such as thick foam, rather than an airbed and plenty of faux furs to drape. Don't forget implements to light a safe fire, such as a spade to dig a fire pit. You may wish to not shower that day so that your natural oils and pheromones are intensified. (So, perhaps clean your teeth!)

You may wish to make love by a fire, under the stars or in a dry cave. If it's still daylight when you arrive at your destination, consider a game of 'catch and kiss' giving your lover a head start to run and hide so you can both enjoy the adrenaline pumping high of 'the thrill of the chase'.

If going bush just isn't possible, decorate your boudoir by draping animal prints and faux fur blankets, cushions and light red candles or if you have a backyard (with a large hedge), turn a mattress into a daybed and light fire torches.

Full Moon Ceremony

Cleanse: Use incense smoke to cleanse each other's energy fields. Sandalwood is good for the base chakra, as it dispels fear. If you're out in the bush you may wish to burn and use the sacred smoke of eucalyptus leaves or dried sage.

Anoint: Anoint each other's feet with a base chakra oil such as sandalwood and honor your beloved's wild self with a blessing, such as '*I honor your inner wild man / wild woman*'.

Exchange of Gifts: Share the gift you created or found at new moon to express your wild self to your beloved. Such as erotic photos of yourself or erotic poetry you have written or found.

Soul to Soul Communion: Sit cross-legged (or on chairs if that's too uncomfortable), so your foreheads are touching and your hands are in a shared prayer position (alternating hands). Visualize the red lotuses of light in your genitals opening and red light emanating so the energy intermingles between you. Then gently pull apart and bless the meal you have prepared. Start by eating with your hands and discussing what your parents found unacceptable about your wild child self. Then share your primal sexual desires with each other.

By firelight silently undress yourselves making eye contact while you do so. Next, start to awaken your own sex organs by caressing and stroking them to stimulate your desire, take your time with this. There is no rush. If we can't relax into our own bodies sensations we can't fully respond to the touch of our lover.

Take turns to relish the pleasure of each other's sex organs orally. Smell them, feel them, taste them, listen to the sounds they make as their energy is stirred and awakened. You may wish to tell them what you love about their cock / pussy (deliberately base terms are good to use when connecting at the base). Tell them your desires; what you'd like to do to them and be done to you, while you touch your lover. As you explore each other's bodies, in your mind's eye, see yourselves as the primal God and Goddess - losing yourselves in the sensations and worship of each other's body. Become drunk on the smells and tastes of your lover's flesh. Allow the heat to rise and give way to your animal lust, with no judgment: lick, suck, fuck, talk dirty, power play, groan, grunt, dribble, come, sweat, moan.

Other Activities to Express and Unify Your Inner Pan and Lilith This Month

- Give self, each other and the sex act, playful porn names that reflect your wild urges.

- Give your own and each other's genitals, porn names that reflect your lusty desires.

- Take each other sexually, by surprise, at least once each this month: (i.e. oral consumption, self-pleasuring, exposing yourself to them or taking them by force to satisfy your lust).

- Dress in a way that expresses your wild self whenever you can.

- Visit a power place to connect with the wild.

The Gift of Sensual Beauty: Sacral Chakra

The Challenge: To take responsibility for one's inner child and emotional needs. To express spontaneous joy and creativity and to take delight in both inner and outer beauty with the innocence of a child.

Archetypes: Ares, the Warrior and Aphrodite, the Beautiful Muse.

Key Words: Sensuality, Creativity, Warrior, Beauty, Play, Inner Child and Elemental Self.

New Moon Rite: Sacred Union Within

1. **Guided Meditation**: Listen to the guided meditation on my '*Sacred Union*' meditation double CD to meet your inner Aphrodite and Ares, the God and Goddess who govern the sacral chakra. (See the resources page).

2. **Art Therapy**: Draw the aspects you saw or felt and write down any information you received so you can share this with your beloved at full moon.

3. **Journaling**: Go within and ask your inner warrior, Ares and Beautiful Muse, Aphrodite what they wish to share at full moon with your beloved. To access what your soul feels to share, I recommend having a ritual bath with bergamot essential oil and orange candles. You may wish to do your guided meditation in the bath. Then journal by writing at the top of the page, '*What Does My Inner Aphrodite / Ares Wish to Share With My Beloved?*' You may wish to create an act of beauty which expresses your love or you may feel inspired to awaken your partner's

senses with a gentle oil massage or natural beauty treatment. Alternatively, you could express the beauty you see in both yourself and them with a love letter. Your warrior may dance for them, showing his strength. For more inspiration read the full moon rite. I also recommend reading the sections on Ares and Aphrodite in volume one.

Creating A Monthly Altar: Create an orange altar with an orange cloth on a small table, decorated with orange candles and a statue of the God / Goddess at this gate or pictures of Aphrodite, the muse and Ares, the warrior. You may wish to also display natural objects from the ocean to honor the element of water, such as sea shells.

Full Moon Rite: Sacred Union with Your Beloved

Full Moon Ceremony Prep: Set up your crystal grid of the six-pointed star with carnelian and rose quartz in the center. (For detailed instructions see volume one). You may also wish to create a circle of rose petals or shells on the floor containing an altar of God / Goddess and two facing cushions. You may like to set this up on a deserted beach or share a bath beforehand scented with bergamot oil and lit with candles.

Full Moon Ceremony

Cleansing: Cleanse each other's auric field with salt water. Simply dip your fingers in a dish of water with sea salt added and then flick it around their body.

Anoint: Anoint each other's belly with bergamot essential oil diluted in jojoba oil and speak a blessing to honor your beloved at the second gate. Such as, '*I honor your beauty / I honor your strength*'.

Soul to Soul Communion: Sit facing each other either cross-legged or on a chair, with your hands in a shared prayer position and your foreheads touching to commune soul to soul. Whilst in that position, visualize or sense orange lotuses of light opening in your bellies and orange light emanating so it merges with each other.

Exchange of Gifts: You each share what your inner self has directed you to share during your new moon practice. For the sacral this might incorporate something to express your creativity such as a painting, floral arrangement or something silly, since this is the gate of joy and play! Alternatively you may wish to gift your lover a home-made pampering treatment to awaken their senses. Such as a foot massage, face masque, body masque, body scrub or bathe them in a flower bath or place flowers in their pubic hair (inspired by the novel, *'Lady Chatterley's Lover'*).

Feasting: Share sensual food such as seafood, or finger foods followed by decadent desserts. You may wish to have a floor picnic on a mat in your lounge room or dine al fresco in the garden under fairy lights to salsa music.

Other Activities to Express and Unify Your Inner Ares and Aphrodite This Month

- Take black and white photographs to capture the beauty you see in each other. You may like to make a montage and set it to music on your laptop and play it for your beloved.

- Buy some charcoal and cartridge paper and draw each other draped in only a scarf, surrounded by beautiful still life arrangements of flowers and fruit while sensual music plays in the background.

- Take a walk in a beautiful garden together or visit an art gallery.

- Paint your toes or each other's, rub oil into each other's skin, wear flowers in your hair or have a picnic.

- Listen to opera or sexy Latin music and cook together naked, save for an apron!

The Gift of Service: Solar Plexus Chakra

The Challenge: To discover, hone and share your inner gifts in service to the greater good.

Archetypes: Athena, the Golden Heroine and Apollo, the Noble Statesman.

Key Words: Self-Worth, Mission / Projects, Inner Gifts, Insight, Strategy and Music.

1. **Guided Meditation**: Listen to the guided meditation on my '*Sacred Union*' meditation double CD to meet your inner Athena and Apollo, the God and Goddess who govern the solar plexus chakra. (See the resources page).

2. **Art Therapy**: Draw the aspects you saw or felt and write down any information you received so you can share this with your beloved at full moon.

3. **Journaling**: Go within and ask your inner heroine, Athena and your inner statesman, Apollo what they wish to share at full moon with your beloved. You may wish to listen to some classical music to hone the mind and then write at the top of a journal page, '*What Does My Inner Athena and Apollo Wish To Share With My Beloved?*' This might be your plan, mission, goals, ambitions and purpose. It may be a book, project, speech or author who has inspired you to serve the greater good. It may be a sharing of your talents and skills or something you have achieved. For more ideas read the full moon rite. I also recommend reading the sections on Athena and Apollo in volume one.

Creating a Monthly Altar: Create an altar for your inner statesman and heroine and the solar plexus chakra which they govern. You may wish to decorate it with golden objects, pictures or statues and sit them atop a table covered with a yellow cloth and yellow candles, perhaps with a black and white yin / yang symbol.

Full Moon Rite: Sacred Union with Your Beloved

Full Moon Ceremony Prep: Set up a crystal grid of the six pointed star. (For detailed instructions see volume one). In the center of the grid place the healing stones: citrine, gold fluorite, clear quartz and/or tiger eye. Create a sacred circle of white and yellow flowers or bay laurel leaves or olive branches on the floor containing an altar of the God / Goddess and two facing cushions.

Full Moon Ceremony

Cleanse: Spray each other's auric field with grapefruit or lime essential oil added to a water spray bottle before you enter the circle.

Soul Communion: Sit facing each other in lotus (either cross-legged or on a chair), with your hands inter-spliced in a shared prayer position and your foreheads touching with eyes closed. Visualize the yellow lotus of light opening in your solar plexus (between your belly and heart) and feel yellow light emanating and intermingling with your beloved as you enter into a shared meditation.

Anointing: Bless each other by saying, '*I honor your divine intelligence*' as you anoint each other's solar plexus with grapefruit or lime essential oil diluted in a base oil.

Exchange of Gifts: You may use your inner light to craft something that expresses what you hold in highest esteem about your lover. Alternatively, whatever you felt moved to share during your new moon communion with self.

Feasting: You may then like to share an elegant dinner for two, while listening to uplifting classical music.

Other Activities to Express and Unify Your Inner Athena and Apollo This Month

- You may like to take it in turns giving each other cryptic puzzles to solve.

- Play strategy games like chess, backgammon or Chinese checkers.

- Lie in bed reading the newspaper and sharing articles of interest.

- Discuss your favorite authors, writers and philosophers while sharing a bottle of wine, with a cheese platter listening to smooth jazz such as Coltrane.

The Gift of Love: Heart Chakra

The Challenge: To touch each other with the milk of human kindness and nurture each other to grow with patience and love.

Archetypes: Green Man, the Earth Emperor / Demeter, the Earth Empress.

Key Words: Growth, Nurturance, Nature, Centering, Home, Patience and Acceptance.

New Moon Rite: Sacred Union Within

1. **Guided Meditation**: Listen to the guided meditation on my '*Sacred Union*' meditation double CD to meet your inner Demeter and Green Man, the God and Goddess who govern the heart chakra. (See the resources page).

2. **Art Therapy**: Draw the aspects you saw or felt and write down any information you received so you can share this with your beloved at full moon.

3. **Journaling**: Go within and ask your inner mother, Demeter and your inner father, the Green Man what they wish to share at full moon with your beloved. This may be a seedling you've potted for them, a jumper you've knitted for them or a batch of scones. I recommend starting by writing a gratitude diary, listing all the things you're grateful for that your partner has brought into your life. To access what your soul feels to share: meditate, journal or have a ritual bath with rose essential oil. I also recommend reading the sections on Demeter and the Green Man in volume one.

Creating a Monthly Altar: Create a green and pink altar for your inner Earth Empress and Emperor and the heart chakra which they govern. You may wish to decorate it with growing things, photos of your children, sacred symbols and drape with a green altar cloth and dress with green candles.

Full Moon Rite: Sacred Union with Your Beloved

Full Moon Ceremony Prep: Set up your crystal grid of the six-pointed star. In the center place rose quartz and aventurine crystals to promote a balance of giving and receiving love. (For detailed instructions see volume one). Create a circle of rose petals on the floor containing two facing cushions.

Full Moon Ceremony

Cleanse: Spray each other's auric field with a rose essential oil added to a water spray bottle.

Soul Communion: Sit facing each other in lotus (cross-legged) or on a chair. Arrange your hands in a shared prayer position, with your foreheads touching and eyes closed. Visualize the green lotus of light opening in your heart and feel green light emanating and intermingling with your beloved as you enter into a shared meditation.

Anointing: Take turns blessing each other by saying, '*I honor your loving heart*' or, '*I honor the Green Man within you*' and '*I honor the Earth Empress within you*' and anointing each other's heart with rose essential oil diluted in jojoba oil.

Exchange of Gifts: Share that which you've prepared, such as your gratitude diary. You may wish to emphasize how your partner has helped you to grow and how they've embodied the positive aspects of particular archetypes which has assisted you. You may then share a physical gift you have made to show your appreciation of them.

Feasting: Share a home-cooked meal, made with love. Such as a slow-cooked dish and traditional dessert like apple pie and custard to ground your energies and commune.

Other Activities to Express and Unify Your Inner Green Man and Demeter This Month

- You may like to plan and start building a 'love garden' bed or veggie patch.

- Take turns cooking breakfast or even a cup of tea in bed for each other.

- Give each other a foot rub or foot bath as a pleasant surprise at the end of a day.

- Rub each other on the back of the heart often to soften and open the heart.

The Gift of Tenderness: Throat Chakra

The Challenge: Can we both speak and honor each other's truth and intention clearly, exposing our vulnerability, wounds and healing abilities?

Archetypes: Artemis, the Medicine Woman / Chiron, the Healer.

Key Words: Healing, Shaman, Animal Medicine, Vulnerability, Boundaries and Truth.

New Moon Rite: Sacred Union Within

1. **Guided Meditation**: Listen to the guided meditation on my 'Sacred Union' meditation double CD to meet your inner Artemis and Chiron, the God and Goddess who govern the throat chakra. (See the resources page).

2. **Art Therapy**: Draw the aspects you saw or felt and write down any information you received so you can share this with your beloved at full moon.

3. **Journaling**: Go within and ask your inner medicine woman, Artemis and your inner healer, Chiron what they wish to share at full moon with your beloved. This may be an energy healing or a sound healing with a drum, rattle, Tibetan bowl, crystal bowl or toning, using your voice. To access what your soul feels to share: meditate or have a ritual bath with lemongrass or pine essential oil. Then journal by writing at the top of the page, '*What Does My Inner Medicine Woman / Healer Wish To Share With My Beloved?*' For more ideas read the full moon rite. I also recommend reading the sections on Artemis and Chiron in volume one.

Creating A Monthly Altar: Create an altar for your inner medicine woman and healer and the throat chakra which they govern. You may wish to decorate it with healing symbols, feathers, pictures of animal totems. Drape with a blue altar cloth and dress with blue candles and a statuette of a symbolic yoni and lingum to honor the joining of opposites at this gate.

Full Moon Rite: Sacred Union with Your Beloved

Full Moon Ceremony Prep: Set up a crystal grid of the six pointed star. In the center place blue crystals such as blue lace agate, lapis lazuli, blue fluorite, chrysocolla and/or turquoise. (For detailed instructions see volume one.) Create a circle of feathers or river stones on the floor containing two facing cushions.

Full Moon Ceremony

Cleanse: Smudge each other's energy fields by burning a sage smudge stick and fanning the sacred smoke through each other's auric fields with your hand or a feather. (Smudge sticks can be bought from health food and holistic stores or you can buy dry sage from a deli or dry your own and bind it together with cotton.)

Soul to Soul Communion: Sit facing each other in lotus (cross-legged or on a chair) Place your hands in a shared prayer position, with your foreheads touching and eyes closed. Visualize a blue lotus of light opening within the throat and blue light emanating out of this energy center and intermingling with your beloved's as you enter into a shared meditation.

Anointing: Bless each other by saying, 'I honor the Healer within you' and anointing each other on the throat with pine or lemongrass essential oil, diluted in jojoba oil.

Exchange of Gifts: You may sing or play each other a song or piece of music that expresses your tenderness or vulnerability. You may like to take it in turns, drumming each other's body, or chant, sing or tone as you feel intuitively inspired to, over your partner as they sit or lie with their eyes closed. You may wish to put on a CD of healing music and place healing stones, or your hands on whichever parts of their body you are guided to, asking that their guides work through you as a clear channel for dissolving past hurts with healing energy. Alternatively, you may wish to play a guided meditation, to assist them to release old hurts, offering forgiveness or an inner journey to meet a medicine totem animal. You may also wish to pull a card from a medicine animal deck and read aloud your lesson.

Feasting: Share cleansing foods such as whole foods, macrobiotic foods, sushi or something clean on the palette like Vietnamese food. You may like to make a fresh juice to drink or refreshing mock tail.

Other Activities to Express and Unify Your Inner Artemis and Chiron This Month

- You may like to spend a night in a teepee or at a health spa or mineral springs complex.

- Consider going on a bush walk or hike with each other in the mountains.

- Spend some quality time with animals.

- Be sensitive to each other as wounds may arise this month, so get a private healing if you feel the need.

The Gift of Wisdom: Third Eye Chakra

The Challenge: Can I transmute past pain into wisdom and do I understand and value my insights and perceptions and those of my partner's?

Archetypes: Hecate / Hermes.

Key Words: Magic, Inner Realms, Plant Medicine, Wisdom, Aging and Death.

New Moon Rite: Sacred Union Within

1. **Guided Meditation**: Listen to the guided meditation on my 'Sacred Union' meditation double CD to meet your

inner Hecate and Hermes, the God and Goddess who govern the third eye chakra. (See the resources page).

2. **Art Therapy**: Draw the aspects you saw or felt and write down any information you received so you can share this with your beloved at full moon.

3. **Journaling**: Reflect upon / journal the major insights you've learnt on your journey to share with your beloved at full moon. These are your toughest, most humbling life lessons to date - your journeys to the Underworld. Go within and ask your inner wise woman and wise sage what they wish to share at full moon with your beloved. To access what your soul feels to share: meditate, journal or have a ritual bath with lavender essential oil. Read the full moon rite for more ideas. I also recommend reading the sections on Hecate and Hermes in volume one.

Creating A Monthly Altar: Create an altar for your inner wise woman and wise sage and the third eye chakra which they govern. You may wish to decorate it with healing symbols, bones and pictures of spirit guides and angels. Drape with an indigo altar cloth and dress with indigo candles and images of hermetic symbols of alchemy or statues of a male sage and a female mystic.

Full Moon Rite: Sacred Union with Your Beloved

Full Moon Ceremony Prep: Set up a crystal grid of the six pointed star. For the third eye you may wish to add amethyst, moonstone, merlinite and/or snow quartz within the center or in front of the clear quartz terminators. (For detailed instructions see volume one.) You may also wish to create a circle of purple fabric / scarves, silver stars or strands of pearls, denoting wisdom. Inside place two cushions so you can sit facing each other.

Full Moon Ceremony

Cleansing: Cleanse each other's auric field with lavender essential oil added to a water spray bottle before you enter the circle.

Soul to Soul Communion: Then sit facing each other, either crossed-legged or on chairs with your hands in a shared prayer position and your foreheads touching and eyes closed. Without speaking, commune soul to soul, sensing this vortex opening and indigo light connecting between both of your brow chakras.

Anointing: Take it in turns to bless your beloved by saying, '*I honor the Sage / Wise Woman within you*' and anoint their third eye with lavender essential oil, diluted in jojoba oil.

Exchange of Gifts: Share what you have brought to the circle from your communion with self at new moon. For third eye this would incorporate sharing the greatest lesson you've learnt from life and from them, in partnership.

Feasting: Share food such as soup you've brewed using fresh herbs and a beverage that you've concocted yourself such as chai tea or mulled wine.

Other Activities to Express and Unify Your Inner Hecate and Hermes This Month

- Write down all that no longer serves you and read aloud to each other and then burn and release.

- To manifest an intention using sex magic you may then like to set a joint intention which you may wish to charge by raising kundalini energy sexually and visualizing your intention when you both climax. Always state the intention aloud first and affirm 'in accordance with highest will'.

- Go to a psychic development class together.

- Light a candle and put on some transcendental music and meditate together.

- Each pull an oracle card and take turns reading your own card and then each other's card by intuiting how it relates to them in their journey.

- Create a compost or worm farm together that honors how we need death and decay to sustain new life.

- Talk about the legacy of those you know who have crossed over, what you have personally learnt from observing how they lived their life.

The Gift of Spirit: Crown Chakra

The Challenge: To experience ecstasy with your beloved by honoring yourselves, your relationship and your time as sacred space.

Archetypes: Ishtar, the High Priestess / Dionysius, the God of Abundance.

Key Words: Spirit, Energy, Soul Union, Crystal Medicine, Devotion and Honoring.

New Moon Rite: Sacred Union Within

1. **Guided Meditation**: Listen to the guided meditation on my 'Sacred Union' meditation double CD to meet your inner Ishtar and Dionysus, the God and Goddess who govern the crown chakra. (See the resources page).

2. **Art Therapy**: Draw the aspects you saw or felt and write down any information you received so you can share this with your beloved at full moon.

3. **Journaling**: Go within and ask your inner High Priestess and Zen Buddha what they wish to share at full moon with your beloved. To access what your soul feels to share

have a ritual bath with Peru balsam essential oil and crystal vibrational essences then do Chakra Toning. (You can simply tone up the notes of a scale, toning the Sanskrit chakra mantras in the next chapter or you can chant along with them on my '*Chakra Workout CD*'. See the resources page). Then to access these aspects, write in a journal, '*What Does My Inner Tantrika and Buddha Wish To Share With My Beloved?*' Read the full moon rite for further inspiration. I also recommend reading the sections on Ishtar and Dionysius in volume one.

Creating a Monthly Altar: Create an altar for your inner Tantrika and Buddha for the crown chakra which they govern. You may wish to decorate it with sacred union symbols and crystals. Drape with a white or rainbow colored cloth and dress with white or rainbow colored candles. You may also wish to create an altar with a statue of God / Goddess or even a mortar and pestle representing the Wand of Light (phallus) in the Grail Cup (womb).

Full Moon Rite: Sacred Union with Your Beloved

Full Moon Ceremony Prep: Set up a crystal grid of the six pointed star. Within the center place selenite, herkimer diamond, opal, sardonyx and/or serpentine. (For detailed instructions see volume one.) Within a circle of rose petals on the floor, place two facing cushions.

Cleansing: Cleanse each other's auric field with frankincense crystals burnt on a charcoal tablet to create sacred smoke. (These can be bought at markets, new age stores and Asian grocers.)

Soul to Soul Communion: Sit facing each other, (cross-legged or on a chair) with your hands in a shared heart salutation, prayer position with your foreheads touching and eyes closed. Commune soul to soul, sensing the thousand petalled lotus of white light in the crown at the top of your heads opening, feeling yourselves connecting higher self to higher self. Now sense all your lotuses of light opening at each of the seven gates so that the seven color rays are emitted, connecting you at every gate. I recommend doing the '*Twin Serpent Activation*' guided meditation. (See the Resources page.)

Joint Practice: Sit facing each other, without words looking into each other's eyes with your right hand facing down and left hand facing up so your hands are touching each other and resting on your knees, sending love out through the right on the out breath and receiving love in through the left on the in breath, creating an energetic current linking our energy fields.

Anointing: Bless each other in turn with words such as, '*I honor the God/Goddess within you*' as you anoint each other's crown with spikenard essential oil, diluted in jojoba oil.

Exchange of Gifts: Take turns sharing what your inner self has directed you to share with your beloved. For example, you may now unveil your body and soul by dancing for your beloved, by doing the 'Dance of the Seven Veils' revealing your personal expression of each of the seven inner Gods or Goddesses as you dance to a playlist of seven pieces of music, removing a different colored veil as the music changes until you are naked, save for seven pieces of jewelry that honor the seven gates you have opened. Alternatively, you may write a poem to your Priest King or Priestess Queen, make a crown or robe for them or have prepared a bed with a canopy in nature and hedonistic delights to take them up the stairway to Heaven!

Feasting: You may then wish to share exotic, aphrodisiac foods and drink a love punch to ground your energy.

Other Activities to Express and Unify Your Inner Ishtar / Dionysius This Month

- Go to a devotional chanting evening or dance meditation to experience an ecstatic communion with Spirit.

- Start each morning rising with the dawn, doing yoga and then toning the Sanskrit mantra for each of the chakras, followed by the affirmation.

- Gift each other Tantric healing. (see following chapters.)

- Write vows to say to your beloved and express them in a place of natural beauty in a sacred space you have prepared.

- Create a piece of art that expresses what you have learn on your hieros gamos journey, this is known as an 'Act of Beauty' and helps you to anchor these gifts.

Sensual and Sacred Rituals for Lovers

How to Keep the Spark Alive!

In our modern lives, it isn't hard for us to become so distracted from the essence of life that we feel literally run down and burnt out. This happens when we don't make time to reconnect with the natural elements: earth, water, air, fire and Spirit which recharge us. When we feel low on energy, we certainly don't feel creatively inspired to express our love for our partner in new and interesting ways, which reignite the spark of interest and delight in each other.

So without needing to fly to Club Med and pay someone to create romance for you in the form of expensive a la carte dining, spa treatments and natural wonders...here are some DIY ways to reconnect with the elements to give your relationship battery a jump-start!

Sacred Elemental Ceremonies for Lovers

FIRE

If the passion has fizzled in your union, try the following simple fire ritual to reconnect with this element together.

1. Build a fire together. This may be in a fire pit, brazier, chimera or fireplace. Alternatively go to the beach and create a huge pile of sand and use your hand to dig out

little caves all around the sides of the sand pile and place a tea light candle in each hole.

2. Sit in silent meditation, staring into the flames and watching the pure element of Spirit dance and change form. If the weather is cold you may want to share a warming liqueur.

3. Close your eyes and visualize a ball of fire getting hotter and larger in your base chakra, awakening your energy as you see this flame engulfing your whole body.

4. Stand up and face each other with your legs hip-width apart and knees slightly bent. Gaze into each other's eyes and see the fire of passion burning in their eyes. Breathe in unison, drawing your fire breath up from the center of the Earth and up your spine.

5. Allow the breath to become faster until you finally release the energy you've built up through a shriek, laughter or roar!

6. Sit opposite each other cross-legged and place your hand on your partner's base chakra, sense it glowing with red vitality. Maintain eye contact, acknowledging with a warm smile, each other's inner fire.

WATER

To connect emotionally, softening and sharing your your deep feelings for each other, try this simple love rite to commune with the element of water.

1. Boil up on the stove fresh sprigs of rosemary in some water and allow to cool.

2. Fill a bath with warm water, lavender essential oil and decorate with freshly picked flower heads.

3. Put on your favorite cinema soundtrack with highly emotive music. I recommend 'Gladiator' with the title track by Lisa Gerrard.

4. Take turns washing each other's hair, using a large jug filled with the rosemary water for the final rinse.

5. Use warm towels to rub each other down.

6. Relax with a really delicious drink such as hot chocolate topped with cream and dusted with cinnamon in winter or cranberry, fresh lime, soda and a sprig of fresh mint in summer.

EARTH

This love rite is designed to get you back into your bodies, enjoying the pleasure of the senses. It is in two parts, one for each of you to gift to the other as a surprise so choose who will read number one or two or draw straws to decide!

1. Partner One: Apply a mud masque over your beloved's entire body and tell them what you love about their body as you apply it. Let it dry and then use a warm soft wash cloth to lovingly wash it off while they are lying down listening to sensual, rhythmic, Earthy music.

2. Partner Two: Prepare a platter of aphrodisiacs. Next blindfold your lover so they have to guess each aphrodisiac using their Earthly senses. I recommend freshly cut mango, strawberries, honey and dark chocolate to tempt their taste buds. Arouse their olfactory sense with spices, essential oils, sprigs of herbs and fresh flowers. For sound, wave a rain stick, chimes and leaves that rustle next to their ears and for touch, caress them with velvet, satin and fur to stimulate their skin all over.

AIR

This elemental love rite is designed to lift their Spirits using inspirations words and sounds. Great if you've been feeling a bit grey. Again, this love rite is divided into two sections, one for each of you to gift to each other so only read one option.

1. Play Native American or sacred Indian flute music. Blindfold your partner and then play then gently blow on their skin and glide a feather boa all over them, wafting incense and smudging their etheric field with a feather.

2. Blindfold your partner and read the poetry of Rumi, Haffiz or passages from 'Song of Songs' from the Bible or read an erotic piece of prose such as an excerpt from a D.H. Lawrence novel.

Chakra Love Rites for Couples

Sacred Chants

Sit facing each other in a sacred circle, on cushions or on an ornamental rug surrounded by a ring of freshly cut aromatic roses and lit tea light candles. Maintain eye contact and start at the base chakra as you tone the following to align and raise the vibration by opening each of your star gates in succession.

Sanskrit Toning and Mantras

Base Chakra:	Lam (pronounced LAH-M)
Sacral Chakra:	Vam (pronounced VAH-M)
Solar Plexus Chakra:	Ram (pronounced RAH-M)
Heart Chakra:	Yam (pronounced YAH-M)
Throat Chakra:	Ham (pronounced HAH-M)
Brow Chakra:	Om (pronounced OH-M)
Crown Chakra:	Aum (pronounced AH-OH-M)

Chakra Stimulation Massage

You can do this with your beloved or on your own. I recommend using, 'Chakra Healing Chants' by Sophia on the Sequoia music label and using a rich, natural oil such as almond or jojoba. Chant along with the sacred chants and lovingly caress the part of the body that relates to each chakra (see below). Ease energetic blocks gently with the awareness that love can move mountains. I recommend either doing a full body massage or choosing either a foot or hand massage, rather than trying to cover all three. (Unless you have evolved to the point of having more than two arms!)

Preparation

N.B. The stroke must turn in the direction that each chakra spins. The feminine meridian, Ida, in the base chakra spins anti-clockwise and then the sacral (one above) alternates and so forth all the way up the spine. The masculine meridian, Pingala, in the base chakra spins clockwise and then the sacral (one above) alternates and so forth all the way up the spine. We have both meridians within us but start with the meridian that corresponds to the foundation physical gender.

Setting Sacred Space

Always take the time to make sure the room temperature is comfortable and you and your beloved are comfortable. Candles, flowers and music always create a soothing ambiance in which to give and receive. Check to see if they have any boundaries they would like to set first, (i.e. so you don't unwittingly digitally rape them by heading straight into their anus with an intention to heal, regardless of their consent.) Similarly, make sure you check the pressure of your strokes are pleasant and relaxing for them to receive. It is also a good idea to have water and tissues at hand and take the phone off the hook.

Cleansing Your Energy Field

Before you place your hands on yourself or your beloved, take a moment to cleanse yourself energetically by visualizing a violet flame spiraling up through your energy field and transmuting all negative energies into white light above your head, which showers down upon you in rainbow sparks of holographic crystalline light.

Chakra Oils and Crystal Grid

You may also like to set up a sacred union crystal grid (see volume one) in the space and anoint each chakra with the Sanskrit symbol before massaging.

Full Body Chakra Massage

Base Chakra:	anus, vulva, perineum, buttocks and legs
Sacral Chakra:	lower back, hips and pelvic area
Solar Plexus Chakra:	abdomen and middle of back (thoracic)
Heart Chakra:	back of the heart, breasts and chest
Throat Chakra:	neck, jaw and shoulders
Brow Chakra:	face: especially the temples and sinus
Crown Chakra:	scalp

Chakra Foot Massage

Base Chakra:	base of the heel
Sacral Chakra:	between the middle and base of the foot
Solar Plexus Chakra:	middle of the foot
Heart Chakra:	just above the middle of the foot
Throat Chakra:	at the metatarsal joint (just under the big toe)
Brow Chakra:	the bottom half of the big toe
Crown Chakra:	the top half of the big toe

Chakra Hand Massage

Base Chakra: an inch below the wrist (where you might wear a watch)
Sacral Chakra: wrist
Solar Plexus Chakra: across the base of the palm
Heart Chakra: across the middle of the palm (extending to the thumb)
Throat Chakra: across the base of the finger joints
Brow Chakra: across the top finger joints
Crown Chakra: tips of the fingers

Seven Tantric Healings: A Feast for the Senses

Consider giving one of the healings below, every month to each other as you journey through the seven gates over the months of autumn / winter. Alternatively, these make a beautiful preparation, exchanged over seven days before you take or renew your sacred marriage vows.

1. Tender Touch Healing

I call this the 'Kiss of Life'. Ask your beloved to lie on a massage table wearing only their underwear or without clothes. Put on some tranquil music and lead them through a guided meditation, asking them to visualize being gently kissed on every inner organ. Next, tenderly kiss them from a place of pure love with no seductive energy all over their body. (Many people haven't been touched in such a tender way since they were a newborn baby so this sense memory is powerful in reverting us back to a deep state of vulnerability, so honor this privilege with deep reverence.)

2. Luscious Scent Healing

To prepare, gather seven flowers, one for each chakra and place them in a shallow basket. Next, ask your beloved to lie on a massage table, recliner or bed. Then, starting with the red flower for the base chakra, invite them to gaze upon its beauty and inhale its scent. Then begin lightly stroking them all over with each bloom to transcendent music such as *'Garden of the Gods'* by Deuter. Repeat this process with seven exotic fruits, giving them a taste of each, before massaging their skin with its nectar and flesh. End by showering them with a cascade of rose petals.

3. Oceanic Sensate Healing

Ask your beloved to choose six crystals from your collection and place them into a sacred union grid around a rubber yoga mat, placed on top of a plastic sheet. Next, heat some jojoba oil so it's warm and not too hot, then use liberal amounts, pouring it onto their body from a jug above them, caressing their skin in one continual flowing movement while singing them into a trance with a repetitive Earth chant, like a mother singing a lullaby to a child. A good chant to use is, 'The River Is Flowing'. The lyrics are below and you can Google it on You Tube to get the melody.

> *The river is flowing, flowing and flowing*
> *The river is flowing back into She*
> *Oh, Mama carry me - your child I will always be*
> *Oh, Mama carry me, back into thee*

4. Butterfly Healing

To prepare, put on the background sounds of the Celtic harp. Apply a few drops of rose essential oil to a powdered body masque clay with some water to form a paste, then apply to your beloved's skin all over as they lie naked on a massage table, using your hands. Then cover them in soft muslin and leave them to meditate upon the wisdom of their heart while the clay of the mother dries. Next, smudge them by burning sweetgrass and sage over them, to clear negative thought forms from their energy field, and then exfoliate away their old psychic armor using a natural body scrub. Gently wash them clean all over with warm water and a soft cloth and dry them with a soft towel. Finally, dip your fingertips in a dish of corn flour to give your hands a silken touch and lightly touch them all over.

5. Sound Healing

Ask your beloved to lie on a massage table or bed, naked or in their underwear. Next, anoint your beloved's chakras with the essential oils recommended for each chapter, diluted in a base oil such as jojoba. Wave each oil under their nostrils, instructing them to inhale before anointing each chakra. As you anoint each chakra, speak the affirmation for that chakra:

Base chakra: You are divine passion (Sandalwood oil)
Sacral chakra: You are divine joy (Bergamot oil)
Solar plexus chakra: You are divine will (Peppermint oil)
Heart chakra: You are divine love (Rose oil)
Throat chakra: You are divine truth (Lemongrass oil)
Third eye chakra: You are divine wisdom (Lavender oil)
Crown chakra: You are divine embodiment (Spikenard oil)

Next, place a crystal over each chakra (use colored stones that correspond to each of the chakras). Sound a gong, hoop drum, Tibetan bowl or crystal bowl seven x times and then using your voice tone into their chakras, the seven x Sanskrit Mantras above.

6. Mind / Body Healing

To prepare, put on deep rhythmic trance invoking music such as 'Shamanic Dream' by Anugama. Ask your beloved to lie on a massage table or bed and then place your hand on their heart and start by gently saying the word, 'Mother' softly in a deep centered voice. Continue to repeat this word as you ask them to notice the sensations they feel in their body. Repeat with the word, 'Father'. If emotion surfaces, just keep repeating the word, slowly and deliberately, varying the intonation, speed and volume. Support their process by intuiting where to place your hands on their body and sending heart light to those areas without speaking. Afterwards, make them a herbal tea and allow them to share what memories, thoughts, feelings or sensations arose in response to the different word associations.

7. Sexual Healing

Bathe separately and wear soft, light robes, meeting in a place in your garden or sacred space to serve each other with a cup of flowering herbal tea. Bless each other's cup with words of intent. (You may wish to put on some traditional Japanese music.)

Next, one of you lights a candle for the Goddess, invoking the energies of Shakti, the divine feminine essence and the other lights a candle for Shiva, the divine masculine essence.

Speak aloud your intention to simultaneously open yourselves to receive the blessings of these universal energies.

Take turns speaking what you love about each other at each of the seven gates.

Then anoint each other at the seven gates with spikenard oil diluted in jojoba oil. (Spikenard opens all the chakras simultaneously.) Honor the names of each deity within them as you anoint each gate.

Bow to each other as thank them for being your divine teacher, muse and mirror for sharing this journey with you.

Sit with one hand on your beloved's heart and the other placed over their genitals, sending heart light to each, then kiss, allowing your hearts to connect through your tongues and enjoy the meeting of the God and Goddess.

The Seven Year Itch

Climbing Jacob's Ladder in Conscious Union

Charting the Chakra Cycles of Commitment

The word, 'chakra' means cycle or wheel. But not only are chakras vortexes of energy within our light body, they also govern cycles of time, as is the true nature of time within our universe. Linear time is a false construct of our rational mind, whereas natural time is cyclic. This is why we unconsciously repeat past patterns, going round in circles like 'Groundhog Day' until we notice the pattern. This awareness changes our awareness, so we make an alternative choice, altering the pattern enabling us to spiral upwards like the double helix.

Like the old saying, '*Show me the boy of seven and I'll show you the man.*' Mystical traditions have taught that over first seven years we develop our feminine aspects by studying our Earth Mother and then for the next seven we develop our masculine aspects by studying our Earth Father. As stated earlier, our Earth parents (or guardians and mentors) become the blueprint for our inner feminine and masculine halves.

Within each seven-year cycle, we experience lessons pertaining to each of the seven gates or chakras, whether we are conscious of it or not. For example, in the first year of life we are focused on survival, as we are governed by the first gate or base chakra. In our second year of life, we become aware of the elemental world of our senses as we are governed by the sacral chakra. In our third year of life we become aware of our will - when kids delight in saying the word, 'No!' My understanding is that each archetype of our feminine and masculine aspects are evoked as the energetic gateways along Ida and Pingala, the inner twin serpents are stimulated. Below is a table that illustrates this pattern:

Age	Chakra	Meridian	Archetype
0-1yrs	Base	Ida	Lilith, the Wild Woman
1-2 yrs	Sacral	Ida	Aphrodite, the Beautiful Muse
2-3 yrs	Solar Plexus	Ida	Athena, the Golden Heroine
3-4 yrs	Heart	Ida	Demeter, the Earth Empress
4-5 yrs	Throat	Ida	Artemis, the Medicine Woman
5-6 yrs	Third Eye	Ida	Hecate, the Wise Mystic
6-7 yrs	Crown	Ida	Ishtar, the High Priestess
7-8 yrs	Base	Pingala	Pan, the Wild Man
8-9 yrs	Sacral	Pingala	Ares, the Warrior
9-10 yrs	Solar Plexus	Pingala	Apollo, the Statesman
10-11 yrs	Heart	Pingala	The Green Man
11-12 yrs	Throat	Pingala	Chiron, the Wounded Healer
12-13 yrs	Third Eye	Pingala	Hermes, the Wise Sage
13-14 yrs	Crown	Pingala	Dionysius, the Zen Master

These cycles would similarly occur in any creative beginning, including our relationships.

My understanding is that the phenomena known as the, 'Seven Year Itch' - coined after a noticeable number of couples parted ways after seven years, is explained through us completion of a full cycle through the seven gates. In the ancient world, a king was only allowed to rule for seven years to ensure virility and a lack of complacency!

So too, despite it being an unconscious process, at the completion of this natural cycle, many couples find themselves reassessing their lives and their commitment to their union. If they elect to stay, they would journey more deeply into the lessons of each of the archetypal marriages at the seven gates with their existing partner. If they decide to move on, they would simply start the process over again with a new partner, albeit unconsciously.

With this understanding, if both parties are committed to creating a conscious partnership, by viewing their relationship as a temple for self-growth, then both can consciously embrace this period of evaluation as natural and necessary, without fearing they'll be replaced by a younger model, as has been the norm during the patriarchal era. Instead, this crossroads every seven years, can be embraced as an opportunity to discuss what each has learnt from their shared journey every seven years. Including, how their values, hope and goals have changed as they've matured and grown, creating an opportunity to discuss their current values, priorities and aspirations. This opens a mature and honest discussion, so together they can amicably discern if they are still on the same page and happy to head in the same direction, toward a common goal. In the new paradigm of sacred union, I see this as an ideal time to renew vows and have another honeymoon! So, what does this pattern look like in relationships?

The First Solar Cycle: (Year One of a Relationship)
The Dance of Pan and Lilith

In our modern 'civilized' culture where we have denied the conscious integration of the wild aspects of Pan and Lilith, the first year of union often proves difficult as each is confronted with each other's shadow aspects and the 'fight or flight' response is heightened. The dynamic often experienced here is - the woman, as Lilith, points out what she sees as the flaws in their dynamic. This is not done to nag or focus on the negative, but to try and bring awareness to that which could jeopardize their union, if not dealt with. If his Pan is mature, he will work with her, to become more self-aware by acknowledging their unconscious words and behaviors when pointed out by the other. If this doesn't occur, they will scapegoat their shadow on to the other and eventually reject each other. As the base governs passion and anger, this can be a very fiery year, with lots of sex and lots of fights. Studies have shown, couples who fight more in the first year of a relationship, statistically go the distance, whereas those who sweep their issues under the rug don't, as their passion dies along with their lack of authenticity. The challenge is to risk rejection by being true to oneself and not persist with a partner who is incapable of owning their own shadow.

The Second Solar Cycle: (Year Two of a Relationship) The Dance of Ares and Aphrodite

In the second year, the aspects of Aphrodite and Ares are evoked, which ushers in a very emotional journey. Since the sacral is also the seat of joy, play, pleasure and beauty, this can be a really romantic time. However, this is also a time of exploring the extremes of love and war. So during this second year, they will each trigger the wounds of their inner child, and may seek emotional security from each other as surrogate parents, to heal the wounds they received in childhood. If these aspects are immature, they may treat the other more like a parent by rebelling against the emotional dependency they feel, spending most of their social time with their friends. If, on the other hand these aspects are mature, the partner with dominant Ares will open to their sensual / creative self more, as they feel inspired by their Aphrodite dominant partner's lead. This willingness will create multiple opportunities to appreciate more beauty in themselves and the world around them. This also helps heal inner conflict, so they don't destroy that which they love the most, with their impatient, self-centered demands and short temper. Similarly, the partner with the dominant Aphrodite aspect will learn to initiate more through pro-active behaviors, empowering their sense of selfhood and personal confidence. Both will also learn to take responsibility for their own emotions, rather than blaming, sulking, withholding or expecting the other to rescue them. This is the year we have the opportunity to stop re-wounding ourselves by recreating the role we played in our family dynamic, through identifying it and making different choices, which dissipates our emotional drama.

The Third Solar Cycle: (Year Three of a Relationship) The Dance of Apollo and Athena

In the third year of relating, the aspects of Athena and Apollo are evoked along with the solar plexus chakra, which highlights whether we are compatible intellectually with our partner. We may make a large financial commitment, such as purchasing a house or business together, since this gate governs our ego ambitions and self-worth. The challenge at this gate is to individuate from how our Father saw us, so how we see and know ourselves is based on our own secure identity and not on other's approval. Without this innate sense of self-worth, based on who we are, rather than what we acquire, do, or earn, many couples can overextend themselves financially during this year, in an unconscious bid to impress their family and friends with how successful they are. This then leads to additional financial pressure, which brings to the surface the underlying issues around self-worth, which the unconscious couple will project onto each other, rather than own their own materialism and need for approval. If a couple is not able to stimulate each other mentally, the initial lust and emotionally co-dependency will fade as it becomes painfully evident that they don't really enjoy each other's company, as they don't have enough in common.

The Fourth Solar Cycle: (Year Four of a Relationship) The Dance of the Green Man and Earth Mother, Demeter

In the fourth year of partnership the aspects of Demeter and the Green Man are evoked by the opening of the heart chakra. This is a time of stabilizing our union, often by investing time and energy on the home front, spurred on by the responsibilities of parenthood, pets, gardening and renovation. If these aspects are mature, both will attune to the natural cycles to grow, harvest and rest in a spirit of patient acceptance, so they sustain growth through consistent effort. This occurs when they have developed the ability to nurture self and what they care about. If these aspects are immature, they will neglect their own needs, jeopardizing the sustainability of the union and everything they sought to build together. When we consider many of us have been under-parented, due to the fact our own parents didn't receive rites of passage to support their own growth into maturity, the greatest boon we can give ourselves at this gate, is to seek out mentoring and support to help us to grow, both individually and together. Otherwise we may resent and rebel against our responsibilities and undermine that which we have seeded. Embracing the annual relationship practice of the hieros gamos is an ideal way to support the growth of the union.

The Fifth Solar Cycle: (Year Five of a Relationship)
The Dance of Chiron and Artemis

During the fifth year of partnership, the aspects of Artemis and Chiron are evoked, along with the throat chakra. This challenges us to take responsibility for healing our own wounds, so we don't shut off from our partner and stop sharing the truth of our inner self with them. These aspects carry the energy of brother / sister, so often this year asks us to be a true friend to our partner above all other desires. If these aspects are mature, they can assist each other to heal, by listening, without shaming each other's vulnerability and encouraging each other to do what they intuitively need to do, to heal their respective wounds. Communication is key, so in this year, it is imperative both spend quality time attuning to their inner truth so they can be really honest with each other, especially about their sensitivities. If these aspects are immature, they stay together to avoid facing their fear of aloneness, but ice each other out and make barbed comments, illustrating how they resent their opposite for not being more like them. During this year, it is helpful to invest in healing modalities, both as a recipient and studying and practicing them so they can transform their wounds into medicine for the journey. When these archetypes are working well together, they encourage each other to see how their wounds have served them.

The Sixth Solar Cycle: (Year Six of a Relationship)
The Dance of Hermes and Hecate

During the sixth year of partnership the archetypes of Hecate and Hermes are evoked, along with the third eye chakra. These aspects often present us with unexpected change or upheaval, challenging our ability, as a couple to journey to the Underworld and not lose faith in ourselves or each other. This can take the form of death of a loved one, job loss, geographical relocation, illness or injury. If these aspects are mature, we surrender to the process of loss, allowing ourselves to grieve what was, and express our fears at the impermanence of life which we must learn to intuitively navigate. As a result, we allow our partner to make this journey of descent in their own way and own time, knowing that it is different for each person. By developing a deeper experiential relationship with the spirit world, studying the psyche and nature of the universe, through esoteric sciences and willingly seeking trance-formation through participating in sacred ceremony, both can grow their experiential wisdom individually and share their pearls of wisdom with each other. If, however, these aspects are immature, they will retract, fearing all change, and become a burden to their partner as they focus upon their fears, creating depression and illness as a way of avoiding life.

The Seventh Solar Cycle: (Year Seven of a Relationship)
The Dance of Ishtar / Dionysius, the Divine Couple

In the seventh year of a partnership, the archetypes of Ishtar and Dionysus are evoked, along with the crown chakra. These archetypes often see unconscious couples polarize between one seeking God and the other hitting the bottle! This happens as both unconsciously wish to expand beyond their old way of being into something more unified with the whole. For a lot of women, during the patriarchal era, this meant getting involved with their local church as a way of dedicating themselves to a search for higher meaning. For a lot of men, their Dionysian community was at the local pub, accessing a different kind of Spirit. Fortunately, more women nowadays are finding states of bliss through ecstatic body practices, such as dance meditation and yoga and more men are finding states of altered perception through shamanic vision quests, including sweat lodges and ayahuasca sacred ceremonies. More importantly, many are experimenting with both as pathways to ecstasy, rather than seeing one as pure and the other as evil. For conscious couples in their seventh year, this gate marks an opportunity to share these transcendent experiences and anchor sacred practices such as Tantra into their union, offering them a deeper connection and higher goal, which renews their inspiration and commitment for the next seven-year cycle.

Resources by Tanishka

Available at www.starofishtar.com

Books

The Inner Goddess Makeover

Sacred Union: Awakening to the Consciousness of Eden:

Volume One. Creating Sacred Union Within

Volume Two: Creating Sacred Union in Partnership

Online Courses

Red Tent online course

Brotherhood Lodge online course

Sacred Union online course for Singles

Sacred Union online course for Couples

Oracle Decks

Sacred Union: Light and Shadow Deck

Sacred Union Oracle Deck

CD's / MP3's

The Inner Goddess Makeover Meditations Double CD

Sacred Union Meditations Double CD

Good Morning Chakra Workout Double CD

Letting Go Meditation MP3

Astrological Updates

Astro Oracle - new moon and full moon astro forecasts

The Moon Woman App - daily lunar cycle updates

Bibliography

Bailey, Alice. *The Labours of Hercules*

Baum, L. Frank. *The Wonderful Wizard of Oz*

Byrne, Rhonda. *The Secret*

Chu, Chin-Ning. *The Secret of the Rainmaker*

Deida, David. *Intimate Communion*

Desilets, Saida. *The Emergence of the Sensual Woman*

Dunne, Claire. *Carl Jung: Wounded Healer of the Soul*

Fontana, David. *The Secret Language of Symbols*

Gawain, Shakti. *Creative Visualization*

Guiley, *Rosemary* Ellen. *The Encyclopedia of Magic and Alchemy*

Hay, Louise. *You Can Heal Your Life*

Kirsch, Jonathan. *Harlot, Forbidden Tales of the Bible*

Lawrence, DH. *Lady Chatterley's Lover*

LePage, Victoria. *Mysteries of the Bridechamber*

Noontil, Annette. *The Barometer of the Soul*

Sams, Jamie. *The Sacred Path*

Shakespeare, William. *A Midsummer Night's Dream*

Sharman-Burke, Juliet and Liz Greene. *The Mythic Tarot*

Shuttle, Penelope and Peter Redgrove. *The Wise Wound*

Tanishka. *Sacred Union: Awakening to the Consciousness of Eden. Volume One*

Vātsyāyana. *Kama Sutra*

Weinstein, Marion. *Positive Magic*

Wolkstein, *Diane* and Samuel Noah Kramer. *Inanna: Queen of Heaven and Earth*

Weblinks

http://www.bibliotecapleyades.net/esp_autor_whenry04.htm

http://www.webmd.com/depression/features/seasonal-affective-disorder

http://www.facebook.com/pages/Running-to-nowhere/212683182110883

http://www.bible-history.com/babylonia/BabyloniaThe_Ishtar_Gate.htm

http://www.islamic-architecture.info/WA-IQ/WA-IQ-014.htm

http://www.crystalinks.com/babylon.html

http://www.universal-tao.com/article/sexual.html

⚕ About the Author

Tanishka has spent the past twenty years as a group facilitator, empowering both men and women to understand and express all their archetypes. She has trained hundreds of women to facilitate Red Tent women's circles in over twenty countries, and is the author of 'The Inner Goddess Makeover' and 'Sacred Union: Awakening to the Consciousness of Eden', which is a trilogy series.

At the time of releasing this edition, she has over 430,000 followers of daily insights on her Facebook page, 'The Moon Woman'. To find out more about her retreats, workshops and speaking tours or range of resources and online courses, visit www.starofishtar.com.

127952